SEMEIA 66

ETHICS AND POLITICS IN THE HEBREW BIBLE

Guest Editor: Douglas A. Knight
Board Editor: Carol Meyers

©1995
by the Society of Biblical Literature

Published by
SCHOLARS PRESS
P.O. BOX 15399
Atlanta, GA 30333-0399

Printed in the United States of America
on acid free paper

CONTENTS

Contributors to this Issue v

Introduction: Ethics, Ancient Israel, and the Hebrew Bible
   Douglas A. Knight 1

THE ETHICS OF ANCIENT ISRAEL AND THE HEBREW BIBLE: THE QUESTION OF METHOD

1. The Basis of Ethics in the Hebrew Bible
   John Barton 11

2. Moral Agency, Community, and
   the Character of God in the Hebrew Bible
   Bruce C. Birch 23

3. Ethics of the Hebrew Bible: The Problem of Methodology
   Eryl W. Davies 43

4. Sources and Methods in the Study of Ancient Israelite Ethics
   Robert R. Wilson 55

POLITICAL ETHICS IN ANCIENT ISRAEL

5. Dominion, Guilt, and Reconciliation:
   The Contribution of the Jacob Narrative
   in Genesis to Political Ethics
   Frank Crüsemann 67

6. *Cui Bono?* — History in the Service of Political Nationalism:
   The Deuteronomistic History as Political Propaganda
   Frank S. Frick 79

7. Political Rights and Powers in Monarchic Israel
   Douglas A. Knight 93

8. Kings and Clients: On Loyalty between
   the Ruler and the Ruled in Ancient "Israel"
   Niels Peter Lemche 119

9. The End of the Omride Dynasty: Social-Ethical
   Observations on the Subject of Power and Violence
   Hannelis Schulte 133

RESPONSES

The Quest for Hebrew Bible Ethics: A Jewish Response
   Peter J. Haas 151

Of Aims and Methods in Hebrew Bible Ethics
   Eckart Otto 161

An Ethicist's Concerns about Biblical Ethics
   Peter J. Paris 173

CONTRIBUTORS TO THIS ISSUE

John Barton
 Oriel College
 University of Oxford
 Oxford OX1 4EW
 Great Britain

Bruce C. Birch
 Wesley Theological Seminary
 4500 Massachusetts Avenue, N.W.
 Washington, DC 20016

Frank Crüsemann
 Kirchliche Hochschule Bethel
 Remterweg 45
 33617 Bielefeld
 Federal Republic of Germany

Eryl W. Davies
 Department of Religious Studies
 University College of North Wales
 Bangor, Gwynedd LL57 2DG
 Great Britain

Frank S. Frick
 Religious Studies Department
 Albion College
 Albion, MI 49224

Peter J. Haas
 Department of Religious Studies
 Vanderbilt University
 Nashville, TN 37240

Douglas A. Knight
 The Divinity School
 Vanderbilt University
 Nashville, TN 37240

Niels Peter Lemche
 Department of Biblical Exegesis
 University of Copenhagen
 1150 Copenhagen
 Denmark

Eckart Otto
 Fachbereich Evangelische
 Theologie
 Seminar für Altes Testament und
 Biblische Archäologie
 Johannes Gutenberg-Universität
 Saarstraße 21
 55099 Mainz
 Federal Republic of Germany

Peter J. Paris
 Princeton Theological Seminary
 CN 821
 Princeton, NJ 08542

Hannelis Schulte
 Theologische Fakultät
 Ruprecht-Karls-Universität
 6900 Heidelberg
 Federal Republic of Germany

Robert R. Wilson
 The Divinity School
 Yale University
 409 Prospect Street
 New Haven, CT 06510

INTRODUCTION: ETHICS, ANCIENT ISRAEL, AND THE HEBREW BIBLE

Douglas A. Knight
Vanderbilt University

While the study of the ethics of ancient Israel and its canonized literary heritage, the Hebrew Bible, is an old discipline, there have been remarkably few comprehensive treatments since early in this century. In contrast, hundreds if not thousands of investigations of individual aspects of this morality have been conducted. The situation appears to be changing now, with several broad treatments already in publication or in preparation. There has been good reason for this relative paucity of full-scale ethical treatises: conducting an analysis of the ethics in this material is not as self-evident an enterprise as might initially be supposed.

The Meaning of "Ethics." First, there is the fundamental question of how "ethics" is to be understood in this context. In the disciplines of philosophical and theological ethics it is normally taken to be a constructive operation. But if the task is to do the ethics of a period in history or of a fixed literary corpus, one would think that it should be more analytical and interpretive than constructive in character, granting of course that interpretation necessarily involves imaginative and creative work as well. Such an undertaking differs quite markedly from an ethical treatise that attempts to make more universal claims concerning moral agency, moral principles and norms, and other common issues. Is there—perhaps on the model of historical anthropology—such an entity as "historical ethics," the study of the ethics of an ancient people who can no longer be interviewed or observed? If so, along what lines should one proceed? Are there comparable examples of, for example, the ethics of ancient Egypt, Greece, Rome, or China? For that matter, how would one even conduct an analysis of the ethics of a *contemporary* culture—whether during only one period or over a longer block of time, perhaps several centuries in the life of that culture? In short, the very notion of ethics seems to require a special definition and approach when one moves away from the usual constructive sense of the term.

The Object of Analysis. Assuming a satisfactory answer to the first question, one then needs to determine the subject matter to submit to ethical scrutiny. Here the problem becomes complex. There are at least two obvious candidates—the Hebrew Bible or the moral lives of the ancient Israelites—and the former can be subdivided into three alternatives. These options are not mutually exclusive, although they do represent rather distinct differences in the way the accent is set. As a rule, they all recognize that the Hebrew Bible is not simply a moral handbook but something more intricate and subtle in character, requiring a carefully developed method of interpretation. And for this very reason, we will refer to these alternatives as constructs or models in order to emphasize that they result from our own reconstructive, interpretive efforts.

Most commonly, the literature of the Hebrew Bible figures as the object of ethical analysis. Focusing on Israel's literary remains may seem at first glance to be quite manageable—but only if one considers the biblical text rather uniform in character. Otherwise, the text emerges as a highly complicated body of literature, with multiple literary forms, diverse strata, varied perspectives, usually unidentifiable authors, and frequent internal conflicts or tensions on moral and other matters. Three angles of approach present themselves, all of which are text-oriented. The first might be termed the *referential construct*. Guided by the various methods that have come to constitute historical-critical exegesis since the Enlightenment, the ethicist operating with this approach takes the text as the point of departure and seeks to interpret it in terms of its prehistory, specifically its literary development, the intentions of its authors and redactors, and the phenomena in the real world to which it, *ex hypothesi*, refers. Any moral problem or principle is thus accounted for and interpreted in light of the historical context(s) in which it arose. For example, texts in Amos or Micah deploring the treatment of the poor are illuminated by our knowledge of eighth-century BCE economic and political conditions; laws concerning agricultural practices are explained in terms of life in the rural countryside; and passages in Genesis depicting the relations with Israel's neighbors may be taken to reflect international politics during the monarchic period. Ethics according to the referential construct relies heavily on extra-biblical information supplied by archaeology, other historical evidence, and ancient Near Eastern literature, but its focus remains on the biblical text itself as the object to be explicated ethically. Most of the comprehensive as well as the more specific studies of biblical ethics over the past century conform to this construct.

Quite different from the historical-critical approach, the *literary construct* is largely interested not in the producers of the literature but rather in the world of the text and the world of the reader, and an ethical analysis along these lines would be similarly defined. By and large, such analysis results directly from a theory of literature that both questions the ability of the critic to get "behind" the text to its cultural and authorial causes, and disputes the value of such information even if it were obtainable. According to this view, what we have is the text, and that is what we must interpret, in its artistry and play of meanings. Here the counterpart to the historical-critical exegete is the interpreter, who must move with great care since the social location and cultural conditionedness of the interpreter—the reader—must be scrutinized as much as the text itself. I know of no comprehensive ethical project along these lines now in print or in process, but on a smaller scale it can be seen in numerous literary studies that attempt to show the ways in which meaning is constituted and conveyed in individual texts, a meaning that bears on the nature of humanity, divinity, and the world. Often the task is to show the ways in which centuries of interpreters, driven by their own prejudices and ideologies, have held tyranny over biblical texts that actually may be conveying quite different meanings. Some of the best work in this area is feminist and liberationist re-readings of long-restrained passages. There is not much in our discipline today to match the newness and freshness of this work.

The third type of approach is the *appropriative construct*, which is most commonly driven by the idea of the religiously authoritative nature of the text within faith communities from the canonization period until the present. Accordingly, ancient moral worlds that were not rendered canonical in the Hebrew Bible have little significance for this model, which attends minimally to the prehistory of the text within the earlier social settings of Israel. The focus falls instead on the usefulness of the biblical material for contemporary moral decision-making. According to this approach, the Hebrew Bible contains or embodies moral principles, standards, directives, or advice that should be influential for postbiblical generations, including us today, in the resolution of our own moral dilemmas. The biblical text is regarded as an authoritative or canonical whole with a special meaning for its subsequent faith communities, mainly Christians and Jews. The appropriative method can range from a static procedure—for example, proof-texting or the strict and unwavering application of selected biblical directives to current situations—to a dynamic process—such as midrash in the rabbinic period or a discriminating combination of biblical values with other moral sensitivities in order to resolve an admittedly complex problem today. But what all of these types of appropriation have in common is the conviction, usually a religious conviction, that the Bible represents a source, and for some the final or—so they believe—the *only* source, of moral direction. Thus when faced with moral problems in the area of, for instance, economic exploitation, sexual practices, family obligations, legal penalties, or animal care, the motive for probing biblical morality is to determine what we, living in the postbiblical period, should do with regard to these matters. According to this approach, the biblical tradition even helps to define what we should consider to be a moral problem, such as the unjust distribution of wealth, or the need for legal order, or the issue of ethics in government. And when we are confronted with a problem that has no precedent in the Bible, such as modern secularity, or the imminent depletion of certain natural resources, or a biomedical conflict, one still relies on the appropriative construct and sounds the biblical text for any values that might apply. Such analysis shows some interest in the historical and social background of the biblical literature, but the agenda is fairly well set by the belief that it is the text that is to one degree or another authoritative for those of us living after the closure of the canon. Biblical ethics thus serves primarily the interests of normative ethics.

These three constructs are often labeled with reference to the literature in its final form: "Old Testament ethics," for Christians; "Hebrew Bible ethics," for Jews as well as for Christians or others seeking a confessionally neutral term; or the more confusing term, "biblical ethics," which can designate the combination of both Old and New Testaments for Christians but only the Hebrew Bible for Jews. These models all involve text-oriented interpretations.

The focal point shifts, however, for the other main option in choice of subject matter, which might be termed the *sociohistorical construct*. Here the object of analysis is not simply the Hebrew Bible against its sociohistorical background, but rather the sociohistorical background itself, the moral worlds of those living within the Israelite territory in antiquity. In a word, such an enterprise would be called "the ethics of ancient Israel," not "biblical/Hebrew Bible/Old Testament ethics." It shares substantial ground in common with the three variations that concentrate on the literature, but the differences are significant. First, the referential, appropriative, and sociohistorical constructs all attend to the setting in which the biblical text arose; but for the first two this historical context is primarily relevant insofar as it enhances our understanding of the text, whereas for the sociohistorical construct the culture itself is the object of study. For the former two the Hebrew Bible holds pride of place; for the latter it provides only one, albeit a very important, line of access to the morality of the ancient Israelites. Second, whereas the literary construct remains with the final, present form of the text and its congeries of meanings, the sociohistorical construct incorporates this level of the literature diachronically as only one of many in the long history of Israel's culture. The final text, the preceding strata, and any hypothesized oral traditions need to be related, where plausible, to the communities, groups, and individuals that expressed in them their values and ideals. The special task of the ethicist employing the sociohistorical construct is to describe the morality of the ancient Israelites—their moral problems, their norms and principles, their conduct, and the character of their community. A lengthy and varied stretch of history is involved, and the termini a quo and ad quem can be variably defined—for example, from the settling of the land at the start of the Iron Age and on through the Persian and Hellenistic periods, if one wants the period under scrutiny to remain relatively coterminous with the period frequently associated with the growth of the biblical traditions and literature. Within this millennium of history, one must attend to the often sharp differences in social, economic, and political structures. Furthermore, the morality of potentially all groups in society must be sought—heterodox and orthodox, peasant and elite, rural and urban, female and male. The task is daunting, limitless, and obviously impossible as well, but the shift of accent is key: from the biblical literature to the proto-Israelite, Israelite, and Yehudite people themselves. The focus falls on the morality not merely of texts but of the people's lives as they might have been played out in the real world. And significantly, the result amounts to a description of Israel's multiple morali*ties*—not just a single, unified, "orthodox" or dominant moral world but the full range of moral values evident in the people's behavior and in the economic and political systems throughout the society.

Design. Following the decision on the subject matter, how should one structure the analysis? An obvious organizational pattern is chronological, normally according to political periods: premonarchical, monarchical, exilic, Persian, and Hellenistic. The sociohistorical model can be divided along these lines, as can also the referential and probably also the appropriative approaches. An option available to the three constructs focusing on the literature is to follow the present order of the text, beginning with the Pentateuch and moving progressively to the historical books, the prophetic literature, and the Writings. A variant scheme might be oriented more toward types of literature: narrative, legal, prophetic, lyrical, and sapiential. In any of these text-oriented cases the ethicist inquires into the moral positions advocated in the respective literary blocks. The social historian, on the other hand, has the option of organizing the discussion according to social groups and constructs: elites and peasants, family and kinship, village and town, region and nation, and the like. An alternative structure might be workable for any of the four models—to key the ethical analysis to moral problems, such as moral agency, worth of life, gender roles, marriage and divorce, sexuality, intergenerational relations, friendship and enmity, inheritance, crime and punishment, political leadership, distribution of wealth, stratification by class, ethnicity, ecology, and many other specific problems. Of course, some combination of these various organizational schemes is conceivable and may in fact be preferable for the various models.

Sources. The problem of sources presents itself for each construct, although in differing ways. For the literary model the text as it stands is quite sufficient, although comparison can also be made to other literature from the region or from other times. A somewhat more complicated situation faces the appropriative model, where interest in the canonization process will necessarily involve knowledge of religious, social, and political happenings during the late periods, especially the Babylonian, Persian, and Hellenistic ages. The ethicist employing the referential model will need an even broader range of information insofar as any period in Israel's history might have left its mark, however slightly, on some part of the literature. The social historian, however, faces the most demanding task since potentially any aspect of life anywhere within the Israelite territory during its millennium of history carries possible interest. The further one moves away from the text, in other words, the more the need increases for additional sources. Archaeology supplies partial but invaluable information about the conditions in which the people lived, from their domestic environments to their political powers, from their relative economic circumstances to their connections with others throughout the region—all data that can help keep the ethical analysis anchored in reality. The wealth of literature from neighboring cultures in the ancient Near East also constitutes a backdrop for Israelite phenomena. Further comparative materials can be cautiously drawn from the discipline of anthropology, and sociology can offer theories for understanding social institutions and group behavior. And we must remember that at all levels of interpretation and analysis our assessments are hypothetical at best, to be regarded as valid according to the test of plausibility in light of all available evidence and to be rejected or modified when another hypothesis manages to account for the evidence in a more convincing manner.

Normative Ethics. A final question poses itself to the ethicist working according to any of these four or other models. What is the relation of these ethical findings to our own moral decision-making today? Stated differently, how can descriptive ethics be employed for normative ethics? It should come as no surprise that very many persons living in our age are inclined—or at least intend to be inclined—to take their cues from biblical morality. They will more often than not be motivated by religious considerations, although a humanistic bent may characterize some. Of the four models, the appropriative approach is most explicitly interested in normative questions, and the referential construct is perhaps close behind insofar as the historical-critical method has often been connected to traditional theological studies. The literary model approaches the issue of contemporary appropriation quite differently in that it deemphasizes the referential character of the text and stresses the interpretive role of the reader, and therein lies the text's potential significance. The social historian, on the other hand, has perhaps the hardest task on this issue: why should anyone today take a lead from the moral lives of people living in antiquity, a culture that expressed itself in heterogeneous, often conflictual ways that are now frequently regarded as unattractive, even objectionable, and certainly out-of-date? One might answer that its pertinence resides precisely in its very diversity and tensions inasmuch as our own world is also pluralistic—in fact much more so—and resists easy resolution of complex problems. According to the sociohistorical approach, then, the very fact of ancient Israel's moral dilemmas and multifarious moral values can thus be regarded as paradigmatic for our own situation, which is similarly marked by conflicted moral worlds, and furthermore many of the specific moral problems faced in ancient Israel may turn out to share substantial ground with the modern versions of the same. To be sure, unless one operates with the notion that the biblical text has a divine origin with only minimal human contributions, it is necessary to regard the Hebrew Bible as the product of that social world.

The question then returns to the point of departure: why consider the Bible or anything else from ancient Israelite culture as a primary resource for contemporary moral decision-making? Moreover, on what grounds should one elevate one moral position in importance and regard another as less than exemplary? For instance, why esteem the Israelite concepts of justice and community but reject their violence and power structures, which appear systemic to their culture? Our standards for judgment stem as much from our own sensibilities as from external, including biblical, sources. For this very reason, in fact, it may be that the sociohistorical construct has wider normative utility than does any of the other models since it can appeal to persons both within and outside of the Jewish and Christian traditions. For instance, Islamic reworking of biblical traditions renders a text-oriented comparison of moral values problematic since one canon becomes set against another, whereas a more fluid, sociohistorical ethic of the Israelite people may conceivably be more easily related to the social contexts and customs of Muslim life. Similarly, others today, from technologically developed societies to more traditionally oriented, small-scale societies, may find in the experiences of the Israelites an easier access to moral alternatives than a fixed and authoritative literary canon would encourage. Yet however the ethic is constructed, whether along these or other lines, those of us living in this age, so long distant from ancient

Israel's existence and from the production of the Hebrew Bible, may find in this heritage principles and standards to inform our own moral dilemmas; we need then only to achieve clarity over our reasons for choosing to be influenced by one and not another moral position from this minute segment within the vastness of human history. This reflection on the grounding of moral norms belongs to the task of the contemporary ethicist, whether philosophical or theological, whether Jewish, Christian, or other in orientation.

* * * * *

The essays in this volume address some but not all of these issues. The first four discuss the conceptual and methodological problems confronting the discipline, introducing many of the specific ingredients and issues that constitute ethical analysis and demonstrating their importance on the basis of various texts and social phenomena. The second part of the volume focuses, by way of example, on one specific area of moral concern—political ethics. Together, the five articles in this section do not attempt to give a full overview of political ethics in ancient Israel or in the Hebrew Bible; rather, they present a close examination of several specific moral topics within this area. Among these nine papers, it will be seen, three of the four models described above are represented in one or more of the discussions; only the literary model has no advocate as such. The approaches and understandings of the task vary, just as might be expected in the discipline at large.

The nine papers were first presented at the International Meeting of the Society of Biblical Literature, convening at the Westfälische Wilhelms-Universität in Münster, Germany, on 26 July 1993. The authors had an opportunity to revise their papers following the meeting, and with one or two exceptions each was modified and amplified, in some cases quite extensively. The respondents did not participate in the sessions at the meeting but wrote their essays after the other manuscripts were completed for publication.

These articles and responses are offered as contributions to an old and on-going discussion in the hope that they will provoke further reactions and reflections concerning the future tasks involved in analyzing and interpreting ancient Israel's moral traditions.

THE ETHICS OF ANCIENT ISRAEL
AND THE HEBREW BIBLE:
THE QUESTION OF METHOD

THE BASIS OF ETHICS IN THE HEBREW BIBLE

John Barton
University of Oxford

ABSTRACT

Alongside the question of the norms of moral conduct in ancient Israel and in the Hebrew Bible, biblical scholars also need to be concerned with issues that in a modern setting might be described as "moral philosophy." Two such questions are investigated in this paper: (a) Why—on what basis or rationale—are certain moral norms regarded as binding? Obedience to God, "natural law," and the imitation of God provide conceivable models. All can be found in the Hebrew Bible, and all were probably known in ancient Israel at some time or other. (b) What is the goal of moral conduct? Should biblical ethics be understood, in modern philosophical terms, as deontological or teleological? To both questions there is an "obvious" answer, since biblical ethics has traditionally been seen as dominated by a sense that human beings have a duty to carry out the declared will of God—in other words, the Bible has a deontological system, and one in which duty derives from positive law given by God. However, the biblical evidence is more complex and varied than this suggests.

It has become something of a cliché in biblical studies that ethics in the Hebrew Bible is a neglected field. This cliché could be called the opposite of a self-fulfilling prophecy—we might call it a self-negating truism. For the more often people say it, the more apparent it is that the ethics of the Hebrew Bible is not quite so neglected as it once was. The recent invaluable survey of the subject by Eckart Otto in *Verkündigung und Forschung* contains six pages of bibliography in small type, and prompts the editor, Werner H. Schmidt (2), to comment that Otto has been able to point to "considerable research activity in this ostensibly neglected field" ("eine reiche Forschungstätigkeit . . . zu dem scheinbar vernachlässigten Thema"). Perhaps ethics is indeed no longer quite the Cinderella of Hebrew Bible study that it once was.

This is not uniformly true, however, of all aspects of the subject. In this paper I should like to draw attention to certain questions within the general sphere of ethics that biblical scholars could perhaps usefully give more thought to, under the umbrella title "the basis of ethics." I have in mind two particular issues that in modern Western culture would be thought of as belonging to the sphere of moral philosophy. The first asks why—on what grounds—the ethical norms acknowledged in the biblical text, or observed in ancient Israel, were regarded as binding. The second asks what *kind* of moral system is represented in the Hebrew Bible: is it, for example, an ethic of obligation or duty, on the one hand, or of goal-directed conduct on the other—deontological or teleological, to use terms sometimes found in moral philosophy? Otto notes that such questions about what he usefully calls "metaethics" are indeed seldom raised in the secondary literature. Whereas in Hebrew Bible theology questions of structure, systematic form, and central theme are firmly on the agenda, he says, "in the realm of Old Testament ethics this discussion is entirely lacking" ("im Bereich der alttestamentlichen Ethik fehlt diese Diskussion vollständig" [11]).

Otto suggests that the study of Hebrew Bible ethics could provide a considerable impetus to moral discussion in the wider theological and philosophical world, but it has tended not to engage with these large-scale questions. Of course it is right to point out, as does Smend (423–24), that ancient Israel was a pre-philosophical culture. In the Hebrew Bible there is no coherent reflection on what is prescribed or proscribed in the manner of Western philosophical thought, and there is no unity such as would justify us in speaking of "an ethic," in the singular. Nevertheless most biblical specialists (including Smend himself) would probably agree that the Hebrew Bible, whether at the level of individual books and sections of books or at the redactional and even canonical level, is more than just a jumble of isolated precepts with no underlying rationale. The surface details of the ethical system or systems in the Hebrew Bible are generated by deeper and more fundamental structures of ethical thinking, even if these are relatively inarticulate by comparison with those of Western moral philosophy.

Where this is denied by biblical scholars, it may be because of their own theological views about the true origins of ethics, rather than because of any empirical examination of the biblical text. When I was first thinking about biblical ethics about twenty years ago, I noticed that many scholars claimed there was no "philosophical" thinking in the Hebrew Bible and hence also no moral philosophy. (This position was centrally important to much in the "biblical theology movement," though it perhaps seems less vital now.) These same scholars, however, commonly made remarks about the centrality of the *covenant* in Israel's moral life, and stressed that all ethical conduct was to be understood as obedience to the will of the God of Israel as laid down in the covenant stipulations. Whether that is true or not, it seemed to me then (and still seems now) to be just as "metaethical" as any other high-level analysis of what holds an ethical system together. To say that ethical obligation is obedience to the declared will of the national God is to say that it is not, for example, the observance of custom or of allegedly universal human norms. Once distinctions like that are possible, we are in the realm of moral philosophy—though no doubt of a fairly primitive kind—whether we like it or not. Better to acknowledge this and try to be sensitive to such systematization and metaethics as there may be in the Hebrew Bible, than to ignore it and uncritically accept one model—usually that of ethics as obedience—as if it were self-evidently the only model with which Israelite thinkers operated.

It was with this conviction that I wrote a short article in 1978 called "Understanding Old Testament Ethics," which was a tentative beginning in a quest for the basis or bases of the ethics of the Hebrew Bible. I should like to suggest some changes of emphasis that may be helpful for the future. It still seems to me that we can identify three basic models in the Hebrew Bible: obedience to God's declared will; "natural law"; and imitation of God. But all three models need closer definition and more subtle analysis.

OBEDIENCE TO GOD'S DECLARED WILL

Obedience to the declared will of God is probably the strongest model for ethical obligation in most of the books of the Hebrew Scriptures. It is methodologically important to distinguish between "ethics in ancient Israel" and "ethics of the Hebrew Bible/Old Testament." But where the obedience model is concerned, I suspect it would appear under both headings in any systematic account of biblical ethics. Many *people* in ancient Israel in various periods seem to have thought (or perhaps better: assumed) that human beings, and Israelites especially, should do as God told them; and many of the *texts* they produced, which now form our Bible, operate with the same assumption. On this issue that particular methodological distinction may matter less than it does elsewhere. Ordinary Israelites and those who wrote the biblical books alike regarded "the good" as that way of life which God enjoined. There were no doubt different levels of sophistication in thinking about the matter, but there was no essential disagreement.

At the same time there is another distinction which is perhaps more important in this case than in some others. That is the distinction between, on the one hand, what the text shows or implies about either ancient Israel or the compilers of Scripture and, on the other hand, how modern Jews or Christians suppose ethics to be grounded. When important writers on Hebrew Bible ethics such as Eichrodt or Hempel emphasized the "theonomy" of biblical ethics, almost to the exclusion of other models, they were of course drawing on much solid evidence from the texts. But they were also surely motivated partly by a dogmatic scheme in which the true theological account of ethics is viewed as divine command. Similarly, when Karl Barth maintained that in placing ourselves under the obligations laid down in biblical ethics we are taking on the obligation to obey God, the divine Commander (see Biggar), he was not primarily saying that an obedience-ethic happens to predominate, as a matter of historical fact, in the biblical documents. He was saying that, seen from the perspective of systematic theology, ethics is obedience to God, and whatever norms are to be found in the Bible should be appropriated (by *us*) on that basis. Although it would look odd in practice, it would not have been inconsistent in theory if any of these writers had found that ancient Israelites in general, or the writers of the Hebrew Bible in particular, did *not* see ethics as a matter of obedience, yet had still argued that we should now accept biblical moral teaching within a framework of obedience. (In a moment I want to mention a case where Barth does argue in something like this way.) But for the most part Hempel and Eichrodt, at least, presented their reading of the texts as correct historically, not just as desirable theologically. And it is possible that they here failed to see how far their own theological preferences might be distorting their judgment about the historical facts.

"Obedience" perhaps suggests to a modern person *blind* obedience. Hempel in particular made much of the secret of the divine will and saw theonomy as a subtype of heteronomy, a system in which the human subject may not question but must simply submit, being in no way autonomous: "He has told you, O mortal, what is good."[1] (But see Birch's essay in this volume for a critique of such a heteronomous interpretation of Mic 6:6.) However, in his presentation of Hempel, Otto stresses that this can be exaggerated. According to Hempel, Otto notes, "die alttestamentliche Ethik sei nicht die Ethik der Unterwerfung unter eine blanke Gotteswillkür" ("Old Testament ethics is not an ethic of submission to pure divine whim" [19]). And this is because Yahweh's own action toward Israel is not arbitrary, but manifests the same moral character that God demands of them: "Spezifikum dieser Ethik sei eine Zusammenbindung von JHWHs mit der vom Menschen geforderten Sittlichkeit" ("Yahweh's own ethical behavior is bound together with that demanded of human beings" [19]). We shall return later to this equation of divine ethics with human ethics.

---

[1] Biblical translations follow the *NRSV*.

NATURAL LAW

The second ethical model that has concerned me I usually call, for convenience, "natural law." The term as I use it is meant to point us in a certain general direction, to draw attention to places in the Bible where ethics is not obedience to revealed or "positive" law, but rather an accommodation of human action to principles seen as inherent in the way things are. It is "a vague phrase which is meant to be suggestive rather than defining" (Barton 1978:60). It is *not* meant to imply, absurdly, that ancient Israelite culture knew about the later Western natural law tradition in all its refinements.

Provided we adopt a fairly loose definition, I do not think a "natural law" model for some biblical ethics should be ruled out in principle. Of course, it is still possible that it does not actually occur; but I sense that the climate of biblical study is a bit more favorable to such interpretations now than it was in the late 1970s. Factors here are the enhanced respect for wisdom literature, in which appeals to the natural order are most at home; the work of H. H. Schmid on "world order," presenting creation rather than *Heilsgeschichte* or covenant as the primary focal point of Hebrew Bible thought and theology; and the development of "green" concerns among biblical scholars, with an attendant interest in a "creation ethic" relevant to ecology (this third point is noted by Otto: 29–30).

One small example of this shift might be the currently increased interest in what Christian theology has traditionally called the "ceremonial" laws—laws about festivals, diet, rituals. Writers like Eichrodt and Hempel follow classical Christian interpretations of these as the very epitome of "theonomous" laws, just as, indeed, much Jewish tradition has also done. There are sayings in the rabbinic literature that make precisely the point that these laws do *not* make sense to any "natural" human understanding; they are given for the very purpose of reminding Israel that, in Eichrodt's words, the "divine will keeps its secret; in its secret hiddenness it remains impenetrable and does not yield itself to his creatures as the ground of being which is accessible to the human spirit" (1951:29). But a theology which centers more on creation and the natural order is likely to find laws about the relation of human beings to the animal world and to the cycles of the seasons far less opaque, and to trace them back to something which might, at least as an interim measure, be called a natural law ethic. Greenberg and Finkelstein have both pursued this from a Jewish perspective, and some impulses in the same direction may be found in the work of social anthropologists, primarily Mary Douglas.

Natural law may also be seen as an aspect of "natural theology," the belief that there can be knowledge of God not dependent on direct revelation. This is the subject of James Barr's most recent book, *Biblical Faith and Natural Theology*, which is hospitable to the idea that there is natural theology and also natural law within the biblical text. Without developing Barr's themes in detail, we may point to his extended discussion of Karl Barth, who is rather the villain of the piece in this work. Barr suggests that Barth was disturbed by the presence in the Bible of passages friendly to the idea of natural law—above all Romans 1 and Acts 17, but also some texts in the wisdom books and the prophets. He presents Barth as wriggling furiously to try to suppress all the "natural" elements in such places. He does, however, also point out that Barth had a theory that could accommodate them, implausible though it looks to anyone who is not already a convinced Barthian. Barth argued that the possibility of a natural knowledge of God and of ethical standards, such as these passages support, is here being made known to us *precisely in passages which are part of Scripture*, that is, part of revelation. It is God who tells us that we have a natural knowledge of the things of God, and to that extent such knowledge is natural only in a rather specialized and, indeed, paradoxical sense.

As one would expect, Barr clearly regards this somewhat contorted line of argument as an unworthy ruse. But whether that is so or not in this particular case, it does remind us how important are the methodological distinctions referred to earlier. We can distinguish *within the biblical text itself* between the plain sense of passages taken in isolation and their meaning as parts of a larger whole: chapters, books, sections of the canon, Scripture as a complete work. There may well be passages which originally reflected a "natural law" ethic but have now been subordinated to a model of obedience. The texts that were a problem for Barth may or may not be examples of this, but others certainly are. In Proverbs, ethical reflections originally based on observation and "natural" reasoning appear, in the final form of the text, as essentially divine revelation about the will of God. "Natural" law thus became a subdivision of "revealed" law. The canonizers of Scripture had succeeded in treating "natural law" elements in the materials they had inherited in a manner not unlike that of Barth. Thus it was with no sense of incongruity that the compilers of the Mishnah were able, in due course, to quote more often from Proverbs than from any other biblical book outside the Torah when they wanted to give divine sanction to the rulings they had made.

Finally, on the question of natural law, it is important to see that the term is not intended to imply an ethic which allows no place for God. There are indeed a few places in the Hebrew Bible where we can point to pure human convention as possibly the source of moral conduct. This is a possibility for the oracles against the nations in Amos 1-2 (see Barton,

1980), and it is certainly a plausible way of interpreting some wisdom sayings, for instance those that belong in manuals of etiquette. No one in ancient Israel is very likely to have thought that the advice to avoid bad table manners when your host can influence your career (e.g. Prov 23:1–3) was a divine injunction, not even when this idea was expressed in the imperative form we find in Ben Sira ("Be ashamed of leaning on your elbow at meals," Sir 41:19). But my own impression is that little genuinely conventional morality has survived in our texts. Otto (17–18) rightly argues that the more we study the redaction of the legal, wisdom, and prophetic books, the more we find that ethical norms, however "natural" in origin, have been "theologized." But—and this is my point—this is not necessarily the same as saying that they have been incorporated into an obedience model. Natural law can perfectly well be theological. It normally was so in the Western legal and ethical tradition until very recent times. Natural law and positive law, in classical theory, are two ways by which ethics flows from God: they are not to be opposed as respectively human and divine. But since this misconception is so common, it may well be that the term "natural law" is often misleading, and a fresh term might be useful.

IMITATION OF GOD

In my 1978 article I mentioned a third possible model for theological ethics in ancient Israel: the imitation of God. I had put this forward with little conviction, but thought it should at least be considered, mainly because Martin Buber had made so much of it. But subsequently I have begun to think that it is more common, and more important, than I then allowed. It is particularly visible in Deuteronomy: "The LORD your God is God of gods and Lord of lords, the great God, mighty and awesome, who is not partial and takes no bribe, who executes justice for the orphan and the widow, and loves the strangers, providing them food and clothing. You shall also love the stranger" (10:17–19); or, classically, "You shall be holy, for I the LORD your God am holy" (Lev 19:2). Although in one sense the desire to be "as God" is reprehensible according to Genesis 3, in another the task of human beings, and especially of Israelites, is to do as God does: to take God's character as the pattern of their character and God's deeds as the model for theirs. This is far less generally recognized as a basis for ethics in the Hebrew Bible than the corresponding ideal of the *imitatio Christi* is in the New Testament and in Christian tradition, but it is there all the same.

Otto (19) notes that Hempel already gave the imitation of God some prominence within his obedience-ethic. As we saw earlier, one reason why obedience to Yahweh is not to be seen as *blind* obedience is that Yahweh is in fact perceived as having a moral character. Yahweh is bound (perhaps voluntarily so) by at least some of the ethical constraints imposed on Israel. As the passage just quoted from Deuteronomy makes clear, the God who enjoins care for the needy cares for them also: Yahweh asks of human agents nothing that is not also self-imposed. "JHWH lege sich Regel und Richtschnur auf, wie er den Menschen an Regel und Richtschnur binde" ("Yahweh applies a rule and measure to himself, just as he binds human beings to a rule and measure" [19]). "Das Handeln Gottes mit dem Menschen kann Modell dafür sein, wie der Mensch mit dem Menschen handeln soll und darin ist dieses Zeugnis Kern einer alttestamentlichen Ethik" ("God's dealings with humans can be a model for the way humans should deal with each other; this testimony is the core of an Old Testament ethics" [20]). Otto himself thinks that this insight of Hempel's could be fruitful in the quest for *the* ethics of the Hebrew Bible, which he sees as the ultimate goal of study in this general area. Let me explore this possibility a little.

At the moment I am not sure how many concrete examples of imitation-ethics can really be found in the Hebrew Bible. But Otto has pointed to one central aspect of this way of thinking, namely its insistence that God is bound by moral laws just as human beings are, even though some of the things God does in the Bible show clearly that the parallelism is not complete. Many texts certainly attest the conviction that God does *not* act like a human agent. David said to Saul, "If it is the LORD who has stirred you up against me, may he accept an offering; but if it is mortals, may they be cursed before the LORD" (1 Sam 26:19). God may persecute David if God chooses, even through the agency of Saul; humans following their own volition may not. Yet in general there is an assumption that God acts according to moral standards that human beings also share. That is why God can be upbraided for failure to do so, as we see so often in the Psalms, in Job, and in Abraham's famous insistence (Genesis 18) that the Judge of all the earth should "do right"—that is, should do the kind of thing Abraham would think himself obliged to do in similar circumstances (cf. Rodd).

This sense of a community of moral perception between God and humanity, which seems inherent in the idea of imitating God, takes us well beyond the few texts which in so many words tell their readers to behave as God does. I think Otto may well be right to see in it a potentially unifying theme for much that the Hebrew Bible has to say about ethics (compare also the comments of Birch in this volume). In a way it can hold together both obedience and natural law models. Hempel proposed that we should follow Luther in seeing the divine commands in the Decalogue as really not arbitrary laws but rather an expression of natural law, spelling out how natural law is to be applied in practice (cf. Schmidt 1993:3-11). He suggested that the same could be said of the ethical message of the prophets, which similarly gives concrete expression to the basic relationships in which men and women need to live. Perhaps we may add to this the idea that the God who utters or underwrites these laws, these ethical principles, is somehow bound by them equally. Yahweh is a *good* God, in some sense which at least is not incompatible with what people in Israel would have meant by good, and whom therefore it made sense for them to try to imitate. This might be one of the many possible senses of being made "in the image of God": that Yahweh and humanity share a common ethical perception, so that God is not only the commander but also the paradigm of all moral conduct (see Biggar). Edmond Jacob was already making fruitful suggestions along these lines in 1960.

Perhaps the "imitation" model can gain some support if we ask our second "metaethical" question about biblical morality. Moral philosophers commonly distinguish deontological systems, the ethics of duty, from teleological systems, the ethics of goal. Applying such terms to the Hebrew Bible once again runs up against the pre-philosophical character of Israelite culture. Yet we may make some progress—and see that this is not just an exercise in anachronism—by noticing ways in which the biblical text seems on inspection to be rather different from its popular image. Intuitively we expect the Hebrew Bible to be primarily about obeying God, and the discovery of natural law and imitation models comes as a surprise. In the same way, we perhaps expect it to be heavily deontological, with Eichrodt's "unconditional ought," *das absolute Sollen*, greatly predominating (see Eichrodt 1967). (This, incidentally, is a hard concept to express in Biblical Hebrew!) But closer acquaintance with the biblical material shows that there is also a strongly teleological character to much of the moral teaching in the Hebrew Bible. Something like this is perhaps implied when we remind ourselves that *torah* is not exactly "law"—directives sent down from on high—but "teaching," advice on how to follow the path that will take the hearer or the reader to the goal God has in mind. The wisdom literature, similarly, is strongly teleological: "do not forget my teaching, but let your heart keep my commandments; for length of days and years of life and abundant welfare they will give you" (Prov 3:1-2). The possibility of moral conduct with no goal in view is, arguably, hardly envisaged before Job; at any rate it is clear that asking where a course of action would lead was normal in Hebrew culture. Laws, where one might most expect to find mere divine commands, are in fact richly provided with motive clauses, many of them oriented toward the future prosperity of the person who is being encouraged to obey the law.

Thus the moral life is envisaged, it seems, as a co-operative venture between God and people. Its commonest image is that of a path, leading to the place where it will converge with the highway trodden by God. And if the teleological character of ethics is clear for Israelites in general, it is even more apparent in the case of those special people who are singled out as having "walked with" God, as Genesis says of Enoch. Any comprehensive treatment of ethics in the Hebrew Bible would need to give some account of the idea of *vocation*, the singling out of people to be God's agents. Such a calling gives them special obligations, which we can certainly understand on an obedience model—hardly, perhaps, on any other model. But it also gives them a special way of life and an insight into the intentions and character of God, and empowers them to be in the place of God for the people at large. The mysteriously godlike character of those with such a vocation, as we see it, for example, in Moses, or Samuel, or other prophets, speaks of the possibility of the divine life and human life running in parallel; and this may be connected with the idea of the imitation of God. To imitate God in *this* sense is not the role of the ordinary person, but is a quite special vocation. Nevertheless, it implies an affinity between the divine and the human; it implies that the human is *capax dei*. And thus it suggests that the imitation of God may indeed lie near the heart of what the Hebrew Bible has to say about human morality.

This paper has presented various partial answers to the quasi-philosophical questions that can be put to the Hebrew Bible. The presentation has made no attempt at completeness, either in the material surveyed or in the questions asked. At best I hope to have suggested fruitful avenues for further investigation. Two methodological points, however, may be made on the basis of our discussion. Scholars inevitably differ over their detailed findings, but they also differ about which questions it is sensible to ask of a given corpus of texts. I have suggested that the study of Hebrew Bible ethics has sometimes suffered from an unwillingness on the part of scholars to contemplate "philosophical" questions at all, on the grounds that the people of ancient Israel simply were not interested in, or could not have understood, questions of such a kind. A case could undoubtedly be made in favor of such a belief, but it *needs* to be made: it should not be asserted as though it were obvious. Secondly, among those who accept that we can ask about the basis of ethics in the Hebrew Bible, some assume that the answer to the question is already known and indeed is obvious: ethics is obedience to God. Again, a case can be made for this, and indeed we have seen that it is undoubtedly true for many biblical texts. But the case is not self-evident. I hope to have convinced the reader that these are at least real questions, and that they can be tackled, even if not always answered, by empirical investigation of the texts. As in many areas of academic inquiry, nothing blocks the way to answering a question so effectively as the belief that the answer is already common knowledge.

WORKS CONSULTED

Barr, James
1993   *Biblical Faith and Natural Theology: The Gifford Lectures for 1991 Delivered in the University of Edinburgh*. Oxford: Clarendon.

Barton, John
1978   "Understanding Old Testament Ethics." *JSOT* 9:44-64.
1979   "Natural Law and Poetic Justice in the Old Testament." *JTS* n.s. 30:1-14.
1980   *Amos' Oracles against the Nations*. Cambridge: Cambridge University Press.

Biggar, Nigel J.
1993   *The Hastening That Waits: Karl Barth's Ethics*. Oxford: Oxford University Press.

Buber, Martin
1933   "Nachahmung Gottes." Pp. 68–83 in *Kampf um Israel: Reden und Schriften (1921–1932)*. Berlin: Schocken. English translation: "Imitatio Dei." Trans. by Greta Hort. Pp. 66–77 in *Israel and the World: Essays in a Time of Crisis*. New York: Schocken, 1948.

Douglas, Mary
1966   *Purity and Danger*. London: Routledge & Kegan Paul.

Eichrodt, Walter
1951   *Man in the Old Testament*. Trans. K. and R. Gregor Smith. SBT 4. London: SCM. German original, 1947.
1967   *Theology of the Old Testament*, vol. 2. Trans. J. A. Baker. Philadelphia: Westminster. German original, 5th ed., 1964.

Finkelstein, J. J.
1981   *The Ox that Gored*. Transactions of the American Philosophical Society 71/2. Philadelphia: The American Philosophical Society.

Greenberg, Moshe
1960   "Some Postulates of Biblical Criminal Law." Pp. 5-28 in *Yehezkel Kaufmann Jubilee Volume*. Ed. Menahem Haran. Jerusalem: Magnes. Reprint: Pp. 18–37 in *The Jewish Expression*. Ed. J. Goldin. New Haven and London: Yale University Press, 1976.

1986 "More Reflections on Biblical Criminal Law. Pp. 1–17 in *Studies in Bible*. Ed. Sara Japhet. ScrHier 31. Jerusalem: Magnes.

Hempel, Johannes
1938 *Das Ethos des Alten Testaments*. BZAW 67. Berlin: Alfred Töpelmann. 2d ed., 1964.

Jacob, Edmond
1960 "Les bases théologiques de l'éthique de l'Ancien Testament." VTSup 7:39-51.

Otto, Eckart
1991 "Forschungsgeschichte der Entwürfe einer Ethik im Alten Testament." *VF* 36/1:3-37.

Rodd, Cyril S.
1972 "Shall Not the Judge of All the Earth Do What is Just? (Gen. xviii.25)." *ExpTim* 83:137–39.

Schmid, Hans Heinrich
1968 *Gerechtigkeit als Weltordnung: Hintergrund und Geschichte des alttestamentlichen Gerechtigkeitsbegriffes*. BHT 40. Tübingen: J. C. B. Mohr (Paul Siebeck).
1973 "Schöpfung, Gerechtigkeit und Heil: 'Schöpfungstheologie' als Gesamthorizont biblischer Theologie." *ZTK* 70:1-19. English translation in abbreviated form: "Creation, Righteousness, and Salvation: 'Creation Theology' as the Broad Horizon of Biblical Theology." Pp. 102–17 in *Creation in the Old Testament*. Ed. Bernhard W. Anderson. IRT 6. Philadelphia: Fortress; London: SPCK, 1984.
1974 *Altorientalische Welt in der alttestamentlichen Theologie*. Zurich: Theologischer Verlag.

Schmidt, Werner H.
1991 "Zu diesem Heft." *VF* 36/1:1-2
1993 *Die Zehn Gebote im Rahmen alttestamentlicher Ethik*. Erträge der Forschung 281. Darmstadt: Wissenschaftliche Buchgesellschaft.

Smend, Rudolf
1982 "Ethik III: Altes Testament." *TRE* 10:423–35.

MORAL AGENCY, COMMUNITY, AND THE CHARACTER OF GOD IN THE HEBREW BIBLE

Bruce C. Birch
Wesley Theological Seminary

ABSTRACT

Recent renewed interest in conversations between biblical scholars and Christian ethicists raises interesting new possibilities for thinking about the role of the Hebrew Bible as a resource for Christian ethics in the life of contemporary communities of faith. This paper focuses on several areas where traditional Christian understandings of the ethics of the Hebrew Bible may be complemented by new areas of investigation: the nature of moral agency, the community as context, and the imitation of God as significant alongside the doing of God's revealed will. A brief treatment of some elements in the moral dynamics of Israelite law attempts to show how these factors affect our understanding of biblical material as moral resources.

From first page to last the Hebrew Bible assumes that all persons are moral agents. Who we are and how we act as individuals and as communities are considered by the Scriptures to be matters of moral accountability. The language of moral agency is currently being widely used in the field of Christian ethics (Birch and Rasmussen: 40–41; Bondi; Hauerwas 1983:38–44) to highlight the moral dimensions of our lives. This language includes both character and conduct, being and doing. Agency encompasses the way in which we act upon the world, and the way in which we incorporate the world's actions into our own story. "To be an agent means I am able to locate my action within an ongoing history and within a community of language users" (Hauerwas 1983:42).

The Hebrew Bible presumes to affect moral agency. The Hebrew canon is not just the fortunately preserved literature of interesting ancient communities. It seeks to form communities of moral agency within which individuals are brought into relationship with the character, activity, and will of God and can then act in particular ways, both individually and corporately, as moral agents in the world. Further, the formation and preservation of this literature as canon imply that its intention is to shape ethical character and conduct in relationship to God and as moral agents in the world for succeeding generations, including our own.

Biblical ethics in the Hebrew Bible cannot be separated from biblical theology. There is no separate, autonomous ethic in the Hebrew Bible that can be simply extracted from explicitly "ethical texts" such as the Decalogue, although there have been many traditional treatments that attempted to do so. Ethics in the Hebrew Bible is inextricably bound up with the entire theological witness of the biblical story to a god who becomes known in relation to the people Israel (see Childs, 1993:676). Although diverse in the forms of its witness, the entire Hebrew canon is concerned with theological/ethical testimony to the character, activity, and will of God on the one hand, and the call to response by God's people on the other hand (see Birch 1991:37–41).

It is gratifying that recent years have shown considerable renewal of scholarly interest in the ethics of ancient Israel and the use of the Hebrew Bible as a resource for Christian ethics (Birch 1991; Barton 1978, 1982; Davies; Wilson; Knight 1985, 1989; Hanson; Kaiser; Wright; Matties; Goldingay: 38–65; Childs 1993). Given the unity of theological and ethical concern in the Hebrew Bible it is, however, puzzling that this area should have suffered such neglect through the middle decades of this century (Hempel and Eichrodt were notable exceptions, but see the critique of Barton 1978:44–51).

Although this paper is concerned to make use of work that, more strictly speaking, describes the ethics of ancient Israel in the literature of particular periods or social groupings, it is primarily focused on the dynamics involved in appropriation of the Hebrew canon as a moral resource for confessing communities of faith, both ancient and modern. In particular, this paper seeks to discuss two areas of recent interest in the field of Christian ethics and the way in which that work illuminates our understanding of the Hebrew Bible as a resource for Christian ethics. These two areas are: 1) the role of community in the moral life, and 2) the character of God as focus for the moral life. A brief treatment of some elements in the moral dynamics of Israelite law will attempt to show how these factors affect our understanding of biblical material as moral resources.

COMMUNITY, CHARACTER, AND CANON

Recent work in Christian ethics has shown a significant shift of interest toward the role of the community as the necessary context for the Christian moral life (Birch and Rasmussen; Hauerwas 1981, 1983; Verhey; Fowl and Jones; Rasmussen). This in turn has fostered particular attention to the role of Scripture in the formation of community and to the locus of biblical authority in the community when the Bible is used as Scripture and not just as ancient text. Lisa Cahill, in a helpful survey, identifies this shift of focus in Christian ethics as a "turn to the community" (386) and describes it as a development in ethics and biblical studies (384):

> First, the concerns of *ethicists* have moved from trying to assimilate biblical morality to the model of deductive argumentation to an interest in Scripture as foundational to the formation of communities of moral agency. Second, *biblical* scholars have become more explicitly aware of the social repercussions of discipleship as portrayed in the New Testament, and also more interested in drawing social and moral analogies between the biblical world and our own.

Cahill's observation holds true for work in Hebrew Bible as well as for New Testament, and studies of community in Christian ethics are of central importance for those interested in biblical ethics. It is the community which serves as the necessary context for our understanding of the biblical text and how it plays its role as Scripture and source of moral authority. We offer several observations in this area.

1. *The text is a product of community.* One of the fortunate developments in recent scholarship on the Hebrew Bible has been the full recognition that every text originates out of a social context. Ethical insight cannot be abstracted from the text as timeless truths or principles, nor attributed to the genius of individual witnesses in isolation from community. "There is no private morality which is not also in its varying commitments, a public morality. The Old Testament knows nothing of the notion that morality could be a purely private and individual affair" (Clements: 13).[1]

To form criticism's early concern with *Sitz im Leben* has now been added scholarly work employing such tools as sociology, social history, cultural anthropology, and socioeconomics. This work has begun to add significantly to our understanding of particular social contexts that gave rise to the voices of the biblical witness and gave impetus to the preservation of those witnesses beyond the social context in which they originated (e.g., Gottwald 1979, 1985; Smith; Smend).

For those interested in the ethics of ancient Israel and of the Hebrew Bible, this affords new possibilities in the area of descriptive biblical ethics. A more complex and less artificial phenomenological description of Israel's social behavior and moral attitudes is emerging. Barton (1978) called attention to "the *synchronic* existence of different social groups in Israel, each potentially capable of holding to a somewhat different set of moral norms" (52) and called for studies that document the way in which

---

[1] For Clements this calls for—and he begins—a full investigation of the moral role of the state as the central administrator of public law, which is the foundation of community moral structure.

particular moral witnesses arise from particular social subgroups in particular time periods, whether "popular morality," prophetic text, or sapiential teaching. To be avoided are the broad, synthetic or developmental attempts to draw theological generalizations concerning all Israel with regard to ethical norms from the Hebrew Bible (Hempel, Eichrodt) or attempts to abstract universal principles expressive of God's will for the moral life of Israel and subsequent generations from the text with little regard for the complex social context out of which the biblical witnesses arose (Kaiser).

More concrete investigations of the particular morality reflected in specific texts (e.g., McKeating) will likely enrich our understanding of the social contextuality of every text. This approach alone, however, "will never produce a normative ethic for the Christian faith, but will only confirm the initial assumptions of cultural and theological relativism" (Childs 1993:676). There are additional dimensions of community relative to the biblical text that will make it available as a resource for normative Christian ethics.

2. *The biblical text is directed to the formation of community.* Throughout the text of the Hebrew Bible the witness of the text is directed to the formation of a community in relation to God that is not limited to Israel or any subgroup of Israel at any given historical time or place. "The contribution of the Bible to ethics is at the level of community-formation, not primarily at that of rules or principles" (Cahill: 395).

It is the work of Stanley Hauerwas (1975, 1981, 1983) that has most influenced the discussion at this point. He bases his understanding of Christian ethics on the concept of the faith community as shaped by the biblical story. It is thus narrative that receives priority as the formative influence on the community and the source of the community's identity. "The narrative renders a community capable of ordering its existence appropriate to such stories" (Childs 1993:664).

We would agree that in the Hebrew Bible narrative is the shaping influence both for Israel at various periods reflected within the canon, for the early church that saw the story of Jesus as a continuation of Israel's story, and for subsequent generations of the church that accepted the Hebrew canon as Scripture, the Old Testament, alongside the New Testament. Of course, the Hebrew Bible contains more than narrative, but it is the narrative framework that still serves to relate the community of faith meaningfully to other types of biblical material. Law, prophecy, and apocalyptic literature all assume a community formed by its memory and reinterpretation of a story which told of God's promise to their ancestors, deliverance out of bondage in Egypt, revelation of the law at Sinai, covenant with the people, Davidic kingship and temple on Zion, and judgment and redemption through the crisis of exile. The story even came to understand the God of Israel as one with the God who created the world and who, when that world became broken, desired the redemption of all creation and peoples. The story is added to and developed but is assumed as the identity-forming, narrative-shaped reality of the community's life. Even wisdom literature, the least reflective of Israel's story, uses Israel's name for God, finds contact with Israel's story in the role of God as Creator, and finally relates wisdom to Torah in Sirach.

Although this story is formative of theological and ethical community, Childs (1993:665) is correct in his criticism of Hauerwas that story as a category does not fully capture the nature of biblical narrative in its function of shaping community. The community is not formed by the text or the story *per se* but by the belief that the narrative witnesses to the reality of the community-shaping encounter with God in historical time and space. Narrative mediates this encounter to new generations of the community but does not create it.

Hauerwas argues that narrative is the most suitable form for the community to remember and reinterpret its own past. In so doing, a community of character is formed. Character refers to the form our moral agency takes through our beliefs and intentions as those are shaped by the remembering and reinterpreting of the biblical story (Hauerwas 1983:39). Israel's character is significantly formed by its remembering and reinterpreting of God's previous actions on its behalf. This is not without its tensions, and there is no harmonious, single, official version of Israel's remembered story. In fact, the text shows the importance of such character formation in relation to the narrative tradition as a dynamic process. The centrally important canonical text of Exodus 1–15 gives evidence not only of originating memory but of community reclaiming and reinterpreting of that memory. The account of Passover (Exodus 12–13) is shaped by liturgical forms of remembering this crucial moment in the story of God's action on Israel's behalf. The community's liturgical way of remembering becomes itself incorporated into the story. Exodus 6 gives witness to the importance of the identity and person of Yahweh ("I am Yahweh") for a generation in Babylonian exile, and that emphasis is now significantly incorporated into a priestly, exilic remembering and reinterpreting of the exodus drama (see Zimmerli).

3. *The biblical text is made available for its task of community formation by the canon.* The canon itself is testimony to the intention of the biblical text as we now have it to transcend its originating social contexts and undertake the dynamic task of community formation through succeeding generations. There has been extensive discussion on the role of the canon in biblical theology and ethics, and we have written in some detail

elsewhere on the moral function of the canon in relating Scripture to Christian ethics (Birch and Rasmussen: 171–81; Birch 1991:43–50). Here we will make only a few additional observations.

The "turn toward community" in Christian ethics heightens the need for attention to the role of the canon in appropriating Scripture for Christian ethics. It seems obvious that recognition of the fact that the literature of Israel is preserved and transmitted in a canonical collection serves to guard against abstracting the text of the Hebrew Bible from the community of faith that preserves, transmits, and values it.

The arrangement of the Hebrew canon does not seem related to realities in the historical life of Israel so much as to the need to make Israel's story, as shaped by the canon, available to future generations. This means that the theological and ethical function of the canon for the church may be enriched by historical and sociological insight into the originating contexts of particular texts, but that function does not depend on detailed descriptive knowledge of the ethics of ancient Israel. Such knowledge, due to the nature of the textual resources, will only be partially available in any case (see Barton 1978:44).

We would agree with Childs (1993:676) "that the task of Old Testament ethics is to acknowledge this canonical corpus as a theological construct which is only indirectly related to an historical and empirical Israel, and to pursue rigorously the theological witness of this biblical witness as the privileged sacred writings of Israel, the people of God."

In the Hebrew canonical corpus, what was experienced as vertical encounter with God in crucial historical moments (e.g., deliverance and commandment) is horizontally redirected (see Childs 1993:677–78; Goldingay: 52–53) through texts to subsequent generations of the community, e.g. "Remember you were a slave . . ."[2] (Deut 15:15); "Not with our ancestors . . . but with us, who are all of us here alive today" (Deut 5:3). This horizontal redirection may create new juxtapositions (the creation stories at the start of Genesis), blur or redirect original historical contexts (Amos), or apply specific witnesses to new contexts (the redirecting of Isaiah's eighth-century witness to new contexts by the addition of chaps. 40–55 and 56–66).

The Hebrew canon only functions as a moral resource to the degree that it is reflected upon and appropriated by contemporary communities of faith. Nowhere does it give rise to autonomous rules and principles, or independent systems of philosophical ethics directed to individual well-being. The canon functions as moral resource only when contemporary communities of faith identify themselves in some authoritative way with the story of Israel as made available in the Hebrew canon.

The Character of God

At several points in our discussion we have already suggested that the relationship between text and community cannot be explained solely in sociological terms. The relationship is theological, and the moral authority of the text is a function of the text as the story of God and God's community, not a function of the community in and of itself.

1. *The focus of the Hebrew canon and of the community formed by the witness of its texts is at every level in response to the reality of God.* Israel as the community of faith is formed in response to its understanding of what God has already done, and who God has already revealed the divine self to be. The canon makes witness to this divine activity and self-disclosure available for the ongoing shaping of faith community. Israel has already "seen what I did to the Egyptians, and how I bore you on eagle's wings and brought you to myself." Now arises the possibility of a new identity as God's "treasured possession out of all the peoples." Now Israel can be shaped in response through covenant to become "a priestly kingdom" and "a holy nation" (Exod 19:4–6).

For the Hebrew Bible the community receives its identity from divine initiative. The shaping of community character is not a human achievement but a divinely initiated gift that calls forth response. Moral character is not the autonomous possession of the community but an ongoing response in relationship to the reality of God. "Rather than viewing ethics as a cultural phenomenon, the Old Testament judges human behavior consistently in relation to God and his creation. Human conduct is therefore evaluated in terms of response, and measured by its conformity to the divine will which is continually making itself known in the world" (Childs 1993:684).

The language of familial relationship used of God's initiative and Israel's response makes clear the dynamic quality of the moral relationship between Israel and God. Israel understands none of its life as self-initiated. Israel is God's "firstborn son," and the appeal to Pharaoh is to "let my son go" (Exod 4:22–23). "When Israel was a child, I loved him, and out of Egypt I called my son" (Hos 11:1).

2. *The knowledge of God is prior to and encompasses the knowledge of God's will.* Traditional uses of the Hebrew Bible in Christian ethics focused on the revealing of the divine will as the basis for ethics. This meant that moral norms were primarily located in commandment, law, or explicit

moral admonitions as in the prophets. At its worst the caricature of ethics in the Hebrew Bible as law set up false contrasts with New Testament ethics as gospel or led to reductionist treatments limited to certain "ethical" texts (e.g., the Decalogue) abstracted from the larger story of Israel's relationship to God. Even more sophisticated and helpful recent treatments of moral resources from the Hebrew Bible have tended to focus on commandment as the primary basis for ethics and therefore to characterize ethics in preexilic Israel as almost entirely deontological (Ogletree).

Although obedience to God's revealed will and the role of commandment are important in the Hebrew canon, a singular focus here separates moral demand from the person of God. In the Hebrew Bible ethics arises not as a matter of obedience to an external model or code of morality but as a result of entering into the life of God. A number of scholars have argued a similar point in the recent literature, and their language paints a much richer picture of the basis for ethics in the Hebrew Bible than previous approaches had accomplished. Barton (1982:128) suggests that "the purpose of the Old Testament is not primarily to give information about morality ... but to provide materials which, when pondered and absorbed into the mind, will suggest the pattern or shape of a way of life lived in the presence of God." He suggests that "ethics is not so much a system of obligations as a way of communion with God" (130). Brueggemann (1982:xv) observes, "Yahweh has no other disclosure to make other than his own person." Childs (1993:677) argues that "divine command rests, of course, on a prior understanding of God ... who continues to make his will known for his people. Nor can this will ever be separated from the person of God."

In the terms of recent discussions in Christian ethics, we are being called to attend more carefully to the character of God alongside the conduct of God ("mighty acts," "commandment"). Who God is becomes important alongside what God does (see Hauerwas 1983:33). The activity and will of God are expressive of the character of God, and knowing God becomes as important as being acted upon or commanded by God (e.g., Jer 22:16). The text of the Hebrew Bible invites us to enter into the life of God as the supreme moral agent in the biblical story. The divine reality over against which community is formed becomes known in character and conduct.

Such attention to the moral significance of the character of God can significantly enrich our understanding of key moments in the biblical story. For example, the theological and ethical significance of the exodus is usually discussed in terms of what God has *done*. But God's act of deliverance is preceded by two remarkable accounts of self-disclosure in

Exodus 3–4 and 6 which make clear that what God does in deliverance is expressive of crucial qualities of God's character which both Israel and Pharaoh (although in different ways) will come to "know" (notice the importance of the knowledge of God throughout the plague stories). Drawing upon the foundational work of Zimmerli, Walter Brueggemann has recently commented on Exodus 6: "As much as any text in the Exodus tradition, this one invites reflection upon the character of the God of Israel" (1994:736). The constant affirmation of the divine name in this chapter—"I am Yahweh"—takes the supreme risk of particularity, and the connection in this chapter between that particularity of identity and the suffering of Israel in bondage (and also in exile since this text is probably an exilic reclaiming of exodus hope) suggests that deliverance is not just an act but an expression of fundamental divine character. "God's very character is to make relationships, bring emancipation, and establish covenants. . . . Israel is now always Yahweh-connected, but . . . Yahweh is always Israel-connected, and will not again be peopleless. . . . The God of Israel is defined by that relatedness" (737).

3. *Moral norms arise as significantly out of imitation of God's character and actions* (imitatio dei) *as out of doing God's will.* The importance of the imitation of God as a basis for ethics in the Hebrew Bible was seen early by scholars such as Buber and Rowley. More recently, a number of important works on biblical ethics have given new attention to this important theme (Barton 1978, 1982; Nasuti; Hanson; Kaiser; Birch 1991).

The life of God models the moral life. God as experienced by Israel and mediated to subsequent generations through the canon is to be imitated as moral agent, in both character and conduct. "A part of Israel's present identity is defined by the need to imitate God" (Nasuti: 17).

This *imitatio dei* can be in reference to particular divine actions. As Barton notes, "for the Old Testament as we have it ethics is a matter of imitating the pattern of God's own actions, in salvation and in creation, because these spring from a pattern which always exists in his own mind and by which he governs the world with justice and mercy" (1982:130). For example, the legal codes urge Israel to act the way God has already acted toward them. "[God] executes justice for the orphan and the widow, and . . . loves the strangers, providing them with food and clothing. You shall also love the stranger, for you were strangers in the land of Egypt" (Deut 10:18–19). The dramatic climax of Micah's oracle in 6:1–8—"He has shown you, O mortal, what is good . . ."—does not seem to imply commandment alone, but a divine demonstration of justice, kindness, and humility.

This already suggests that we imitate God not only in actions of significant ethical importance but in qualities of life that are ethically significant. "You shall be holy, for I the Lord your God am holy" (Lev 19:2). Israel is asked to love God (Deut 6:4) and the neighbor (Lev 19:18) because God has already loved them (Deut 7:8). The prophets in urging justice, righteousness, and compassion as attributes of the moral life also attribute such qualities of character to God (Jer 22:16). As God's actions reflect and flow out of these qualities of character, so too should Israel's (and ours). "Yahweh asks of men that they shall reflect His own character, so far as it can be reflected within the limitations of human life.... When the prophets denounced harshness and oppression and called for compassion for the unfortunate they were calling men to reflect the character which was uniquely expressed in God's deliverance of His people" (Rowley: 25).

Barton (1978, 1982) has argued that alongside the imitation of God and obedience to God's will there is a third basis for ethics attested in the Hebrew Bible which is akin to "natural law." He describes it as "conformity to the patterns and orders of the world" (1982:121), and although God created the world this moral order operates as a given framework into which one can place the moral life without reference to revealed morality (seen primarily in wisdom, e.g., Job 31:13–15). The point is well taken that especially in the wisdom literature we see a rather different mode of ethical thought. Yet, we would observe that in the present arrangement of the canon we are asked to reflect upon God's creation of an orderly universe (Genesis 1) as the first witness of the canon. We are further asked to see the human role in that created order in terms of *imago dei*. Our role in creation is to be like God, to imitate God in sovereign responsibility for a "good" creation. One wonders if reading of divine order in wisdom texts does not presuppose that Writings have already been preceded by Law and Prophets in the process of canon formation.

There are, of course, limits to the community's imitation of God (see Patrick 1981). We cannot duplicate God's deeds of sovereign power; we cannot perfectly embody the moral attributes toward which we strive.

In spite of this recent helpful work on the imitation of God as a basis for biblical ethics, not much of these considerations is yet reflected in the work of Christian ethicists or in the church's understanding of biblical ethics. An exception to this is the work of Stanley Hauerwas and some who have been influenced by his work (Bondi; Fowl and Jones). "Therefore the task for Israel, indeed the very thing that makes Israel Israel, is to walk in the way of the Lord, that is, to imitate God.... To love God meant to learn to love as God loved and loves" (Hauerwas 1983:77–78; see Birch 1992). Hauerwas has stressed that character formation requires emulation as a necessary part of its dynamic. "We learn what the moral life entails by imitating another" (1981:131). In moral development this process might focus on parents, friends, leaders, communities, or even the mediated example of persons in novels or biographies. For the Christian community we must attend to and follow Jesus. Here a difference between the two Testaments becomes clear. In the New Testament, imitation of Jesus and, to some extent, of the apostles gives us human models of the moral life. Because of the incarnation, imitation of Jesus as moral model includes imitation of God as revealed in Christ. In the Hebrew Bible there are no human models in this manner. At every point the role of emulation in the development of the moral life is focused on God. We might learn from, identify with, or react to various characters or the community of Israel at various points, but it is God who models the moral life in the quality of the divine life. It is not Israel we are to imitate, although often we do. It is God.

THE MORAL DYNAMICS OF ISRAELITE LAW

In light of our discussion of community and the character of God in relation to the ethics of the Hebrew Bible, we might turn to a specific concrete area of interpretive interest in biblical ethics. How might our discussion above bring new perspective to our understanding of the moral authority of Israelite law?[3]

Law and Community

Israelite law is handed on to us in a narrative setting, and there is increasing attention to the importance of this narrative context in the interpretation of Israel's law (Jackson). All the legal material in Exodus and Leviticus appears now in the context of Israel's experience in the encampment and covenant-making at Sinai. This is interpretively important in spite of the fact that much of this material originated historically at a much later time. It has become important in the canonical arrangement that these laws be read through the norm of the Sinai covenant. Even the laws themselves often include a narrative reference to Israel's experience or tradition (e.g., the sabbath commandment reference either to creation, Exod 20:8–11, or to the exodus, Deut 5:12–15). The narrative context makes clear that for Israel all law receives its authority

---

[3] This discussion is based on and develops further the material that originally appeared in Bruce C. Birch, *Let Justice Roll Down: The Old Testament, Ethics, and Christian Life*, 1991:164–68. ©1991 Bruce C. Birch. Used by permission of Westminster/John Knox Press (7/93).

from the belief that it has been divinely revealed as a part of the solemn covenant established by God with Israel and agreed to by Israel at Sinai.

Legal codes invariably reflect and derive some measure of their authority from the communities out of which they come. Israel's law codes are no exception. The legal materials reflect an understanding of Israel as a community that was initiated by the saving activity of God and that continued in ongoing covenant relationship with God.

With such a dynamic understanding of community, it would be odd if the law codes were regarded as static, fixed, authoritative codes. There is ample evidence that the authority of Israel's law was not regarded in this way. The *Shemaʿ* (Deut 6:4) is already treated in the text as a summary of the law in terms of loving God, and it is this central quality of relationship to God to which the law points and which is to be passed on to future generations.

> The ability of Deuteronomy to summarize the Law in terms of loving God with heart, soul and mind is a major check against all forms of legalism. According to Deuteronomy, the whole Mosaic law testifies to the living will of God whose eternal purpose for the life of his people provides the only grounds for life and salvation. (Childs 1985:56)

Recent studies of biblical law suggest that the laws are not considered the expression of ideals or timeless truths which are then enforced to define the community. Community is already formed in relation to Yahweh, and the laws are for guidance and instruction in apprehending and living out the implications of such a community.

> For the period during which the legal tradition was in formation, the law of God was an unwritten Law. It was the sense of justice and right shared by the legal community and sharpened by lawgivers and judges. . . . The precepts and judgments of the codes were not prescriptions with statutory force but testimony to God's just and righteous will. . . . The lawbooks were intended not for judicial application but for instruction in the values, principles, concepts, and procedures of the unwritten divine Law. (Patrick 1985:189–90, 198)

In a sense, the law codes in their narrative setting are themselves witnesses to the journey of the community Israel, constantly discovering God's will for itself in an ongoing relationship. This is a very different notion of authority for the law than that which sees the law as an authoritative end in itself.[4]

---

[4] Hauerwas (1983:119), writing on the formation of character in community, notes: "For the telos in fact is a narrative, and the good is not so much a clearly defined 'end' as it is a sense of the journey on which that community finds itself."

Law and Moral Identity

It has been customary to think of Israel's laws as specifying actions (frequently moral actions), but Israelite laws often specify, even advocate, a particular identity for the reader (Nasuti: 12). Their function is not just in the shaping of community conduct, but in the formation and maintenance of a particular community character (see Hauerwas: 77f.).

The sojourner formula and the slave formula serve as examples of the function of the law to specify identity for the reader (Nasuti: 12–14). The sojourner formula ("For you were sojourners [*NRSV*: 'resident aliens'] in the land of Egypt," Exod 22:20 [Engl. 22:21]; 23:9; Lev 19:34; Deut 10:19; 23:7) appears in motive clauses (Gemser; Sonsino) within individual provisions of the law. As a motive for receiving the law authoritatively the reader is reminded of an identity with a people who themselves were once sojourners. The slave formula ("Remember that you were a slave in the land of Egypt," Deut 5:15; 15:15; 16:12; 24:18, 22) appears primarily as a separate and distinct command. There are various other references in the laws which serve to remind the Israelite reader of an identity. For example, in a law specifying the use of unleavened bread in the cultic feast of Passover the identity statement is made: "because you came out of the land of Egypt in great haste" (Deut 16:3). All these identity statements serve not simply to seek compliance with laws on slaves or sojourners or Passover, but to establish and perpetuate a community of memory (Birch, 1988a).

This role of the law in identity formation is especially evident in the credo statement of Deut 26:5–10, to be recited at the offering of firstfruits. It begins with memory in the third person regarding the ancestor of the promise: "A wandering Aramean was my ancestor; he went down into Egypt"; but with the beginning of the exodus recital the language shifts to the first person: "When the Egyptians treated us harshly . . ., we cried to the Lord. . . . The Lord brought us out of Egypt. . . . Now I bring the first of the fruit of the ground." Clearly the commandment for this cultic recital serves to establish an identity between the bringer of the offering and the faith memory of Israel brought to birth in God's deliverance.

In addition to identity with those who were former slaves and sojourners, the intended Israelite reader of the laws is asked to identify with and imitate God who acted with justice and compassion toward them when they were slaves: "For the Lord your God is God of gods . . . who executes justice for the orphan and the widow, and who loves the strangers, providing them food and clothing. You shall also love the stranger, for you were strangers in the land of Egypt" (Deut 10:17–19). Exod 20:8–11 calls for Israel to rest on the sabbath because God rested on the seventh day of creation. These are commands to act as God has acted, an *imitatio dei* (Nasuti: 16–18; Hanson: 44). The imitation of God extends in the law codes beyond actions to qualities of character which God models for Israel to emulate. "You shall be holy, for I the Lord your God am holy" (Lev 19:2).

Thus, the laws function not simply to specify actions appropriate to the covenant relation but to establish and preserve an identity with Israel's memory of themselves as delivered slaves, and an identification with (imitation of) God in certain specified ways (identifying with the oppressed, resting on the Sabbath, embodying holiness). The need to urge this specificity of identity may itself imply that the actual reader whom the law codes have in mind is someone in the land, possibly someone holding slaves and in a position to oppress the vulnerable. The need to establish an identity for such people is as morally urgent as the specification of particular actions. In light of the identity-shaping function of the law, the role of the law in formation of community, and the wider significance of relationship to the covenant, it would seem we should avoid characterizing Israelite ethics prior to the exile as primarily deontological in character (contra Ogletree: 47–48).

Law and Divine Will

It is important to stress that the covenant relationship and the law as an expression of that relationship are presented in the Hebrew Bible as the revealed will of God. The laws of the Pentateuch cannot be reduced to sociological evidence for the structures of ancient Israel. They are also evidence for the theological priority given in that community to the revelation of God's will as a central moral focus. "To know God is to know his will. . . . Israel does not first know God and then later discover what God wants. Knowledge of his person and will are identical, and both are grounded in his self-revelation" (Childs 1985:51). Thus, the law cannot be fully understood if it is wrenched out of its context in theophany at Sinai.

For those who claim the Hebrew Bible as Christian Scripture and seek resources there for the theological and ethical reflection of the church, the biblical community's own claim that its life has been initiated by the revelatory activity of God is of central importance. This biblical claim has, however, been subjected to modification in some recent sociological approaches to the Hebrew Bible (e.g., Gottwald 1979, 1985).

For many who have taken this cultural-materialist approach, religion is as much the symbolic expression of underlying social realities as it is the product of divine revelation. These social realities can be recovered to a certain degree using social-scientific methods, and a sociohistorical account of Israel's traditions can be written. The danger is that this approach can reduce theology (ideology) to a secondary symbolic expression intended to support prevailing social values or institutions, and give too little credence to the biblical community's own testimony to the priority of divine revelatory experience. This would reduce the theological dimension of the text to realities no different from the realities that stand behind other ancient religions (see Childs, 1985:25). For Christian ethics this would leave little reason to look to the Bible for moral resources in any way distinguishable from the broad resources of human history.

For our discussion of covenant and law, we must take seriously the community's own claim that something new has altered the course of their existence, and that this new reality, God, has shaped their lives and community in ways they could not have shaped themselves. This does not, however, take place in a vacuum. Covenant and law, as these concepts develop in Israel, reflect a variety of social contexts that must be described and assessed in understanding the vocabulary and institutions that give expression to Israel's perceived relationship to God (Gottwald, 1992:87–88). The laws of Israel are both influenced by many socio-cultural factors (see Clements: 12) and at the same time constantly bear testimony to a sense of the transcendent reality of God as a formative influence in the very heart of Israel's social structures. It is our awareness of this testimony to God's self-revealing activity that helps create openness to such transforming realities beyond the sum of social forces in our own world.

* * *

The current stage of renewed conversation between biblical scholarship and Christian ethics is still relatively limited although richly promising. These reflections on moral agency, community, and the character of God are offered in the hope of stimulating further and wider reflection across these disciplinary lines.

WORKS CONSULTED

Barton, John
    1978   "Understanding Old Testament Ethics." *JSOT* 9:44–64.
    1982   "Approaches to Ethics in the Old Testament." Pp. 113–30 in *Beginning Old Testament Study*. Ed. John Rogerson. London: SPCK; Philadelphia: Westminster.

Birch, Bruce C.
1988a "Memory in Congregational Life." Pp. 20–47 in *Congregations: Their Power to Form and Transform*. Ed. C. Ellis Nelson. Atlanta: John Knox.
1988b "Old Testament Narrative and Moral Address." Pp. 62–74 in *Canon, Theology, and Old Testament Interpretation: Essays in Honor of Brevard S. Childs*. Ed. Gene M. Tucker, David L. Petersen, and Robert R. Wilson. Philadelphia: Fortress.
1991 *Let Justice Roll Down: The Old Testament, Ethics, and Christian Life*. Louisville: Westminster/John Knox.
1992 *To Love As We Are Loved: The Bible and Relationships*. Nashville: Abingdon.

Birch, Bruce C., and Larry L. Rasmussen
1989 *Bible and Ethics in the Christian Life*, revised and expanded edition. Minneapolis: Augsburg.

Bondi, Richard
1984 "The Elements of Character." *JRE* 12:201–18.

Brueggemann, Walter
1982 "Introduction." Pp. ix–xvii in Walther Zimmerli, *I Am Yahweh*. Atlanta: John Knox.
1994 "The Book of Exodus: Introduction, Commentary, and Reflections." Pp. 677–981 in *The New Interpreter's Bible*, vol. 1. Nashville: Abingdon.

Buber, Martin
1948 "Imitatio Dei." Trans. by Greta Hort. Pp. 66–77 in *Israel and the World: Essays in a Time of Crisis*. New York: Schocken. German original, 1933.

Cahill, Lisa Sowle
1990 "The New Testament and Ethics: Communities of Social Change." *Int* 44:383–95.

Childs, Brevard S.
1985 *Old Testament Theology in a Canonical Context*. Philadelphia: Fortress; London: SCM.
1993 *Biblical Theology of the Old and New Testaments: Theological Reflection on the Christian Bible*. Minneapolis: Fortress.

Clements, Ronald E.
1992 *Loving One's Neighbour: Old Testament Ethics in Context*. London: University of London Press.

Davies, Eryl W.
1981 *Prophecy and Ethics: Isaiah and the Ethical Traditions of Israel*. JSOTSup 16. Sheffield: JSOT.

Eichrodt, Walther
1967 "The Effect of Piety on Conduct (Old Testament Morality)." Pp. 316–79 in *Theology of the Old Testament*, vol. 2. OTL. Philadelphia: Westminster. German original, 5th ed., 1964.

Fowl, Stephen E., and L. Gregory Jones
  1991 *Reading in Communion: Scripture and Ethics in Christian Life.* Grand Rapids: Eerdmans.

Gemser, Berend
  1953 "The Importance of the Motive Clause in Old Testament Law." VTSup 1:50–66. Leiden: E. J. Brill.

Goldingay, John
  1990 *Approaches to Old Testament Interpretation.* Rev. ed. Downers Grove: InterVarsity; Leicester: Apollos.

Gottwald, Norman K.
  1979 *The Tribes of Yahweh: A Sociology of the Religion of Liberated Israel, 1250–1050 BCE.* Maryknoll: Orbis.
  1985 *The Hebrew Bible: A Socio-Literary Introduction.* Philadelphia: Fortress.
  1992 "Sociology (Ancient Israel)." ABD 6:79–89. New York: Doubleday.

Hanson, Paul D.
  1986 *The People Called: The Growth of Community in the Bible.* San Francisco: Harper & Row.

Hauerwas, Stanley
  1975 *Character and the Christian Life.* San Antonio: Trinity University Press.
  1981 *A Community of Character: Toward a Constructive Christian Social Ethic.* Notre Dame: University of Notre Dame Press.
  1983 *The Peaceable Kingdom: A Primer in Christian Ethics.* Notre Dame: University of Notre Dame Press.

Hempel, Johannes
  1938 *Das Ethos des Alten Testaments.* BZAW 67. Berlin: Alfred Töpelmann. 2d ed., 1964.

Jackson, Bernard S.
  1985 "Law." Pp. 548–51 in *Harper's Bible Dictionary.* Ed. Paul J. Achtemeier. San Francisco: Harper & Row.

Kaiser, Walter C., Jr.
  1983 *Toward Old Testament Ethics.* Grand Rapids: Academie Books, Zondervan.

Kelsey, David H.
  1975 *The Uses of Scripture in Recent Theology.* Philadelphia: Fortress.

Knight, Douglas A.
  1985 "Moral Values and Literary Traditions: The Case of the Succession Narrative (2 Samuel 9–20; 1 Kings 1–2)." *Semeia* 34:7–23.
  1989 "The Ethics of Human Life in the Hebrew Bible." Pp. 65–88 in *Justice and the Holy: Essays in Honor of Walter Harrelson.* Ed. Douglas A. Knight and Peter J. Paris. Atlanta: Scholars.

McKeating, Henry
- 1979 "Sanctions against Adultery in Ancient Israelite Society, with Some Reflections on Methodology in the Study of Old Testament Ethics." *JSOT* 11:57-72.

Matties, Gordon H.
- 1990 *Ezekiel 18 and the Rhetoric of Moral Discourse.* SBLDS 126. Atlanta: Scholars.

Nasuti, Harry P.
- 1986 "Identity, Identification, and Imitation: The Narrative Hermeneutics of Biblical Law." *Journal of Law and Religion* 4:9-23.

Ogletree, Thomas W.
- 1983 *The Use of the Bible in Christian Ethics.* Philadelphia: Fortress.

Patrick, Dale
- 1981 *The Rendering of God in the Old Testament.* OBT. Philadelphia: Fortress.
- 1985 *Old Testament Law.* Atlanta: John Knox.

Rasmussen, Larry L.
- 1993 *Moral Fragments and Moral Community: A Proposal for Church in Society.* Minneapolis: Fortress.

Rowley, H. H.
- 1953 *The Unity of the Bible.* Philadelphia: Westminster.

Smend, Rudolf
- 1982 "Ethik III: Altes Testament." *TRE* 10:423-35.

Smith, Daniel L.
- 1989 *The Religion of the Landless: The Social Context of the Babylonian Exile.* Bloomington: Meyer Stone Books.

Sonsino, Rifat
- 1980 *Motive Clauses in Hebrew Law: Biblical Forms and Near Eastern Parallels.* SBLDS 45. Chico: Scholars.

Verhey, Allen
- 1984 *The Great Reversal: Ethics and the New Testament.* Grand Rapids: Eerdmans.

Wilson, Robert R.
- 1988 "Approaches to Old Testament Ethics." Pp. 62-74 in *Canon, Theology, and Old Testament Interpretation: Essays in Honor of Brevard S. Childs.* Ed. Gene M. Tucker, David L. Petersen, and Robert R. Wilson. Philadelphia: Fortress.

Wright, Christopher J. H.
- 1983 *An Eye for an Eye: The Place of Old Testament Ethics Today.* Downers Grove: InterVarsity.

Zimmerli, Walther
1982   *I Am Yahweh*. Ed. and with an Introduction by Walter Brueggemann. Trans. Douglas W. Stott. Atlanta: John Knox. German original of essay, "Ich bin Jahwe," in 1953.

ETHICS OF THE HEBREW BIBLE: THE PROBLEM OF METHODOLOGY

Eryl W. Davies
University College of North Wales

ABSTRACT

This paper outlines some of the methodological problems that beset any examination of the ethics of the Hebrew Bible. Its primary focus is on biblical law since this is often regarded as the starting-point of any ethical inquiry. It is shown that it is methodologically unsatisfactory to read off our account of Israel's ethical values on the basis of the laws contained in the Hebrew Bible since these laws were not intended as a comprehensive guide to Israel's ethical conduct and ethical obligations may demand actions that go beyond strictly legal requirements. The importance of distinguishing between the ethics of the Hebrew Bible and the ethics of ancient Israelite society is underlined, and consideration is given to the phenomenon of popular morality. The possibility that a "natural law" type of ethic was operative in Israel is discussed and found to be appealing, although it is pointed out that the concept is laden with ambiguity and needs further clarification.

The subject of ethics has, for some considerable time, remained a much neglected area in the research of the Hebrew Bible. One reason for this undoubtedly lies in the very nature of the raw material which is the object of study, for ethics is a notoriously amorphous subject which does not lend itself very readily to scholarly analysis. The material available is by no means easy to identify or classify, for nowhere does the Hebrew Bible present a unified or coherent body of ethical principles; on the contrary, it contains a wide variety of moral values and moral norms, preserved in books which date from different periods and which have frequently been subjected to a long process of editing. To complicate matters further, the ethical principles enshrined in the Hebrew Bible are not always self-consistent, and thus scholars who have attempted to analyze the subject in any depth have inevitably been confronted with the unresolved tensions that exist between various ethical demands. To explicate the significance of specific ethical principles is easy enough; the problem arises when one tries to do justice to the whole range of biblical material relating to any particular issue. Quite apart from these difficulties there is, also, the hermeneutical problem of applying the ethics of the Hebrew Bible to the exigencies of the present age, for our own society and culture seem so far removed from that of ancient Israel that the ethical ideals contained in the Hebrew Bible must appear to many to be outmoded, obsolete, and irrelevant.

The study of ethics is thus a very complex task, and it must be recognized at the outset that it is a task for which comparatively few scholars are well prepared. As James M. Gustafson (430) has remarked, "those who are specialists in ethics generally lack the intensive and proper training in biblical studies, and those who are specialists in biblical studies often lack sophistication in ethical thought." This may well explain why scholars have tended to occupy themselves with other areas of Hebrew Bible study, such as the literary, theological, sociological, and anthropological aspects of research. However, the significant advances made in these spheres have merely compounded the difficulty for those concerned with the study of biblical ethics, for they are made increasingly aware that due account must be taken of the complex interaction of historical, sociological, and theological factors which attend any serious examination of their subject. In view of these difficulties, the paucity of studies relating to the subject of Hebrew Bible ethics is, perhaps, understandable. There have, it is true, been studies of key ethical words and concepts, such as "righteousness" and "holiness," and there can be no doubt that clarifying the meaning of such terms is a significant aspect of any ethical inquiry. But even these studies have not always exhibited an appreciation of the complexity of the task involved, for what these words mean in one context may be quite different from what they mean in another. Writers on the ethics of the Hebrew Bible have constantly to be sensitive to the fact that many of the words with which they deal may, indeed, have a wide variety of connotations, and that it simply will not do to abstract a word from its contextual background and make unwarranted generalizations. Clearly, then, attempts to analyze the basis of Hebrew Bible ethics involve navigating the most treacherous waters, and it is hardly surprising that the subject has been either widely ignored or subsumed under the broader theme of the theology of the Hebrew Bible. In view of this, the current resurgence of interest in the field of Hebrew Bible ethics is warmly to be welcomed, notwithstanding the reservations expressed by some scholars that the writing of an "Ethics of the Hebrew Bible" may well prove to be a pointless or impossible task (Barton 1978:44; Rodd: 208–9). The purpose of the present paper is to outline some of the methodological difficulties that have beset scholars who have made incursions into this particular field of study.

Hebrew Bible Ethics and the Law

All who have attempted to analyze the ethics of the Hebrew Bible have immediately been confronted with the wide variety of material available, for moral principles are contained in the law, the narratives, the psalms, and wisdom-sayings, and it has been by no means easy to decide which literary *genre* should serve as the starting-point for their ethical inquiry. Exigencies of space will clearly not allow a discussion of each of these literary forms, and we shall therefore limit our remarks to the role of law in the study of Hebrew Bible ethics.

Since the heart of the ethical teaching of the Hebrew Bible has traditionally been found in the commands of Yahweh and since few have doubted the value of the law as a source of normative ethical guidance in Israel, many scholars who have sought to examine the basis of Hebrew Bible ethics have naturally focused their attention upon the Torah. Their tacit assumption is that the law furnishes a reliable guide to the generally accepted norms of behavior embraced by the people of Israel. But it is precisely this assumption that must seriously be questioned. In the first place, the law can hardly be regarded as a comprehensive guide to Israel's ethical behavior. Even aside from the possibility that the laws emerged from an elite group attempting to maintain a status quo favorable to the existing power structure, the law as recorded in the Hebrew Bible seems to contain only the minimum standards of conduct required of every morally decent person. Precepts safeguarding life, marriage, and property such as those found in the Decalogue of Exodus 20 were probably never intended to provide a complete system of rules governing all aspects of human behavior. On the contrary, such stipulations contained only the absolute minimum of God's requirements of his people, and since such demands involved merely some measure of forbearance on their part, they must, in general, have been regarded as precepts which could easily be obeyed. To refrain from killing another person, for example, was a duty which was presumably regarded as easy to discharge, requiring no extraordinary moral heroism. There probably existed in Israel—as in every society at any given time—a system or systems of generally binding moral requirements, enforced by the law, which defined what that society regarded as the minimum conditions of a tolerable social life. However, within the sphere of life circumscribed by these commandments, there undoubtedly lay a wide area of moral action that remained completely unregulated, for a good deal of what was important in morality was simply not expressible in terms of obedience to rules. In many areas of life conduct had to be governed by mutual trust and respect rather than by strict compliance with defined obligations. Even though the stipulations of the law were binding and any infringement of them would presumably be duly punished, it was the voluntary participation of people in acts which they themselves believed to be good, right, and proper that ultimately made it possible for the social order to function equitably. Certainly, many of the practices against which the eighth-century prophets inveighed came within that area of moral action that was not regulated by law; their concern was often not so much with activities that were illegal *per se*, but simply with actions that tended to corrupt the ethos of society, whether in the form of cruelty, inhumanity, or merely a failure to recognize where one's duty lay in relation to one's fellow-citizen. Such offenses could not always be defined in precisely formulated legal terms and had to be left to the jurisdiction of public opinion and individual conscience. Clearly, then, the law contained in the Hebrew Bible cannot be regarded as a full or comprehensive statement of the ethical imperatives incumbent upon the people of Israel, for many ethical obligations demanded actions that went far beyond strictly legal requirements.

Some of the dangers implicit in regarding the law as a guide to the generally acknowledged norms of behavior of the ancient Israelites have recently been emphasized by Henry McKeating. His article is primarily concerned with the sanctions against adultery in the Hebrew Bible, but in fact he raises profound methodological issues which are important for the study of Hebrew Bible ethics generally. McKeating observes that a wide variety of sanctions against adultery are found in the Hebrew Bible: in the Decalogue and Leviticus 18, they take the form of exclusion from the cultic community; in Deuteronomy and the Holiness Code, adultery is regarded as a capital offense; in the wisdom literature, on the other hand, the adulterer is merely warned to beware of the wrath of the husband and to take due cognizance of the damage that may be done to his own reputation, and the unpleasant consequences which would inevitably follow upon his detection; in the prophetic literature, the punishment is different again, for it is here implied that the adulteress would be subjected to public disgrace and humiliation. It seems most unlikely that these texts reflect a development in the sanctions applied against adultery in Israel—that, for example, what was once regarded as a capital offense later came to be regarded as something which involved the far milder penalty of humiliation or public reprobation. Rather, it is probable that a wide variety of sanctions applied to adultery (and, by implication, to any given offense) at any one time. From this, some important observations arise (McKeating: 65–71). In the first place, it is clearly methodologically unsatisfactory simply to read off our account of a society's ethical values from the laws which it produced, for we simply do not know how often or, indeed, how rigorously, those laws were applied. The severity of the penalty attached to a law need not be a reliable guide to the seriousness with which its infraction was viewed, for if the sanction was not applied on a regular basis (as seems to have been the case with the death penalty for adulterers), the offense may have been one which was, to some extent, tolerated if not condoned; furthermore, we might add, the severity of penalties may well have fluctuated in practice according to economic or other conditions among the people. Secondly, as numerous recent studies of ancient and modern societies illustrate, the status of the law and its function in ancient Israel need to be assessed carefully: Was the rule of law something that was actually implemented, or was it merely a statement of the principles or ideals of behavior generally considered to be desirable? If it is deemed to be the latter, then the law cannot be regarded as an accurate reflection of the actual behavior of the Israelites—or certainly not all of them. This, in turn, leads to a third consideration, namely, the ultimate purpose of any ethical inquiry: Is it intended to delineate the actual behavior of a given society or the ideals of behavior to which that society subscribes? In the context of Hebrew Bible studies, are we to be concerned with how the Israelites *did* behave in practice or how they believed they ought to behave in principle?

The issue of determining the actual behavior of the Israelites, as opposed to the behavior that was expected of them, itself raises a serious methodological problem, for the documents contained in the Hebrew Bible merely reflect the "official" religion of Israel, and the thoughts of the "ordinary Israelites," i.e., those not belonging to groups possessing significant political, economic, or religious power, may not always have coincided with the perspectives of those who had a hand in producing the biblical canon. It is often tacitly assumed by modern scholars that, for the Israelites, religion was *the* decisive influence in moral matters, but due allowance must be made for the fact that the Hebrew Bible is largely a body of religious documents produced by a people for whom religion was presumably a dominant interest. Of course, Israel's ethic appears to demand a religious interpretation, but, as McKeating (70) observes, this is only because it has already been given one in the documents at our disposal. This leads to an important observation, the implications of which have not always been fully appreciated: the ethics of the Hebrew Bible and those of ancient Israelite society do not necessarily coincide, and the former may not always be an accurate representation of the latter. Indeed, the indictments of the prophets against their contemporaries testify to the fact that everyone did not always share their enlightened views on the ethical issues of the day. We must constantly beware of the temptation to regard the ethical values embraced by the prophets as somehow representative of the values accepted by the nation as a whole, for this will only distort our view of the actual situation. As John Barton has observed (1978:48), if the ethics of the eighth-century prophets are regarded as normative for that period of Israel's history, then we will inevitably find ourselves playing down the originality of the prophetic contribution and at the same time exaggerating out of all proportion the ethical sophistication attained by the populace at large. In order to do justice to the ethical diversity which was present in ancient Israel, account must be taken not only of the utterances of the prophets but also of the conventional morality, or popular morality, embraced by the "ordinary Israelite." The study of ethics must entail more than an examination of the official religion which seems to be advocated by the Hebrew Bible; it must also encompass an examination of the public ethos, the manners and mores of society at large. But here the question inevitably arises: is the evidence available for ascertaining the moral life of the person-in-the-street in biblical times? Barton (1978:57–59) believes that some idea of the nature of popular morality in Israel between the eighth and sixth centuries BCE can be gleaned, in part, from the quotations in the prophets that allude to the beliefs of the people. But as Barton himself recognizes, this evidence must be used with considerable caution; for although some of the prophetic quotations may have a ring of authenticity about them, which might justify their acceptance as the genuine popular views of the people at large, there can be little doubt that in many such sayings the prophets were presenting a caricature of the beliefs of those whom they opposed. Moreover, the concept of the "ordinary Israelite" is in itself rather vague and obscure, for the fact is that Israelite society consisted of diverse groups, and it cannot be assumed that all groups, or even all members within a single group, shared the same ethical values. To embark on a study of Israel's "popular morality" is thus bound to be an endeavor fraught with difficulties, for the evidence at our disposal is hardly complete, and it is most improbable that anything but a very general, impressionistic picture of popular morality will emerge.

NATURAL LAW

Finally, some consideration must be given to the possibility that a "natural law" type of ethic functioned in ancient Israel. This idea was, in fact, mooted in an article published over forty years ago by Friedrich Horst, but it generally met with little response in the scholarly world. More recently, however, the notion has been resuscitated by Barton in a series of articles, and by James Barr in his book, *Biblical Faith and Natural Theology*. The theory of natural law, according to Barton, implies "a way of looking at ethics which stresses that certain moral norms are felt to be *natural*, in tune with the way things are, or likely to be held by all men in virtue of some innate moral sense" (1979:1). Scholars have, of course, long recognized that some such ethic undergirds much of the wisdom literature in the Hebrew Bible, but Barton finds traces of it also in the prophets and in the priestly writers. Barr casts his net wider still, for he begins with passages in the book of Acts and the epistle to the Romans and traces the concept of natural theology through the Wisdom of Solomon, some of the Psalms, the wisdom literature, the prophets, and the law. By his own admission, Barr started out as one who was instinctively "distrustful of the entire box of tricks that makes up traditional natural theology" (103), but upon examination of the evidence he was forced to concede that the phenomenon was a prominent one in the Hebrew Bible and that it formed a continuous tradition which could be traced from Hebrew Bible times down to the period of the post–New Testament church.

But what are the criteria to indicate that a "natural law" type of ethic is operative in a particular passage? Barton (1979:9–14) suggests that one possible clue is that the passage in question may well indicate that the punishment for a particular offense will correspond to the crime. Those who offend against the norms of society will receive their just deserts, for a kind of "poetic justice" is regarded as operative in the world. A good example of this retributive justice is found in Isa 5:8-10, where the prophet condemns those who dispossess the poor of their patrimony: the punishment which awaited those who "join house to house" is that "many houses shall be desolate"; the punishment in store for those who add "field to field" in an attempt to increase their crops is that the expected produce will be drastically diminished: "ten acres of vineyard shall yield but one bath, and a homer of seed shall yield but an ephah." If such an ethic can be shown to exist in the prophetic literature, then its appeal to the prophets is easy to comprehend, for it was a system of law that presupposed the notion of an immutable justice. Its precepts could not be altered, repealed, or abolished, and there would be little point in resorting to casuistry in order to escape its obligation, for its principles were binding at all times and in all places.

The possibility that a natural law type of ethic undergirds some of the material in the Hebrew Bible may well open up significant new perspectives in our understanding of Hebrew Bible ethics, and it may force us to question some of the presuppositions which have hitherto been regarded as axiomatic. For example, the tendency to regard the ethics of the Hebrew Bible as exclusively revelational may need to be reconsidered, for it may well be that Scripture bears witness to principles of right conduct which are rationally discoverable. Moreover, the view, often adumbrated, that the type of ethic evinced in the wisdom literature is to be regarded as something of an aberration within the Hebrew Bible may need to be revised, for the ethic of the sages may have been far more orthodox and "normative" than has hitherto been allowed. Further, the existence of a natural law ethic serves as a potent reminder of the fact that a plurality of models must be considered as furnishing the basis of Hebrew Bible morality; these may include imitation of God and obedience to God's revealed will as well as conformity to a pattern of natural order.

The presence of a natural law ethic in the Hebrew Bible undoubtedly has interesting hermeneutical possibilities. As has often been observed, one of the difficulties of applying biblical commands to the circumstances of the present age is their specificity (cf. Goldingay: 51–55); after all, many of the enactments found in the Hebrew Bible were formed in particular historical, cultural, and social situations and were, by and large, designed to function in those situations. The advantage of natural law, on the other hand, is its universal applicability, for its appeal is to common human experience, and its principles are those which rational reasoning dictates to all humans. Moreover, in an age that is becoming increasingly secular in outlook, the emphasis upon the place of reason in making moral judgments would probably be very appealing. Unlike revealed law, which demands unconditional obedience to divine commands, natural law evinces a deliberative approach to the formation of the moral norm and provides a rational justification for the ethical imperative.

While the evidence for the existence of some type of "natural law" ethic in the Hebrew Bible seems convincing, however, one aspect of the subject requires further clarification, namely, the problem of definition. The fact is that there is not one tradition of natural law, but many, and those who have encountered this phenomenon will have been confronted with a wide variety of definitions, and may well have wondered why they should accept one rather than another. Is natural law a concept that originates from the nature of the universe, from the being of God, or from human reason? In this regard there seems to be something of a difference of opinion even among the few who have seriously entertained the possibility of the existence of a natural law ethic in the Hebrew Bible. Barton (1979:1–2) accepts as a working definition one that is suggested in the *Dictionary of Christian Ethics*, where one type of natural law is said to comprise "a set of ethical judgments obtained by reflecting on man's ordinary experience, *as contrasted with* the divine laws that may be supernaturally revealed" (Bourke: 224; my italics). Barton himself, in the course of his article on natural law, claims that it is a phenomenon that appeals to "a human consensus about what sort of acts are just and unjust, which is not logically derived from the revelation of moral norms by God, but rests on ideas about ethics formed by reason" (1979:13; cf.

1978:60). James Barr, on the other hand, is able to speak of "a kind of revealed natural law" (90), and believes that this was one of the ways in which the faith of ancient Israel articulated itself from the very beginning. It is not my purpose here to discuss the possible origin of the concept of natural law as it functions in the Hebrew Bible, but merely to point out that it is a complex phenomenon and that it is by no means easy to trace the infinite variety of its manifestations. At the very least, those who discuss natural law in the context of the ethics of ancient Israelite society will have to decide how (if at all) it is to be related to the concept of revelation.

Conclusion

In this paper, we have been concerned to explicate some of the difficulties which inhere in regarding the law as the point of entry into the study of Hebrew Bible ethics. In view of the methodological problems outlined, it is not difficult to appreciate why any attempt to provide a clear, systematic account of the subject has proved to be such a difficult undertaking.

The emphasis of recent sociological studies on the pluralistic nature of Israelite society is a reminder of the fact that the nation consisted of diverse groups which probably adhered to a wide variety of ethical ideals, and it is thus perilous to suppose that anything like a "moral consensus" existed in Israel. Israelite society almost certainly spoke on the moral issues of the day with a divided voice, and the ethicist must constantly be aware of the possible dissemblance between the thoughts and perspectives of the "ordinary Israelite" and those of the writers who formed the biblical canon. Further, the need to consider afresh moral problems was ever present in Israel, especially in periods of rapid social and economic change, and this undoubtedly led to a diversity of ethical standards and ethical viewpoints from one period to another. Now these factors must all be taken into account by those who are concerned to examine the ethics of the Hebrew Bible. If the subject is to be studied in a comprehensive fashion, the ethical perspective must be broad enough to include all of the central and distinctive moral insights represented by all groups in all periods; but since the evidence for this is no longer available, the picture of Israel's ethic must, inevitably, be fragmentary and incomplete. But just as Israelite society was pluralistic, so, also, must a plurality of models be considered in any examination of the rationale which underlies the ethic of the Hebrew Bible. One such model, which has recently been the focus of attention, is that of "natural law." Of course, nobody who argues in favor of the concept of "natural law" in the

Hebrew Bible would wish to deny or denigrate the value of ethical insights derived from other spheres (e.g., divine revelation); it is merely that the notion of Hebrew Bible ethics as basically revelational needs to be kept in its proper perspective. The need to consider a plurality of models further complicates the task of the ethicist and serves to underline the fact that Hebrew Bible ethics admits of no easy solutions. In this regard, recent attempts to untangle the intricate web of Hebrew Bible ethics must be viewed as an important contribution to the debate, if only in the negative sense of setting sensible limits to the ethical inquiry and warning of the dangers inherent in over-simplifying what is, after all, a most complex phenomenon.

WORKS CONSULTED

Barr, James
    1993   *Biblical Faith and Natural Theology: The Gifford Lectures for 1991 Delivered in the University of Edinburgh.* Oxford: Clarendon, Oxford University Press.

Barton, John
    1978   "Understanding Old Testament Ethics." *JSOT* 9:44-64.
    1979   "Natural Law and Poetic Justice in the Old Testament." *JTS* n.s. 30:1-14.
    1981   "Ethics in Isaiah of Jerusalem." *JTS* n.s. 32:1-18.
    1982   "Approaches to Ethics in the Old Testament." Pp. 113-30 in *Beginning Old Testament Study.* Ed. John Rogerson. London: SPCK; Philadelphia: Westminster.

Bourke, Vernon J.
    1967   "Natural Law." Pp. 224–25 in *Dictionary of Christian Ethics.* Ed. John Macquarrie. Philadelphia: Westminster.

Davies, Eryl W.
    1981   *Prophecy and Ethics: Isaiah and the Ethical Traditions of Israel.* JSOTSup 16. Sheffield: JSOT.

Gehman, Henry S.
    1960   "Natural Law and the Old Testament." Pp. 109-22 in *Biblical Studies in Memory of H. C. Alleman.* Ed. J. M. Myers, O. Reimherr, and H. N. Bream. Locust Valley, NY: J. J. Augustin.

Goldingay, John
    1990   *Approaches to Old Testament Interpretation.* Rev. ed. Leicester: Apollos; Downers Grove: InterVarsity.

Gustafson, James M.
  1970   "The Place of Scripture in Christian Ethics: A Methodological Study." *Int* 24:430-55.

Horst, Friedrich
  1950/51   "Naturrecht und Altes Testament." *EvT* 10:253-73. Reprint: Pp. 235–59 in *Gottes Recht: Gesammelte Studien zum Recht im Alten Testament*. Ed. Hans Walter Wolff. TBü 12. Munich: Chr. Kaiser, 1961.

McKeating, Henry
  1979   "Sanctions against Adultery in Ancient Israelite Society, with Some Reflections on Methodology in the Study of Old Testament Ethics." *JSOT* 11:57-72.

Rodd, Cyril S.
  1990   "Ethics (Old Testament)." Pp. 208-10 in *A Dictionary of Biblical Interpretation*. Ed. R. J. Coggins and J. L. Houlden. London: SCM; Philadelphia: Trinity Press International.

SOURCES AND METHODS IN THE STUDY OF ANCIENT ISRAELITE ETHICS

Robert R. Wilson
Yale University

ABSTRACT

In spite of the recent increase in scholarly interest in the subject of ancient Israelite ethics, there is still no consensus on the question of how the Hebrew Bible should be used in ethical reflection. Scholars have advanced a number of proposals, ranging from simple descriptions of ancient Israelite ethical norms to full-scale theological prescriptions for the behavior of modern communities of faith, but lack of methodological clarity continues to hamper efforts to advance the discussion. As a contribution to the ongoing debate about method, this paper considers several recent methodological proposals and pays particular attention to the role that the study of ancient Israelite society has played in the discussion. This survey of recent work serves in turn as the basis for formulating some suggested methodological guidelines for future research.

Just over ten years ago, Douglas Knight, writing in *The Christian Century*, noted that during the previous fifty years biblical scholars had produced only one monograph dealing with the subject of ethics in ancient Israel (Knight 1982:55). While the reprinting of Johannes Hempel's *Das Ethos des Alten Testaments* in 1964 (1st ed., 1938), the publication in 1976 of Bruce Birch and Larry Rasmussen's *The Bible and Ethics in the Christian Life*, and the appearance of Eryl Davies's *Prophecy and Ethics* in 1981 do necessitate some modification of Knight's gloomy picture, the fact remains that for most of this century biblical scholars have had little to say about this crucial topic, a point already noted in Brevard Childs's 1970 assessment of the crisis in biblical theology (Childs 1970:124). However, scholarship never tolerates a vacuum for very long, and since Knight's article at least four major books and numerous articles have appeared on various aspects of ancient Israelite ethics. Although the output of the past ten years can hardly be considered a flood (one recent survey estimates the total bibliography on the topic to contain fewer than 200 items [Kaiser 1992:289; cf. Otto: 3–9]), enough work has accumulated to suggest that the field is still in some disarray. There is as yet no general agreement about the proper focus of the inquiry, and methodological difficulties—sometimes unrecognized and unexamined—still abound. Indeed, the problem of method is so serious that Childs has recently characterized the field with the comment that "the study of Old Testament ethics has frequently been paralyzed by the sheer complexity of the methodological problems" (Childs 1993:674). Nevertheless, these problems must be faced squarely if there is to be any progress at all. Therefore, in the essay that follows I will first sketch in broad strokes some recent approaches to the study of Israelite ethics. My intention in this survey is neither to be comprehensive nor to offer a detailed critique of recent work, but rather I hope that the sketch will provide the grounds for a consideration of methodological issues. Following the survey of recent work, I will turn to a consideration of method and indicate some of the methodological issues that must still be resolved.

I.

Discussions of ancient Israelite ethics often begin by noting that the Hebrew Bible nowhere outlines a comprehensive ethical system and that even the explicit statement of ethical principles and commands is relatively rare. Furthermore, contemporary scholars who approach the text from a historical-critical perspective also tend to recognize the historically and culturally conditioned character of the Bible's ethical norms and to be keenly aware of the diversity of ethical views to be found in Scripture. All of these factors taken together have caused scholars to appreciate anew the enormous difficulties involved in using the Hebrew Bible in contemporary ethical reflection and have encouraged the field to move in two somewhat different directions.

First, without giving up completely on the problem of the use of the Bible in modern communities of faith, a growing number of scholars are simply focusing their attention on describing the varieties of ethical norms and behaviors to be found in ancient Israel. Following the seminal suggestions of John Barton (Barton 1978:44–64), research of this sort often moves in a sociological direction and attempts to uncover the various social forces that shaped the ethical perspectives and actions of particular groups in ancient Israel. The focus of the research is relatively narrow and is usually confined to specific groups, problems, and pieces of literature. Seldom is there any claim to have uncovered overarching ethical principles or norms. In addition, the inquiry is rarely confined only to the biblical text. Rather the whole picture being reconstructed is much larger than what is available in the Bible, and use is often made of comparative material from anthropological and sociological research and from ancient Near Eastern texts. The object of the enterprise is not to contrast Israel's moral world with that of other ancient and modern cultures but rather to elaborate by comparison the material found in Scripture. Examples of this sort of descriptive and historical approach to the topic can be found in Henry McKeating's study of the problem of adultery, in Douglas Knight's treatments of Jeremiah and the Succession Narrative (Knight 1980, 1985), and in my own preliminary attempts to reexamine Deuteronomistic ethics (Wilson 1988). However, this rather restrained approach to ancient Israelite ethics is still in its infancy, and so far nothing has been produced to match the scope of Wayne Meeks's recent study of the moral world of the early Christians. Meeks's work is important at this point in the discussion because it attempts to integrate the historical, sociological, and conceptual dimensions of ethical inquiry in a comprehensive way. By examining the diverse forces that helped to shape the moral world of the first Christians, he provides the sort of integrated study that has so far been lacking in recent approaches to ancient Israelite ethics. Although it is not at all clear to me that Meeks's perspective can successfully be applied to the study of ancient Israel (Wilson 1990), he does provide a sophisticated research model that deserves to be explored further.

However, alongside this renewed interest in what the Hebrew Bible has to say about ethics, a second line of inquiry is emerging with increasing vehemence. Scholars pursuing this second set of questions are concerned with the observation that both church and synagogue have always viewed Scripture as a source of moral direction. Furthermore, communities of faith have traditionally done this in spite of their clear-eyed recognition that much of the biblical text does not seem to be *about* ethics (Clements). While contemporary Christians and Jews no longer universally read the Bible as a reliable guide to history and theology, for the most part they still do assume that the text has something valid to say about what faithful people ought to do (Rogerson: 28–29). Much of the recent interest in Israelite ethics has therefore focused not only on what ancient Israelites thought and did about moral behavior but on the vexing question of how these descriptive observations might inform the efforts of contemporary believers to shape their moral lives. In contrast to scholars simply interested in the descriptive task, scholars focusing on the use of the Bible in contemporary ethical reflection normally confine their work to the biblical text in one way or another and do not resort to comparative studies of any sort. Among the various participants in this broader discussion, recent studies by Walter Kaiser, Jr., Bruce Birch, and Brevard Childs are both representative and illustrative of the variety of approaches being taken to the subject.

After providing a useful discussion of the ways in which earlier scholars approached Hebrew Bible ethics and the methodological problems involved in these approaches, Kaiser suggests that the modern discussion of ethics can best proceed by seeking direction from the central tenets which give Hebrew Bible ethics organization and coherence. These tenets are first of all the character of God, which Kaiser understands particularly to involve God's holiness, the trait which undergirds all of the Hebrew Bible's moral imperatives and ethical directions. The second tenet, which is extremely important in Kaiser's overall investigation, is positive law, direct divine commands to engage in particular types of moral behavior. Finally, Kaiser highlights what he calls "creation ordinances," by which he seems to mean a sort of moral structure built into creation and visible primarily in the creation stories and wisdom literature of the Hebrew Bible (Kaiser 1983:29–31). Within this general framework, Kaiser then concentrates on interpreting the specific commands of God as they appear in the text. Kaiser thus focuses much of his attention on law in the Hebrew Bible, a subject usually avoided by modern discussions of biblical ethics. Using an explicitly stated set of hermeneutical guidelines, Kaiser extracts moral principles from the laws and provides examples of how these principles might be applied in contemporary situations. Although the great strength of Kaiser's work is his attempt to wrestle with the problem of law, he is less successful in dealing with other types of biblical literature that are often thought to be relevant to modern ethical reflection: narrative, prophecy, and wisdom.

Some of the omissions in Kaiser's treatment are remedied in the recent monograph by Bruce Birch (1991). At the other end of the theological spectrum from Kaiser, Birch in this volume does not undertake a description of ancient Israelite ethics but concentrates instead on relating "the testimonies and stories of Israel's faith as recorded in the Hebrew canon to the character and conduct of Christians and the Christian community in our own time" (18). His focus is therefore the narrative texts of the Hebrew Bible, and from these he extracts theological principles that help to form Christians within the community of faith and to shape their behavior as moral agents. Specific divine commands, such as laws and prophetic exhortations, which play such a large role in Kaiser's discussion, are treated by Birch primarily in the context of "Israel's story." Specific laws, for example, are seen within the theological framework of Israel's covenant with God and within the narrative context of God's liberation of the oppressed Israelites from Egyptian bondage. Like Kaiser, Birch understands the Bible as authoritative for the Christian community, but unlike Kaiser, who seems to believe that the Bible is the Christian's sole moral authority, Birch views the text as a primary but not sufficient authority, although he does not work out in detail the way in which the Bible relates to other forces that help to shape the Christian life.

Brevard Childs has considered the problem of Hebrew Bible ethics in several works (Childs 1970:123–38; 1985:51–91, 204–21) and has usually focused the debate on what he considers the central ethical problem of the Bible: knowing the will of God. His most recent work on the topic continues this emphasis, but he also engages in an ongoing dialogue with current scholarship and provides some hints about how ethics might be dealt with in a canonical context, although as in his previous works he does not offer a comprehensive treatment of the problem (Childs 1993:673–85). In his survey of current research, Childs rejects both what he considers to be the traditional approach of Kaiser and the newer sociologically oriented approach advocated by Barton, Meeks, and myself. The former approach he finds unsatisfactory because it does not deal adequately with the way in which the biblical text developed over time, while the latter approach represents for Childs a turning away from Scripture and an attempt to locate ethical discussion in a reconstructed setting outside the biblical text. As an alternative, Childs argues that "the task of Old Testament ethics is to acknowledge [the] canonical corpus as a theological construct which is only indirectly related to an historical and empirical Israel, and to pursue rigorously the theological witness of this biblical witness as the privileged sacred writings of Israel, the people of God" (1993:676). A canonical approach of this sort will recognize both the diverse historical settings in which God's will was revealed to Israel and also the great variety of ethical witnesses in the Hebrew Bible. Rather than resolving the conflicts among these witnesses, the interpreter's task is to work within the general arena created by them. Childs does not provide concrete examples of how this process would work, but he does note that different contributions are made by the various types of witnesses. He then discusses the perspectives of the narratives, the Torah, including the legal material, the prophets, the psalter, and the wisdom writers. He strongly resists privileging any one of these witnesses over the others, and on this point he presumably would disagree strongly with the legal focus of Kaiser and the narrative approach of Birch.

II.

Setting aside for the time being general hermeneutical problems that have recently been raised in connection with any sort of historical-critical research—problems that are particularly severe for any scholar who attempts to describe ancient Israel's moral world—we may now briefly summarize some of the methodological issues raised in current research on Israelite ethics, particularly by the work of Kaiser, Birch, and Childs.

Although these issues are interrelated, they can usefully be considered under three headings.

Hermeneutical Issues

At the outset, the recent discussion raises a whole host of hermeneutical issues related to the use of the Hebrew Bible in ongoing ethical discussion. Particularly important is the question of the goal of the enterprise. Is the scholar's task a rather traditional one of first reconstructing the moral world of ancient Israel, making full use of all of the comparative and historical-critical tools available (i.e., determining what the text meant) and then attempting to explore the relevance of this reconstruction for modern believers (i.e., determining what the text means)? Or is the historical description in some sense irrelevant to the theological use of the Bible's ethical materials, whatever those materials are finally determined to be? The recent work of Kaiser, Birch, and Childs shows signs of moving in this latter direction, although these scholars make this move to different degrees and in very different ways. In particular, Childs's very sharp polemic against the sort of sociological approach represented by Meeks, among others, indicates a clear divergence in the field which needs to be examined, even if it cannot be resolved.

Recent research also suggests the need to examine more thoroughly the interpretive processes involved when a particular scholar uses the Bible to do ethics. To be sure, most scholars are quite clear about the guidelines they are following when they deal with particular texts, but there are other dimensions to the process that are not so transparent. Among other things, the diversity of approaches currently being employed is surely related to the particular interpretive traditions out of which the interpreters come. Interpretation does not take place in a vacuum but is part of a particular history of interpretation, the influence of which requires more documentation and study. Exploration of this dimension of hermeneutics would move in both a theological and sociological direction, although one very different from current sociological descriptions of ancient Israelite ethics.

The Authority of Scripture

A second set of methodological issues focuses on the authority of Scripture for contemporary ethical reflection. Both Kaiser and Childs seem to imply a principle of *sola scriptura* when it comes to shaping modern ethical consciousness, while Birch candidly admits that Scripture is only one, although perhaps the most important one, of a number of forces shaping the Christian life. What those other forces might be and how they relate to Scripture is an issue still to be resolved. Particularly problematic is the role that societies and groups within them play in influencing behavior. In spite of Childs's protests to the contrary, it is likely that the discipline as a whole would benefit from a more systematic examination of how groups, including Christian groups, shape the behavior of their members.

The Diversity of Biblical Ethics

Finally, there is an important and highly complex set of methodological issues raised by the diversity of ethical materials and positions within Scripture. Virtually all contemporary scholars recognize this diversity, but they understand different things by it, and they deal with it in different ways. To begin with, scholars do not always mean the same thing when they speak of the diversity of the Bible's ethical witness. Sometimes the reference is to the diverse and even conflicting ethical views or beliefs contained in the text. Childs seems to have this in mind when he speaks of the canon as an arena within which a variety of theological and ethical positions can legitimately be held by faithful people. Kaiser seems also to have this in mind when he notes conflicts within the legal corpus. The primary methodological problem raised by diversity of this sort is the question of what to do with it. Should it be allowed to continue to exist, as Childs suggests, or should it be resolved in some way, as Kaiser, and in fact most scholars, do? If the latter approach is taken, then what methods are appropriate to resolve the tension? In the past it has often been popular to appeal to theories of historical development in order to deal with diversity and conflicts of this sort, but this approach to the problem has come under heavy fire in recent years. Clearly this is an area where more research is needed.

However, when scholars speak of ethical diversity within Scripture, they sometimes refer not to ethical norms but to the diverse sorts of biblical materials which have played a role in ethical discussion. To mention simply the most common ones, over the centuries faithful Jews and Christians have used biblical narratives as didactic examples of moral or immoral behavior, appealed to laws as divine ethical commands, seen prophets as giving specific instructions or general moral guidance, discovered in the psalter patterns for molding the obedient life, and taken the wisdom writings as distillations of common sense or as inspired insights into the ethical structure of reality. Within the current scholarly discussion, however, there is a clear tendency to emphasize one sort of material at the expense of the others. Kaiser, for example, clearly privileges law, while Birch focuses on narrative. Only Childs insists on letting each of these different types of material have its say, but he does not clearly indicate how to resolve tensions among the various perspectives involved. Clearly, more work is required in order to determine whether or not an even-handed treatment of all of this material is either possible or desirable. In the end the enormous volume of the material and the complexity of the methodological problems involved may have the practical effect of discouraging all but the bravest from attempting the sort of comprehensive treatment of the subject advocated by Childs. If so, then perhaps the enormity of the problems will have the unexpected benefit of forcing biblical scholars to cooperate more closely with their colleagues in theology and ethics. Perhaps we will finally be forced to admit that biblical ethics is not solely the province of biblical scholars.

WORKS CONSULTED

Barton, John
    1978   "Understanding Old Testament Ethics." *JSOT* 9:44–64.

Birch, Bruce C.
    1991   *Let Justice Roll Down: The Old Testament, Ethics, and Christian Life.* Louisville: Westminster/John Knox.

Birch, Bruce C., and Larry L. Rasmussen
    1976   *Bible and Ethics in the Christian Life.* Minneapolis: Augsburg. Revised and expanded edition, 1989.

Childs, Brevard S.
    1970   *Biblical Theology in Crisis.* Philadelphia: Westminster.
    1985   *Old Testament Theology in a Canonical Context.* Philadelphia: Fortress; London: SCM.
    1993   *Biblical Theology of the Old and New Testaments: Theological Reflection on the Christian Bible.* Minneapolis: Fortress.

Clements, R. E.
    1984   "Christian Ethics and the Old Testament." *The Modern Churchman* n.s. 26/3:13–26.

Davies, Eryl W.
    1981   *Prophecy and Ethics: Isaiah and the Ethical Traditions of Israel.* JSOTSup 16. Sheffield: JSOT.

Hempel, Johannes
    1964   *Das Ethos des Alten Testaments.* 2d ed. BZAW 67. Berlin: Alfred Töpelmann. 1st ed., 1938.

Kaiser, Walter C., Jr.
  1983 *Toward Old Testament Ethics.* Grand Rapids: Academie Books, Zondervan.
  1992 "New Approaches to Old Testament Ethics." *JETS* 35:289–97.

Knight, Douglas A.
  1980 "Jeremiah and the Dimensions of the Moral Life." Pp. 87–103 in *The Divine Helmsman: Studies on God's Control of Human Events.* Ed. James L. Crenshaw and Samuel Sandmel. New York: Ktav.
  1982 "Old Testament Ethics." *The Christian Century* 99/2:55–59.
  1985 "Moral Values and Literary Traditions: The Case of the Succession Narrative (2 Samuel 9–20; 1 Kings 1–2)." *Semeia* 34:7–23.

McKeating, Henry
  1979 "Sanctions against Adultery in Ancient Israelite Society, with Some Reflections on Methodology in the Study of Old Testament Ethics." *JSOT* 11:57–72.

Meeks, Wayne A.
  1986 *The Moral World of the First Christians.* Library of Early Christianity. Philadelphia: Westminster.

Otto, Eckart
  1991 "Forschungsgeschichte der Entwürfe einer Ethik im Alten Testament." *VF* 36/1:3–37.

Rogerson, J. W.
  1982 "The Old Testament and Social and Moral Questions." *The Modern Churchman* n.s. 25:28–35.

Wilson, Robert R.
  1988 "Approaches to Old Testament Ethics." Pp. 62–74 in *Canon, Theology, and Old Testament Interpretation: Essays in Honor of Brevard S. Childs.* Ed. Gene M. Tucker, David L. Petersen, and Robert R. Wilson. Philadelphia: Fortress.
  1990 "Ethics in Conflict: Sociological Aspects of Ancient Israelite Ethics." Pp. 193–205 in *Text and Tradition: The Hebrew Bible and Folklore.* Ed. Susan Niditch. SBLSS. Atlanta: Scholars.

POLITICAL ETHICS
IN ANCIENT ISRAEL

DOMINION, GUILT, AND RECONCILIATION: THE CONTRIBUTION OF THE JACOB NARRATIVE IN GENESIS TO POLITICAL ETHICS[*]

Frank Crüsemann
Kirchliche Hochschule Bethel

ABSTRACT

The peoples Israel and Edom, neighbors and twins, had a long history characterized by bloody hatred. If one attempts to read the Jacob narrative of Genesis against this background, then it is not sufficient to relate the promise of dominion in chaps. 25 and 27—as is usually done—solely to conditions prevailing in the early monarchic period. Rather, one must examine the whole narrative sequence of promise, culpable attempt to realize the promise through deceit, and ultimate reconciliation of the brothers. At the end they dwell together in peace, a condition which is, however, not an exact fulfillment of the promise. Thus the Jacob story becomes an important contribution to a (narrative) ethic of the political sphere.

Conflicts between related and neighboring peoples can oftentimes be especially brutal, both in our contemporary world and in biblical times. The demarcation that seems necessary for the consolidation of one's own identity can assume frightful forms. With Edom, its twin, Israel shared an almost indistinguishably close relationship from the very outset, as well as a long history characterized by bloody hatred (Bartlett; Knauf 1988, 1991; Weippert 1971, 1982a, 1982b). The scornful participation of the Edomites in the destruction of Jerusalem and in the exile of God's people led to a hatred of Edom, which lasted for centuries and gave rise to some of the most brutal texts of the Hebrew Bible (Psalm 137; Isaiah 63). Eventually Edom became the symbolic name of all inimical and destructive worldly powers. However, this is only the latest and most well-known chapter in an older and equally brutal story. David and Joab are said to have slaughtered 12,000 or 18,000 Edomites (Ps 60:2; 2 Sam 8:13 and 1 Chr 18:12), an atrociously high number even by the standards of larger contemporary populations. The report that Joab liquidated all the male inhabitants of Edom (1 Kgs 11:15–16), probably after an uprising, smacks of genocide. In so doing he took more drastic measures than did

---

[*] Translated by Carl S. Ehrlich.

the pharaoh of the exodus against the Israelites, or than did Herod in Bethlehem. Whatever the historical reliability of such reports may be, the fact that they were handed down and remained fixed in the memories of the peoples is indicative of the depth of the conflict.

This is the background against which the tale of Jacob and Esau in Genesis is to be read. The patriarchs whose stories are recounted in Genesis represent their descendants (Blum: 478ff.). If the central theme of the Joseph narrative is the dominion of Joseph over his brothers, i.e. the question of inner-political dominion and its legitimation (Crüsemann: 143ff.; Westermann 1982; Blum: 234ff.), then the central themes of the Jacob narrative are the foreign conflicts with the closely related Edomite and Aramean peoples. The main thread of the narrative of the conflict between Jacob and Esau is thus of direct relevance for an understanding of the ethical aspects of conduct toward inimical neighboring peoples. Admittedly this ethic is not stated explicitly. It is to be found solely in the narrative development. Methodologically the following arguments thus deal with aspects of a *narrative ethics* in an area about which the legal texts of the Torah make only few and indirect statements.

I.

As is well known, the conflict between Jacob and Esau already began before their births. According to Gen 25:22 they struggled in their mother's womb. The verb employed in this context (רצץ hithpol.; see Ringgren) should actually be translated with more force: "they abused each other." This leads directly to suicidal thoughts on the part of their mother: "If so, why do I exist?"[1] She then receives a YHWH-oracle, in which God says to her:

Two nations are in your womb,
Two separate peoples shall issue from your body;
One people shall be mightier than the other,
And the older shall serve the younger. (25:23)

This divine word with its clear political message hovers over the whole continuation of the story. Everything that follows revolves around the question of its fulfillment.

I will contrast the beginning of this story directly with its ending, omitting for the time being what comes between these two poles. When

---

[1] Biblical quotations are cited according to *Tanakh: A New Translation of the Holy Scriptures according to the Traditional Hebrew Text* (Philadelphia/New York/Jerusalem: The Jewish Publication Society, 1985).

the brothers see each other again after a separation of more than twenty years, it is Jacob, the younger one, who bows before his brother (33:3) and refers to himself as the latter's slave (32:19; 33:5) and to Esau as his master (32:19; 33:8). Jacob gives Esau a large part of his possessions as a reconciliatory present (32:14ff., 21) and begs him to accept "my blessing" (ברכתי; 33:11). Esau, who runs to greet him, embracing and kissing him (33:4), appears to Jacob as the face of God himself (33:10). The reconciliation of the two brothers is followed by their peaceful separation and return to their respective territories (33:12ff.). In short: At the end, neither one has dominion over the other. The brothers live as equals and in freedom next to each other. The divine word has *not* been fulfilled.

The whole of the Jacob narrative lies between this beginning and this ending. Almost all of its motifs deal with the basic theme of fraternal conflict. The reversal of the status of the brothers, as announced in the divine oracle, takes place in two stages. Jacob convinces his brother to sell him his birthright, spontaneously taking advantage of an emergency situation and of Esau's contempt for his status in order to secure the birthright for himself (25:29–34). And then in chap. 27, the blind Isaac is tricked into giving the firstborn's blessing to Jacob rather than to his beloved Esau (25:28). On this occasion Isaac repeats the divine oracle:

> Let peoples serve you,
> And nations bow to you;
> Be master over your brothers,
> And let your mother's sons bow to you. (27:29a)

Even though the father does not curse his twice-cheated older son (27:36), he is only able to provide him with a greatly reduced blessing (Willi-Plein: 319ff.), in which his subservience to Jacob is in fact reiterated:

> Yet by your sword you shall live,
> and you shall serve your brother. (27:40a; see below on v. 40b)

Fraud and deception are thus intended to lay the foundation for the future realization of the divine word. The immediate results are Esau's desire to kill Jacob (27:41) and the latter's flight from his promised land.

What happens between the flight and the reunion serves, with many indirect references to the fraternal conflict, to explain the turn of events. In Aram the deceiver himself experiences deceit.[2] He must learn that the younger one is not always preferred to the elder (29:26) and that sibling

---

[2] On this point see most recently Zakovitch: 140f., with reference to *Gen. Rab.* 70:19.

rivalries can be settled in other ways. A mutually accepted border treaty concludes the conflict with Laban (31:44ff.). Above all, however, it is the two encounters with the divine, after Jacob's flight (28:10ff.) and before the reunion (32:22ff.), which set new accents. The promise of blessing is renewed in the dream at Bethel, but there is no mention of dominion over his brother. Jacob leaves the nocturnal battle at the Jabbok, that life-or-death wrestling match, stricken (32:32). Face to face with God, he again wins life and blessing—but in such a manner that dominion over his brother, who bears the face of God (33:10), is no longer conceivable.

II.

In previous scholarly studies, the political aspects of the Jacob–Esau narrative have hardly ever been applied to the *whole* of the composition.[3] For example, in most commentaries the explicit declarations of the divine oracle and the paternal blessing are examined and applied to the ascendancy of Israel in the Davidic period. The possibility alluded to in 27:40b, that Edom/Esau can cast off the "yoke" of his brother, is explained on the basis of the deliverance of Edom in the days of Joram of Judah (2 Kgs 8:20–22). While the testimony of chaps. 25 and 27 about the individuals Jacob and Esau is related to the political history of their descendants, the end of the narrative with its account of the reconciliation of the brothers almost always lacks a political interpretation, nor is it related to the beginning of the story.

This raises a methodological problem, which can be only briefly considered in this context. It concerns the relationship of individual and national history in the ancestral traditions. I assume that already in the earliest strata Abraham, Isaac, and Jacob were viewed as representatives of all Israel (Blum: 478ff.). A simple family history without national and political dimensions[4] cannot be isolated. On the other hand, this does not mean that all particulars of the stories can or must be related to the history of the nation as a whole. We are *not* dealing with allegories here. Interpretation cannot proceed mechanically. Rather, it must always be derived with concrete reference to the texts since they are what was relevant for the world of the descendants, to whom the tales were without doubt told.

Most commentaries do not substantiate the putative difference between a national beginning and a purely individual ending.

---

[3] An exception is Blum: 175ff., esp. 185f.; see the discussion below, Part III. Also see Gammie: 129ff.

[4] The Jacob narrative is interpreted in this manner by Albertz, following Westermann 1989.

Interpreters clearly assume that the stories originally existed separately and that therefore the statements in chaps. 25 and 27 are to be associated with the history of the nation, while the reconciliation in chaps. 32–33 is not. If one looks at the complete and interconnected Jacob narrative as a whole, then such a line of argumentation cannot be upheld. Above all others, Benno Jacob recognized this problem in his Genesis commentary. However, he denied any application of the testimony of the divine oracles or of the paternal blessing to the concrete individuals mentioned. In reference to 25:23 he wrote: "Wichtig ist aber, daß רב und צעיר *nicht auf Esau und Jakob gehen können, sondern nur auf die eben genannten Völker. Keiner der beiden Brüder hat dem anderen 'gedient'"* (543). In like manner he wrote in reference to 27:29: *"Dieser Segen ist lediglich politischer Natur und hat nichts mit Jakob als einem Stammvater Israels zu tun. Den Patriarchen als solchen wird niemals Herrschaft verheißen"* (567). But does this do justice to the texts? The expression צעיר "the younger," which is employed in 25:23, appears especially in Genesis in contexts which describe the relationships between siblings (19:31ff.; 29:26; 43:33; 48:14), and not between nations. In 27:29, as well as in the summary of the blessing in 27:37, the word גביר "master" is used. This expression appears elsewhere in Genesis only in its feminine form in reference to the personal relationship of Sarah to her servant Hagar (16:8–9). Throughout the blessings, therefore, one finds references both to the personal relationship between the individuals and to the nations which derived their ancestry from them.

The account of the reconciliation in chap. 33 is not filled with explicitly political expressions, yet it contains features that do not fit into the lives of the individuals mentioned. This applies in particular to Gen 33:12ff. The story does not end with the brothers' embracing, but rather with a renewed separation. Jacob turns down (33:13–14) Esau's invitation to journey with him (33:12). Even though mention is made of an intent to visit Seir (v. 14), Jacob travels instead to Succoth and Shechem (vv. 17ff.). Jacob even rejects Esau's offer to leave behind some people as protection (v. 15): "Oh no, my lord is too kind to me!" (v. 15b) is Jacob's peculiar answer to Esau's offer. Each one returns to his own territory. Neither one makes claim to the other's territory nor protects the other. This ending does *not* represent the ideal situation "when brothers dwell together" (Deut 25:5; Ps 133:1). Nonetheless, it is not appropriate to follow Coats and speak of "strife without reconciliation," that is, to see a beginning of a new conflict instead of a reconciliation.[5] Rather, what is reflected here is

---

5 Compare Coats (103): "What good is reconciliation if the brothers do not live together? . . . The framework story ends, therefore, at the same point it begins. The brothers are separated. And the strife between them becomes permanent division."

clearly the relationship of the two nations: Each lives in its own territory. Neither one rules over the other, makes claims on the other, needs or dispatches "Schutztruppen."

III.

Concerning the abundant problems of literary strata and their dating, it should be emphasized that the opposition of promised dominion and fraternal reconciliation is *not* dependent on source-critical analysis and its results. It underlies each text and must be considered and explained as part of *every* interpretation. Even the—in my opinion unlikely—assumption that the political formulations of chaps. 25 and 27 were inserted later (see most recently Boecker: 17f., 44f.) has to confront the same problem.

The most convincing literary analysis, in my view, and the one with which I agree is that of E. Blum (66–270). Blum speaks of a unified "Jacob story" ("Jakoberzählung"), found in Genesis 25B (= 25:19–34) and Genesis 27–33.[6] The revisions, which are later than the original composition, are clearly identifiable.[7] Blum (190ff.) has identified a few older, preexisting traditions which have been reworked in the originally literarily-independent Jacob story.[8] The "imperial" promises of Genesis 25 and 27 belong to these traditions.

Blum (175ff.) dates the independent Jacob story on the basis of a number of references to the early history of the Northern Kingdom under Jeroboam I, and he regards it virtually as "eine *'Programmschrift'* für das um seine politische Konsolidierung bemühte Nordreich" (Blum: 203, cf. 183f.). The conflict and reconciliation of the brothers must thus be viewed against the background of Israel's or Judah's continuing dominion over Edom in this period. Blum is one of the few who has attempted to understand politically the whole of the Jacob story, with its opposition

---

[6] Particularly in the Jacob story, the documentary model has been unable to stand the test of time, and it can be considered to be disproved in a number of important texts: Concerning 28:10ff., see Rendtorff; Blum: 7ff. Concerning chap. 27, which has been the subject of a number of unsuccessful attempts to distinguish sources (Schmidt; Fabry; Vermeylen), see Westermann 1989:530f. (E.T.: 1985:436); Blum: 79ff.; Willi-Plein: 317f.

[7] In addition to the P-passages of Gen 25:19, 20, 26b; 26:34, 35; 27:46 – 28:9 (see on the one hand Weimar, on the other Blum: 263ff.), Blum (152ff.) also identifies a D-stratum (28:15; 31:3; 32:10–13). Moreover, the arena of the Jacob–Laban stories has been shifted from the nearby East-Jordanian mountains to faraway *Haran*. This Haran recension is responsible in particular for the geographical terms in 27:43; 28:10; and 29:4 (Blum: 164ff.).

[8] These include in particular both stories about the fraternal conflict in 25:29ff. and chap. 27, the sanctuary legend in 28:10ff., and the treaty accord in 31:43ff.

between the promises of chaps. 25 and 27 and the "Friedfertigkeit der Brüder" (Blum: 185) in chaps. 32–33. Blum is of the opinion that "die politisch-militärische Unterwerfung Edoms für einen Erzähler in Nordisrael . . . kein Thema (mehr) [war], so daß gleichsam aus einem potentiellen Eroberungszug (wie er 27,29.40 entspräche) die Zusage des Besuches Jakobs bei Esau werden konnte (33,12ff)" (185). Furthermore, Blum (185) wants to understand the "Umkehrung der . . . zugewiesenen Rollen" against the background of a confrontation with the "imperialen Machtanspruch" of the Davidic empire.

However, the tension between the grand promises in the divine oracle and in the paternal blessing and the completely different ending is not done full justice in this interpretation. Instead of leading toward a domination as promised, the main thrust of the narrative moves in the direction of reconciliation and peaceful coexistence. In the period to which Blum assigns the narrative, this would represent a challenge to the prevailing political reality. Therefore, it would be more appropriate to date the stories to a later time. According to 2 Kgs 8:20ff., Edom was finally able to free itself from Israel's or Judah's domination in the time of Joram of Judah (851/0–845/4 BCE). If one were to assume this occurrence as the background of the Jacob story,[9] then the text would reflect the people's coming to terms with the collapse of a dominion that had been viewed as divinely legitimated. This would be more in accord with the main thrust of the narrative. However, the question of dating cannot be treated fully in this context. Nor does it need to be since what is at stake has been neither concealed nor contradicted in later strata. Indeed it was especially in later times that fierce hatred of Edom was current.

IV.

In this final section I will attempt to work out the meaning of the Jacob narrative for political ethics. The narrative will be read as a literary unit in the context of the bloody and hate-filled history of Israel and its neighbor.

I would first like to refer to a certain type of interpretation of Genesis 27 in particular, which has shown itself to be of a questionable nature. In the most recent German commentary to Genesis, Boecker has written about chap. 27: "Der Weg der Verheißung Gottes ist nicht von der moralischen Qualität von Menschen abhängig, vielmehr verläuft dieser Weg immer wieder auch über höchst zweifelhafte Gestalten und

---

[9] This depends to a great extent on whether one views Gen 27:40b, which is most often linked with 2 Kgs 8:20ff., as an original component of the Esau blessing or as a later addition.

Machenschaften, deren Bedenklichkeit das Alte Testament in keiner Weise verharmlost" (52).[10] This type of interpretation was championed especially by G. von Rad, according to whom Genesis 27 "reckons with an act of God that sovereignly takes the most ambiguous human act and incorporates it into its plans. The guilty one becomes the bearer of the promise" (280; German: 225). The narrator's "view of what God has decreed and accomplished keeps him from being ruffled before the question of the personal guilt and subjective motives of the individual persons" (280; German: 225). Already in regard to Genesis 25 he had written: "In the final analysis, only what God had already determined from the beginning (v. 23) comes to pass, not without the guilt of all concerned" (268; German: 214). However, can this theology, which is borrowed from Gen 50:20 where it is employed in the context of the Joseph story, simply be applied in turn to the Jacob story? It is certainly correct that Israel never concealed the guilt and dubious actions even of its greatest figures, and that in the person of Jacob it is also dealing with its own. Nonetheless, the question arises whether such an understanding does justice to the Jacob story. The ways of dealing with questions of guilt and election, of God's plans and human actions, are *in essence* more nuanced. To view deceit and hate as irrelevant with regard to God's plans is to understand belief in a manner which must end in a "suspension of the ethical" (Kierkegaard).

To begin with, one must assume, on the basis of the generous conciliatory presents given by the culpable party to the one deceived, that the final reconciliation between Jacob and Esau is of immediate relevance for the political attitude toward the fraternal nation. The seed of Jacob can behave no differently than Jacob himself did. This is the core of the political message. Such a reconciliation with the fraternal nation does not merely take place against the background of a history saturated with guilt. On the contrary, it happens in light of an existing divine promise, which has assured Jacob/Israel permanent dominion over Esau/Edom. Precisely what the narrative does *not* show is such a divine promise being carried out irrespective of human behavior. On the contrary, the divine pledge is *not* realized, and the reason why events happened differently is explicated.

The two main factors leading to the brothers' reconciliation, in which the original divine word was *not* fulfilled, are guilt and the way this guilt is handled by Jacob himself and by Rebekah, whom he indulges. Both of them try on their own to realize God's pledge through questionable

---

[10] See also, for example, Scharbert: "Gott läßt sich durch die Sünde der Menschen seine Pläne nicht stören. Wen Gott als Werkzeug seiner Heilspläne erwählt hat, den läßt er nicht fallen, sondern lenkt auch das Böse, das er getan hat, zum Guten" (194).

means. Their attempts to put into effect that which was said in the divine oracle include a problematic exploitation of momentary weakness in chap. 25 and out-and-out deceit in chap. 27. Yet that is exactly how it cannot be fulfilled. Coming to terms with the guilt, a process that stretches over many years, has as its result that neither Esau's murderous intentions nor Jacob's claims become reality. Reconciliation becomes *necessary* on account of the guilt; it becomes *possible* through renouncing that which was promised.

However, one must make a distinction here. Both the divine and the paternal blessings continue in effect with respect to the wealth and fertility of the land. They are abrogated, however, in regard to one brother's domination of the other.

This reversal (*peripeteia*) comes about not only through Jacob's own experiences as one deceived, but decisively through his two encounters with God at Bethel and Penuel. That a divine word is not realized, that it also does not simply continue to endure as a promise but rather is lost through culpable human attempts to realize it—this constitutes an important and exciting theological statement. It touches on the very concept of God: God is engaged in dialogue and is capable of change. It also has very much to do with political ethics, for the basic problem is that of the dominion of nations over nations. The dominion of Israel over Edom, which began historically with David and continued until the mid-ninth century BCE, was undoubtedly also legitimated theologically and prophetically. In 2 Sam 8:14, i.e. in the account of the conquest of Edom, it is said that YHWH helped (ישע hiph.) David wherever he went. The Jacob story is, after all, also a confrontation with such prophetic traditions. Guilt and its resolution are viewed as an ingredient of reconciliation between inimical fraternal nations. Renunciation of dominion, even in a case which appears theologically legitimate, is the basis of reconciliation. And a renewed and difficult encounter with God is the decisive precondition for it.

Works Consulted

Albertz, Rainer
    1990   "Die kleinen Schritte zur Versöhnung wagen—Streit und Versöhnung in den Jakob-Esau-Erzählungen Genesis 25–33." Pp. 132–44 in *Der Mensch als Hüter seiner Welt: Alttestamentliche Bibelarbeiten zu den Themen des konziliaren Prozesses*. Calwer Taschenbibliothek 16. Stuttgart: Calwer.

Bartlett, John R.
    1989   *Edom and the Edomites*. JSOTSup 77. Sheffield: Sheffield Academic.

Blum, Erhard
    1984   *Die Komposition der Vätergeschichte*. WMANT 57. Neukirchen-Vluyn: Neukirchener Verlag.

Boecker, Hans Jochen
    1992   *1. Mose 25,12 – 37,1: Isaak und Jakob*. Zürcher Bibelkommentare 1/3. Zürich: Theologischer Verlag.

Coats, George W.
    1980   "Strife without Reconciliation—A Narrative Theme in the Jacob Traditions." Pp. 82–106 in *Werden und Wirken des Alten Testamentes: Festschrift für Claus Westermann zum 70. Geburtstag*. Ed. Rainer Albertz, Hans-Peter Müller, Hans Walter Wolff, and Walther Zimmerli. Göttingen: Vandenhoeck & Ruprecht.

Crüsemann, Frank
    1978   *Der Widerstand gegen das Königtum: Die antiköniglichen Texte des Alten Testamentes und der Kampf um den frühen israelitischen Staat*. WMANT 49. Neukirchen-Vluyn: Neukirchener Verlag.

Fabry, Heinz-Josef
    1989   "Erst die Erstgeburt, dann der Segen: Eine Nachfrage zu Gen 27,1–45." Pp. 51–72 in *Vom Sinai zum Horeb: Stationen alttestamentlicher Glaubensgeschichte*. Ed. Frank-Lothar Hossfeld. Würzburg: Echter.

Gammie, John G.
    1979   "Theological Interpretation by Way of Literary and Tradition Analysis: Genesis 25–36." Pp. 117–34 in *Encounter with the Text: Form and History in the Hebrew Bible*. Ed. Martin J. Buss. Philadelphia: Fortress; Missoula: Scholars.

Jacob, Benno
    1934   *Das erste Buch der Tora, Genesis*. Berlin: Schocken. Reprint, New York: Ktav, 1974.

Kellermann, Ulrich
    1975   *Israel und Edom: Studien zum Edomhaß Israels im 6.–4. Jahrhundert v.Chr.* Habilitations-Schrift. Münster: Westfälische Wilhelms-Universität.

Knauf, Ernst A.
    1988   "Supplementa Ismaelitica 13: Edom und Arabien." *Biblische Notizen* 45:62–81.
    1991   "Edomiter." Cols. 468–71 in *Neues Bibel-Lexikon*, vol. 1. Ed. Manfred Görg and Bernhard Lang. Zürich: Benziger.

Rad, Gerhard von
    1972   *Genesis: A Commentary*. Trans. John H. Marks. OTL. Philadelphia: Westminster; London: SCM. German original: *Das erste Buch Mose, Genesis*. 9th ed. ATD 2–4. Göttingen: Vandenhoeck & Ruprecht.

Rendtorff, Rolf
 1982   "Jakob in Bethel: Beobachtungen zum Aufbau und zur Quellenfrage in Gen 28,10–22." ZAW 94:511–23.

Ringgren, Helmer
 1992   "רָצַץ rāṣaṣ." Cols. 663–65 in TWAT, vol. 7. Ed. Heinz-Josef Fabry and Helmer Ringgren. Stuttgart: W. Kohlhammer.

Scharbert, Josef
 1986   Genesis 12–50. Neue Echter Bibel, Lieferung 16. Würzburg: Echter.

Schmidt, Ludwig
 1988   "Jakob erschleicht sich den väterlichen Segen: Literarkritik und Redaktion von Genesis 27,1–45." ZAW 100:159–83.

Vermeylen, Jacques
 1990   "Le vol de la bénédiction paternelle: Une lecture de Gen 27." Pp. 23–40 in Pentateuchal and Deuteronomistic Studies: Papers Read at the XIIIth IOSOT Congress, Leuven 1989. Ed. Christian Brekelmans and Johan Lust. Leuven: Leuven University Press and Uitgeverij Peeters.

Weimar, Peter
 1974   "Aufbau und Struktur der priesterschriftlichen Jakobsgeschichte." ZAW 86:174–203.

Weippert, Manfred
 1971   Edom: Studien und Materialien zur Geschichte der Edomiter auf Grund schriftlicher und archäologischer Quellen. Dissertation/Habilitations-Schrift. Tübingen: Eberhard-Karls-Universität.
 1982a "Remarks on the History of the Settlement in Southern Jordan during the Early Iron Age." Pp. 153–62 in Studies in the History and Archaeology of Jordan. Ed. Adnan Hadidi. London: Routledge.
 1982b "Edom und Israel." Pp. 291–99 in TRE, vol. 9. Ed. Gerhard Krause and Gerhard Müller. Berlin and New York: Walter de Gruyter.

Westermann, Claus
 1982   Genesis 37–50. BKAT I/3. Neukirchen-Vluyn: Neukirchener Verlag. English translation: Genesis 37–50: A Commentary. Trans. John J. Scullion, S.J. Minneapolis: Augsburg, 1986.
 1989   Genesis 12–36. 2d ed. BKAT I/2. Neukirchen-Vluyn: Neukirchener Verlag. English translation: Genesis 12–36: A Commentary. Trans. John J. Scullion, S.J. Minneapolis: Augsburg, 1985.

Willi-Plein, Ina
 1989   "Genesis 27 als Rebekkageschichte: Zu einem historiographischen Kunstgriff der Vätergeschichte." TZ 45:315–34.

Zakovitch, Yair
 1993   "Through the Looking Glass: Reflections/Inversions of Genesis Stories in the Bible." Biblical Interpretation 1:139–52.

Cui Bono? — History in the Service of Political Nationalism: The Deuteronomistic History as Political Propaganda

Frank S. Frick
Albion College

ABSTRACT

This paper is concerned with the nature of political propaganda in the Deuteronomistic History (DH), especially in that part of the DH that deals with the transition from tribal confederation/s to a monarchic form of government. In particular, the vocabulary of poverty in the DH is examined as an indicator of its treatment of political weakness and the injustice of oppression, the concrete socioeconomic forms of poverty. The notable lack of poverty language suggests that the DH writers distanced themselves from the issues of socioeconomic injustice and were not concerned with a critique of the government's role in creating and fostering systemic poverty and injustice.

The Latin phrase in the title of this paper, *Cui bono?* ("Who would profit from this?," or literally, "For whom for good?"), comes from a speech by Marcus Tullius Cicero (*Pro Milone* XII.xxxii), the renowned Roman diplomat, politician, and ethicist, who lived in the first half of the first century BCE. In Cicero's time the Roman Senate was more and more openly acclaiming Pompey as the champion of the status quo and of the narrow and selfish system of world exploitation for which they themselves stood. The expression *Cui bono?* appears in a speech Cicero made on behalf of one Titus Annius Milo. In this speech Cicero cites L. Cassius Longius whose custom it was, when presiding in court, to urge the jury to guide their deliberations by the maxim *Cui bono?* Besides being an author of philosophical and rhetorical treatises, Cicero also wrote several works on ethics that had considerable influence on liberal political thought in the nineteenth century.[1]

Cui bono? This is a fundamental question to ask when inquiring about the degree to which a government deals ethically and justly with the people under its authority. The ideal to which governments should aspire

---

[1] *De amicitia, De officiis, De finibus, De senectute, Tusculanae disputationes,* and *De natura deorum.*

is aptly stated in the final line of the pledge of allegiance to the flag of the United States of America: "With liberty and justice *for all*!" Of course no government ever realizes such an ideal, and most nation states fall far short of it. Instead, in order to camouflage their shortcomings, governments characteristically engage in efforts to "massage" the information that is disseminated to the public about the level of their performance. In this connection, we have recently seen a new connotation attached to the word "spin." Governments "put a spin" on information through press secretaries and other officials. One who in earlier times might have been called a minister of propaganda is now known as a "spin doctor."

Propaganda, defined as the "deliberate (albeit mostly dissimulated) spreading of ideas, information, rumors, etc. in order to support one's own political (or religious) cause . . ., and in the last analysis to gain more power" (Liverani: 474), may have developed into a fine art in our time, but it is certainly not something that has only recently arrived on the stage of world history. With the rise of states and the socioeconomic stratification that accompanied them, ruling elites have consistently sought to maintain their power through persuasion and propaganda as well as repression. The "despotic" states in the riverine civilizations of the ancient Near East were certainly the sources of many species of political propaganda (Williams 1964). While some species of propaganda are directed at external audiences, most often propaganda is intended for internal consumption. One type of propaganda in the ancient Near East is illustrated by the royal inscriptions of the New Kingdom in Egypt and of imperial Assyria, which, according to Liverani (474), "reveal all the biased deformations typical of propaganda in all times: only the successes are reported, and never the losses or defeats; 'our' reasons are always good, while those of the enemies are wicked; the king who is author of the text constitutes the apex (in glory, bravery, power, justice, and the gods' favor) in the course of history for his own country and for the empire world."

Propaganda in antiquity was certainly not limited to royal inscriptions. It assumed various other forms, some written, some oral, and some even architectural—e.g., the monumental buildings in the capital cities of Egypt and Mesopotamia.

If we measure it against the standards of the "despotic" states of the ancient Near East, ancient Israel may seem to be exceptional for the absence of the kinds of explicit propaganda that were commonly practiced by her neighbors. This might especially appear to be the case in premonarchic Israel, where the lack of marked socioeconomic stratification obviated the necessity of overt forms of propaganda. But it seems also to have been the case in the United Monarchy and in the kingdoms of Israel and Judah. To date, Syro-Palestinian archaeology has not discovered any royal inscriptions, no iconic representations of kings, and only rather modest public buildings from the ancient Israelite monarchies. While these species of political propaganda may still be missing from the archaeological record of ancient Israel, propaganda is certainly *not* missing from the Hebrew Bible. Keith Whitelam has quite successfully applied the kind of literary and sociological analysis developed for the study of propaganda in modern times to the study of the Hebrew Bible, in particular to those narratives that deal with liminal periods like the problematic rise of David and the struggle for power throughout 1 Samuel – 1 Kings 2. As Whitelam observes: "Obviously one of the most fertile areas for the propagandist is a time of social upheaval, especially where the fragmentation of the population leads to isolation from traditional reinforcing environments. Such would have been the case during the period of David's rise to power and the establishment of the Davidic dynasty: the all-important period of the transition from egalitarian society to dynastic state" (67).

In the balance of this paper we shall examine the Deuteronomistic History (hereafter referred to as DH), which comes from such a period of social upheaval, as a species of political propaganda. In particular, the vocabulary of poverty in the DH will be surveyed as one possible indicator of the DH's treatment of political impotence and the injustice of oppression, which are concrete socioeconomic expressions of poverty. We shall suggest that the notable lack of poverty language, together with the peculiar usage of such language as does appear, indicates that the DH writers intended to distance themselves from the issues of socioeconomic injustice and were not concerned with criticizing the government's role in creating and fostering systemic poverty and inequity.

The theory of the DH as a literary unit within the Hebrew Bible originated with the publication of Martin Noth's *Überlieferungsgeschichtliche Studien* in 1943. The main point of Noth's monograph, that Deuteronomy through Kings represents an original literary unit that could be dated to the middle of the sixth century BCE, gained wide approval. "The acceptance of this viewpoint has continued such that, to the extent that any position in biblical studies can be regarded as the consensus viewpoint, the existence of the DH has achieved almost canonical status" (McKenzie: 161). While Noth's conception of the scope and nature of the DH has been widely accepted, his idea of the *purpose* of the DH has not, however, enjoyed equivalent status. Noth's idea was that the purpose of the DH was an entirely negative one: to demonstrate to the exiles in Babylon that their suffering was their just recompense for a long history of disloyalty to Yahweh. In place of Noth's notion of the purpose of the DH, however, Frank Cross has argued that there was a primary edition of the DH that was written to support the reform of Josiah (284–88). The bulk of the DH, from Cross's perspective, was political propaganda from Josiah's reign. Cross's suggestion has taken on new meaning in the light of recent work that concentrates on the social location of the Deuteronomist/s (Dutcher-Walls; Steinberg; Nakanose). While earlier discussions of the reform tended to focus on the religious dimensions of the reform abstracted from its social class matrix, these recent studies emphasize the primacy of the economic issues at stake.

By the time of Josiah, Judah had already been under Assyrian hegemony for three-quarters of a century, with the inevitable consequences of economic stress that such foreign domination brings. The members of the ruling class were attempting to buffer themselves from this stress and maintain their privileged position by putting increasing pressure on the peasant economic base. The rapid decline of Assyrian power early in Josiah's reign, however, disturbed the class balance of power. The Jerusalem elite saw the Assyrian decline as presenting them with the opportunity to expand their economic base to include the former Northern Kingdom of Israel. Josiah's politics of state centralization, though supported by the DH, doubtless received a mixed reception outside elite circles, ranging from indifference to open hostility. Gottwald has described the reform as "a draconian reconstitution of government and cult from above, drastically extracting surplus and severely disrupting culture in all major areas of the common life" (14).

This understanding of the DH undergirds the notion that what we have in biblical literature are the perceptions and interests of *both* the dominant and dominated classes, predominantly the former. On occasion, the DH shows the dominant class taking action to reduce the grievances of the exploited, but usually doing so in ways that only further solidified their political control over them (Chaney: 127–39). Similarly, we sometimes see in the DH the members of the dominated classes cooperating with such programs. Overall, however, the DH when viewed as propaganda presents the ideas and programs propagated by state officials and their clients as resting on the self-perception that their superior wealth and power were justified by the improved production, domestic peace, freedom from foreign aggression, and divine blessings that the state and its client elites provided (Gottwald: 9). Those disparities in wealth and power that existed were not, according to this perspective, systemic in nature but simply the result either of random idiosyncratic personal differences in ability or industry, on the one hand, or the inordinate greed and moral corruption of particular individuals, on the other. It seems evident, however, that poverty and powerlessness were systemic. As Gottwald has suggested: "An important service of a sociological reading of the Bible is to plot the contours of class consciousness and class strategy—when and how they are expressed, ignored, or suppressed—in order to give a convincing social context to the diversities of biblical texts and religious developments" (10). So, how does the vocabulary of poverty in the DH illustrate the dominant class's attitudes toward the poor and, at the same time, mask the systemic nature of poverty in ancient Israel?

As we shall see, certain facts in this regard are constituted by their absence. Eagleton makes this point when he says (89–90): "The task of criticism, then, is not to situate itself within the same space as the text, allowing it to speak or completing what it necessarily leaves unsaid. On the contrary, its function is to install itself in the very incompleteness of the work in order to *theorise* it—to explain the ideological necessity of those 'not-saids' which constitute the very principle of its identity. Its object is the *unconsciousness* of the work—that of which it is not, and cannot be aware" [italics Eagleton's]. The so-called "scientific method" might demand that we say *only* what is supported in a statistically significant way by the evidence. Certainly, evidential support is a rhetorical device used in certain kinds of arguments. It is by no means, however, completely or exclusively determinative for a critical reading of biblical texts. Ideological material is concealed, but may be exposed. Uncovering the concealed agenda of a text is an important part of the interpretive process. What then is expressed, ignored, or suppressed in the language of poverty in the DH?

Various strands of the biblical text reflect on the plight of the poor in different ways, offering differing analyses of their situation. As J. David Pleins has observed (402–3), legal texts in the Hebrew Bible seek to regulate the treatment of the poor. Prophetic texts concern themselves with the poor as victims of the economic exploitation by the large landowners and ruling members of ancient Israelite society. In the wisdom tradition, Proverbs, in a somewhat condescending and possibly censorious tone, promotes the traditional wisdom (still quite popular today) that poverty is the undesirable consequence of laziness. Job, and to a lesser extent Ecclesiastes, echoes the prophetic understanding of poverty as the result of political and economic exploitation. In the Psalter it is difficult to determine to what extent the language has moved away from concrete cases of poverty to a more spiritualized, abstracted consideration of it. Outside these blocks of literature, the topic of poverty is treated only occasionally in the Hebrew Bible. In particular, it receives the least attention of all in the narrative literature of the Pentateuch and in the DH.

When examining the vocabulary of poverty we believe that it is the semantic field of these words as they actually appear in the biblical text that is critical (Wittenberg). It is also important to note, as Pleins does, the distribution of the vocabulary throughout the Hebrew Bible. No one biblical writer or text uses all the Hebrew terms for "poor"/"poverty." The distribution thus reveals a selectivity on the part of the biblical authors. For the statistics and much of the analysis of individual words in what follows, we are indebted to David Pleins (1992). In the present study, references to the poor in the Deuteronomic laws are counted together with those in the other Pentateuchal laws. We should also note that the Deuteronomic law code includes serious attempts to deal with poverty where the actual terms for poverty may not be prominently used—as in provisions for remission of debts, release from debt servitude, return of immovable property, and exceptions for charging interest on loans. While in all likelihood the DH inherits significant perspectives and orientations from the Deuteronomic legal tradition, we must remember that the DH composition of Joshua, Judges, 1-2 Samuel, and 1-2 Kings represents a discrete narrative and political stage and therefore deserves the special focus it will receive here.

There are six Hebrew words for "poor"/"poverty" that collectively appear a total of 248 times in the Hebrew Bible (see table). In order of their frequency these terms are:

1. עני / ʿānî (104)
2. אביון / ʾebyôn (59)
3. דל / dal (46)
4. רש / rāš (22)
5. מחסור / maḥsôr (13)
6. מסכן / miskēn (4)

Terms for "Poor" in the Hebrew Bible

Hebrew Term	Prophetic Lit.	Psalms	Prov.	Job	Eccl.	Pent. Narrative	DH	Pent. Legal	Totals
עני / עניים	32	44	11	8	1	0	1	7	104
אביון	17	23	4	6	0	0	0	9	59
דל	12	5	15	6	0	1	3	4	46
רש	0	1	15	0	2	0	4	0	22
מחסור	0	1	8	0	0	0	3	1	13
מסכן	0	0	0	0	4	0	0	0	4
Totals	61	74	53	20	7	1	11	21	248

1. עני / ʿānî // ענוים / ʿănāwîm

The term ʿānî is the most common term for "poor" in the Hebrew Bible, occurring a total of 104 times.[2] It appears 32 times in the prophetic literature, where it connotes economic oppression, unjust treatment, and victimization. One of the most instructive uses of ʿānî in the prophets occurs in Isaiah 40–66. When speaking of the "poor," these chapters make exclusive use of ʿānî in all but one passage, and even there it is combined with ʾebyôn. This nearly exclusive emphasis on ʿānî in Isaiah 40–66 represents a deliberate word choice, as the writer attempts to transform the prophetic notion of the "oppressed poor" to apply it to the situation of the upper-class exiles in Babylon. The pervasive assumption of the prophet is that the exiled elite had been purified by the experience of exile and, upon their return to Palestine, would rule with justice and equity over a passively receptive peasantry (Gottwald: 16).

In the Psalms ʿānî occurs 44 times and represents the preferred term for "poor," appearing most often in the psalms of lament. It is used a total of 20 times in wisdom literature. In legal texts in the Pentateuch it appears only rarely. As with other terms for poverty, the word ʿānî is *completely* absent from the narrative portions of the Pentateuch. The only appearance of the term in the DH is in the poetic text of 2 Samuel 22, which is also preserved as Psalm 18 and is a passage that is clearly secondary to its context. The contrast between the large number of occurrences of this word throughout the other sections of the Hebrew Bible and its striking absence from the Pentateuchal narrative and the DH give us our first clue about the lack of a "conscience" regarding the issue of the systemic nature of poverty and the government's responsibility toward the poor on the part of Israel's "official" historians.

2. אביון / ʾebyôn

The next most frequently occurring term for "poor" in the Hebrew Bible is ʾebyôn, which occurs 59 times in the Hebrew Bible, denotes severe economic deprivation, and probably came into use during the monarchy (Humbert: 1–6). Like ʿānî it is used frequently in the prophetic corpus and in the Psalter. The high proportion of instances of ʾebyôn in the Psalter contrasts markedly with its rarity in Proverbs and its complete absence in the narrative literature of the Pentateuch and the DH—texts which certainly reflect royal literary traditions. Indeed, the general scarcity of

---

[2] For purposes of this paper it is assumed that ʿănāwîm, which occurs 24 times in the Hebrew Bible, is a plural form of ʿānî. Thus the statistics for word distribution of these two terms have been combined. On the arguments for ʿănāwîm as a plural of ʿānî see Pleins: 412, and the references cited there.

any of the terms for "poor" in these extensive bodies of narrative material is noteworthy, suggesting that ancient Israel's historians were quite reluctant to take up the topic of poverty. For the DH this means a rejection (or at least suppression) of the prophetic contention that both Israel and Judah were destroyed, at least in part, because they mistreated the poor. This historian instead attributed the collapse of the kingdoms to the failure of kingship and to cultic abuses. Similarly, the Deuteronomistic editor attributed the fracturing of Solomon's kingdom to Solomon's being oversexed and idolatrous, whereas one might conclude from the narrative that Solomon's imposition of the corvée on the people, deepening their poverty, was a principal cause of the schism. In the DH, the term *ebyôn* occurs only in the Song of Hannah (1 Sam 2:8), which again is a later psalm that has been inserted into the narrative. Indeed, the Song of Hannah, with its radical sentiments regarding poverty, stands in very sharp contrast to the DH's narrative, which all but avoids the topic of poverty. Clearly the radical sentiments regarding poverty in the Song of Hannah have little to do with the overall agenda of the DH.

3. דל / *dal*

The term *dal* is used 48 times in the Hebrew Bible. Half of these occurrences are in prophetic texts and the book of Proverbs. In the prophetic corpus it appears 12 times and clearly refers to the politically and economically marginalized elements of society. Its use concerning such things as "levies of grain" (Amos 5:11) and the lack of sufficient grazing and farmland (Isa 14:30; Jer 39:10) suggests an agricultural background for this word. The term *dal* appears only 5 times in narrative portions of the Pentateuch and only three times in the DH, not surprisingly in contexts that are concerned with issues other than poverty. Twice the word is used to indicate the relative political strength of one group in relation to another (Judg 6:15; 2 Sam 3:1), not powerlessness. Its other use in the DH is to describe Amnon's gaunt appearance, which was the result of his frustrated sexual obsession with Tamar (2 Sam 13:4). Thus, none of the occurrences of the term *dal* in the DH carries with it the notion of "poverty," which sets it apart from the term's usage anywhere else in the Hebrew Bible.

The frequent use of *dal* in Proverbs (15 times) and Job (6 times) suggests that, at least in part, this was a wisdom term. It cannot be argued that *dal* was an early term that fell into disuse in the postexilic period. The fact that it appears 11 times in Sirach/Ecclesiasticus confirms the notion that *dal* continued to be a word that was still in use even in very late periods (at least by wisdom writers).

4. רש / rāš

The word rāš occurs 22 times in the Hebrew Bible, mainly in wisdom texts. It does not appear at all in the Pentateuch or the prophetic writings. In wisdom literature it frequently refers to someone who is lazy. The wisdom analysis that traces the origins of poverty to personal laziness diverges radically from other streams of biblical tradition, such as the prophetic and legal, which see the problem of poverty in terms of social structures and power arrangements. Despite its use in the wisdom books of Proverbs and Ecclesiastes, the word rāš never appears at all in Job. This may suggest that the book of Job bears more resemblance to the prophetic books, at least in its perspective on poverty.

Like *dal*, *rāš* is unusual among the words for "poor" in that it appears a few times (4) in the DH. In its first occurrence in the DH (1 Sam 18:23) it is used in much the same way as the DH uses *dal*, referring to relative political strength (in this case David is said to be weaker than Saul). The other three occurrences of *rāš* in the DH are all found in Nathan's parable in 2 Sam 12:1-4. Here the *rāš* is the character in the parable who "had nothing but one little ewe lamb" (12:3) in contrast to the wealthy person who had "very many flocks and herds" (12:2). While Nathan's parable seems to recognize the ruthlessness of the rich when they seize what little the poor possess, in the larger context of the DH its purpose here is *not* to offer a systemic critique of an economic system that oppresses the poor, as do many prophetic texts and parts of the book of Job. Instead, the DH as political propaganda uses Nathan's confrontation with David to explain a moment of political weakness in David's career, in the context of the DH's overall support of the Davidic dynasty. It is curious that *rāš* here is put in the mouth of a prophet by the DH, since it *never* appears in the prophetic corpus. Thus, in its use of both *rāš* and *dal*, the DH comments on relative political strength, not powerlessness or poverty.

5. מחסור / maḥsôr

The word *maḥsôr* occurs only 13 times in the Hebrew Bible, mainly in Proverbs. Its rarity throughout the rest of the Hebrew Bible would seem to mark it off as a wisdom term. In Proverbs its use is in contexts that commend hard work and condemn laziness, the ethic of the bureaucratic elite. Significantly, this term does not appear in Job or Ecclesiastes. It appears only once in the Pentateuch, in the legal materials of Deuteronomy (Deut 15:8), where it commends the charitable act of lending to the needy. It appears only once in the Psalter (34:10).

In the DH, *maḥsôr* is found 3 times, all in Judges. In Judges 18, the narrative about the migration of the tribe of Dan to the far north of

Galilee, *maḥsôr* describes the fact that the environment of Laish lacks nothing (18:10). The other two occurrences are in the story of the Levite and his wife in Judges 19. In 19:19 *maḥsôr* describes the fact that the Levite's party is adequately provisioned: "There is no lack (*maḥsôr*) of anything." In the following verse, the elderly man of Gibeah answers: "I will care for all your wants (*maḥsôr*)." There is thus a uniformity in the use of *maḥsôr* in the DH. It factually describes a situation relating to what could be a shortage of material goods but is not, and is *never* used to editorialize or comment on that situation.

6. מִסְכֵּן / *miskēn*

The word *miskēn* is a late Hebrew term for "poor" that appears only 4 times in the Bible, all in Ecclesiastes.

CONCLUSIONS

Close attention to the usage and distribution of the vocabulary of poverty highlights the different ideologies regarding poverty that are reflected in the Hebrew Bible. Some streams of the biblical tradition are clearly concerned about the ethical issues raised by the presence of poverty in society, although their theologies and analyses of poverty differ. Parts of the legal, prophetic, wisdom, and liturgical traditions see poverty as a matter of grave ethical concern for the community. The philosophies that drive these streams of tradition, in part, derive and explain their social visions in light of their confrontation with the realities of poverty in ancient Israelite society.

One conclusion from this study, however, is that the plight of the poor was hardly a vital issue for the DH. A notable lack of poverty language distances the Pentateuchal and DH writers from the issues of socioeconomic injustice. It is true that narratives such as those describing Solomon's use of the corvée (1 Kgs 5:27–32; 9:15–22; 12:1–17), Samuel's critique of kingship (1 Samuel 8), and the story of Ahab's appropriation of Naboth's vineyard (1 Kings 21) are potentially useful for developing sociological perspectives on the treatment of the poor in ancient Israelite society. But the language of poverty is not present in these narratives, and it would seem that this is deliberately the case. In the few cases where words for "poor" are used, they either take on different nuances or are used to discuss matters that have nothing to do with the systemic causes for the situation of the poor and the government's ethical responsibility toward them. It would seem, then, that the writers of the DH are not concerned with a critique of poverty and injustice.

The small, transformed vocabulary of poverty in the DH suggests an alternative analysis of these texts that argues that the author/s of the DH were concerned with developing a critique of kingship and foreign domination, but not with an analysis of the structures of poverty within their society. There is in the DH an assumption that national identity is the key, rather than factors such as class, race, or gender. It assumes a coherent Israelite ideology that is independent of other nations. It also sees outsiders as ruthless oppressors. The ideology of the DH is similar to the one that Itumeleng Mosala suggests guided the process of the various editions or recompositions of the book of Micah. Using criteria proposed by Robert Coote, Mosala (123–53) develops a structural reclassification of the text of Micah into Micah A (1:10–16; 2:1–5, 8–9; 3:8–12; 5:9–14; 6:9–15), Micah A B (1:8–9; 4:3–4), Micah B (1:5b–7; 2:6–7, 10–11; 3:1–7; 5:1, 4–6; 6:1–8, 16; 7:1–7), and Micah C (1:1–5a; 2:12–13; 4:1–2, 5–13; 5:2–3, 7–8; 7:8–20).

In Micah A the oracles are unambiguous about the crimes of the ruling classes. They are economic exploiters who accumulate wealth by underhanded means. The class or group of people on whose behalf the Micah A oracles speak is not sympathetic with the economic, political, and ideological interests of the class under attack. Yahweh devises evil for this class and its political and ideological structures. There is *none* of this perspective in the DH.

The B-stage materials in Micah most closely resemble the DH in their social analysis. According to Mosala, the B-stage oracles "derive their identity from a certain kind of incompleteness: they are eloquent by their silence on the struggles of poor and exploited peasants in the Israelite monarchy. Although these oracles condemn evil and injustice and exhort people to good and justice, they do not name the actual actions of oppressors, except vaguely, and the resistance of the oppressed is present only by its absence" (141). The original message of Micah (Micah A), which condemned the injustice of the unethical system in place in eighth-century BCE Judah, has been abstracted by Micah B from its concrete context, where it concerned the condition of the poor and exploited. In Micah B it is applied to the Judahite ruling class in its relationship with their foreign oppressors. The problem in view is no longer the struggle between exploited peasants and exploiting latifundiaries but the conflict between other nations and Judah. The DH, in our analysis, reflects similar interests. By abstraction the DH forces its interpretation on a wide spectrum of particular events. More significantly, abstraction helps the DH to conceal its designs. That which existed as the ethical center of other texts becomes marginalized in the DH.

The latest layer in Micah, the C-stage texts, provides the dominant ideology of the book. At this level the world of meaningful action lies in the future, not the past or the present. The God of the C-stage material is the God of restoration, who reconstructs the citadel of power of the former ruling classes of Judah. The interests of the powerful are the focus, not an interest in building democratic structures to guarantee the protection and liberation of the oppressed. If, as we have suggested, the DH served as a propaganda prop for Josiah's reform, it also reflects interests similar to those of Micah C. The firm base of the reformation proponents consisted of the king and his court officials, army commanders, priests and prophets attached to Jerusalem, and landowners and merchants of Judah—all of whom had a stake in seeing greater wealth and power flow to Jerusalem (Gottwald: 12). Since Josiah's reform program demanded an increase in revenues from his subjects, his propaganda program included appeals to his subjects' patriotism and religiosity. Internal contradictions were suppressed, and the struggle was couched in terms of Yahweh versus Assyrian foreigners and apostate Israelites. The only evidence we have of real social reforms that fundamentally addressed the question *Cui Bono?* is the oracle of Jeremiah that praises Josiah for having "judged the cause of the poor (*ʿānî*) and the needy (*ʾebyôn*)" (22:16), which may actually be a reference to wage laborers on royal construction projects who replaced corvée workers and who were the only group of the depressed populace that profited from the reforms (Gottwald: 14).

The DH thus stands in support of one of those periodic attempts to correct abuses and close the gulf between exploiters and exploited which had been instituted since the beginning of the monarchy with its state taxes and state-sanctioned indebtedness that enabled a concentration of wealth in a small elite of state functionaries and their cronies. By the time of the DH, the tributes demanded by foreign powers meant that the peasant cultivators had to bear the double burden of foreign and domestic exploitation. In this situation, interest in their welfare was lost or suppressed, and the question *Cui Bono?* was answered: "For those who have, not those who have not!"

WORKS CONSULTED

Chaney, Marvin L.
    1991   "Debt Easement in Israelite History and Tradition." Pp. 127–39 in *The Bible and the Politics of Exegesis: Essays in Honor of Norman K. Gottwald on His Sixty-Fifth Birthday*. Ed. David Jobling, Peggy L. Day, and Gerald T. Sheppard. Cleveland: Pilgrim.

Coote, Robert B.
1981   *Amos among the Prophets: Composition and Theology*. Philadelphia: Fortress.

Cross, Frank Moore
1973   *Canaanite Myth and Hebrew Epic*. Cambridge: Harvard University Press.

Dutcher-Walls, Patricia
1991   "The Social Location of the Deuteronomists: A Sociological Study of Factional Politics in Late Pre-Exilic Judah." *JSOT* 52:77–94.

Eagleton, Terry
1980   *Criticism and Ideology*. London: Verson.

Gottwald, Norman K.
1993   "Social Class as an Analytic and Hermeneutical Category in Biblical Studies." *JBL* 112:3–22.

Humbert, Paul
1952   "Le mot biblique èbyôn." *RHPR* 32:1–6.

Liverani, Mario
1992   "Propaganda." Pp. 474–77 in *The Anchor Bible Dictionary*, vol. 5. New York: Doubleday.

McKenzie, Steven L.
1992   "Deuteronomistic History." Pp. 160–68 in *The Anchor Bible Dictionary*, vol. 2. New York: Doubleday.

Mosala, Itumeleng J.
1989   *Biblical Hermeneutics and Black Theology in South Africa*. Grand Rapids: Eerdmans.

Nakanose, Shigeyuki
1993   *Josiah's Passover: Sociology and the Liberating Bible*. Maryknoll: Orbis.

Noth, Martin
1943   *Überlieferungsgeschichtliche Studien: Die sammelnden und bearbeitenden Geschichtswerke im Alten Testament*. Halle: Max Niemeyer. 3d ed., Tübingen: Max Niemeyer, 1967. E.T. in two parts: *The Deuteronomistic History*. Trans. Jane Doull et al. Foreword by E. W. Nicholson. JSOTSup 15. Sheffield: JSOT, 1981; 2d ed., 1991. *The Chronicler's History*. Trans. and with an Introduction by H. G. M. Williamson. JSOTSup 50. Sheffield: Sheffield Academic, 1987.

Pleins, J. David
1992   "Poor, Poverty." Pp. 402–14 in *The Anchor Bible Dictionary*, vol. 5. New York: Doubleday.

Steinberg, Naomi
1991   "The Deuteronomic Law Code and the Politics of State Centralization." Pp. 161–70 in *The Bible and the Politics of Exegesis: Essays in Honor of Norman K. Gottwald on His Sixty-Fifth Birthday*. Ed. David Jobling, Peggy L. Day, and Gerald T. Sheppard. Cleveland: Pilgrim.

Whitelam, Keith W.
1984   "The Defence of David." *JSOT* 29:61–87.

Williams, Ronald J.
1964   "Literature as a Medium of Political Propaganda in Ancient Egypt." Pp. 14–30 in *The Seed of Wisdom: Essays in Honour of T. J. Meek*. Ed. W. S. McCullough. Toronto: University of Toronto Press.

Wittenberg, G.
1986   "The Lexical Context of the Terminology for 'Poor' in the Book of Proverbs." *Scriptura: Tydskrif vir bybelkunde* (Stellenbosch) 2:40–85.

POLITICAL RIGHTS AND POWERS IN MONARCHIC ISRAEL

Douglas A. Knight
Vanderbilt University

ABSTRACT

While the presence of a centralized state in agrarian Israel meant severe restraints on the general populace, the question of political rights and privileges must be considered in two contexts, the macro- and the micro-level of social organization. At the national level, political and economic power was seated in a very small group of people—the royal family and the royal court, high civil and military officials, large landowners, wealthy merchants, leaders in the priesthood, and others. This governing class controlled the economic well-being as well as the legal and political viability of the rest of the country's inhabitants, who fell into a range of classes or professions with diminished status and power. However, at the local level the situation shifted, albeit not structurally. While the presence of the centralized state and its governing class was recurrently felt, social and political life continued along traditional lines in villages, lower-class urban neighborhoods, artisan enclaves, and similar contexts. Here the customs and norms inherited from the past determined an individual's political status and power. As was the case at the national level, the structure at the local level was predominantly hierarchical, even though the group in power was proportionately larger in the latter context than in the former. On the other hand, it might be argued that power exerted—often subtly and according to traditional warrants—in the local contexts was more determinative of social viability than were the egregious acts of the state and the wealthy. In neither instance is there evidence of a "rights theory." Nonetheless, the power, privileges, and political options present in Israelite society can be indicative of prevalent moral values.

The subject of "rights" is not a topic natural to the study of ancient Israel, nor is it for other cultures prior to the French Revolution. There is a general sense in legal and philosophical scholarship that before the latter part of the eighteenth century neither law nor politics was based on a principle of the rights with which all humans by nature were endowed. Anticipated by natural law theory, the passage of the Bill of Rights in England in 1689, and the writings of Hobbes, Rousseau, and Locke, the political revolutions in the United States and France gave concrete form to the question of what humans by their very being are due in terms of legal and political protections. France's Déclaration des droits de l'homme et du citoyen (1789) and the U.S. Constitution's Bill of Rights (proposed

1789, ratified 1791) became the watershed for subsequent developments in democratic polity and human rights. To be sure, those articulations of rights were not without their limitations: they were enunciated largely as a reaction to monarchialism rather than as a philosophical affirmation of human nature; their focus on government leaves unrestrained the power of social mores, which can be enormously effective in oppressing individuals or groups (note, for example, the impact of racism and sexism when unchecked by positive law); and they essentially envisioned only white males—in France largely bourgeois at that—as the ones who were endowed with such rights. It has taken events and discussions over the past two centuries to extend these rights logically into truly universal properties, and political experiments have been necessary to test their meaning and implications. All such developments are recent phenomena, and it is inevitably difficult for moderns—at least those in the democratic West—to conceive of societies not based on a doctrine of universal human rights.

Yet if rights are modern issues in the debate, the pre-modern world is not merely to be eliminated from the discussion. As has been recently demonstrated (Wiltshire), virtually every one of the numerous rights affirmed in the U.S. Bill of Rights has ample precedent in terms of legal protections in ancient Greek or Roman law. To be sure, such protections were not expressed as inalienable and universal endowments of humans, but the potential for risk and violation was perceived and prevented by positive law. Jewish law, which is often cast as obligation-based, has also been interpreted as being founded, at least implicitly, on rights by virtue of humanity's relation to the divine realm and divine command (Wolfson; Nahmani; Cohn; Cover). Nonetheless, finding precedents or implied principles is not the same as speaking of rights, just as one cannot logically infer rights from obligations or commands (Hart 1955; but cf. Stoljar: 36–50). The issue might be put starkly in the following form: if one was fully unaware of the rights discussion of the past two centuries, one would never think to describe the legal systems of the Jews, the Romans, the Greeks, or the ancient Israelites in terms of inalienable and universal human rights. Having stated that, there is nevertheless more that can be said. The entrée, we will find, occurs through the disciplines of the anthropology of politics and the anthropology of law. For ethics, the results can be related to moral values that pertain to the worth of humans and the communitarian ideal.

At an even prior level, however, one might ask whether it is legitimate at all to inquire about rights in ancient Israel if such notions were foreign to that society. Are we not inappropriately imposing modern categories on an ancient society, thereby introducing distortion and confusion in our effort to understand it? The answer would be affirmative if we were prematurely to posit a rights-theory in that culture, either in its political structures or in its legal provisions. However, asking the question is not illegitimate. Interpreters must necessarily draw on their own concepts, categories, and perspectives if they are to function as historians, attempting to recover the character of the past in terms understandable by the present. An endless variety of other examples either anachronistic to or differently understood in antiquity appear in contemporary discussions about the history and religion of ancient Israel, such as the idea of history itself, historiographical criteria, theology, myth, literature, text, society, class, and the like. In all such cases we invest these terms with meanings alien to the ancient Israelites. For us today, "rights" constitutes a notion with which we are intimately familiar, and if we fail to investigate it—both the theory and the practice of rights—we run the risk of presuming precisely what needs to be established: whether the theory was explicitly or even implicitly present in Israel and whether their practices, even in the absence of such a theory, were conducted in a manner consistent with what we understand as rights.

RIGHTS, POLITICS, AND POWER

We need first to establish a way to think about rights, and to this end we will begin by focusing on the general area of legal rights before turning to the specific realm of politics.[1] The complex debate lasting from the eighteenth century until the present has resulted in two primary perspectives concerning legal rights, the first rooted in the theories of

---

[1] As may be evident, political rights and legal rights are not identical, although they can share some common ground. Legal rights, just as political rights, involve liberties and protections, but their domain is law and juridical procedures. Political rights, conflicts over which might indeed end up in court, represent a subset of rights that focuses on political activity and expression. Actually, political activities, especially when they occur as subtle maneuvers within a political system, often do not result in legal conflict simply because they are not perceived to be political, or because they are effectively reinforced by social sanctions or brute force, or because they seem to be so entrenched within the given social system that opposition to them appears fruitless. Our focus in the present discussion is limited to investigating whether the Israelites sensed and exercised any "rights" in the determination of their political well-being. The extent to which any legal rights were recognized or were implicit in Israel's laws will remain unaddressed in the present discussion, except to reiterate that, while certain fundamental values and norms probably existed in ancient Israel, rights in the modern sense should not be expected. For discussions relevant to the question of legal rights or values in ancient Israel, see Horst; Greenberg 1960; Harrelson; Barr 1989; Crüsemann 1992.

natural law and social contract and the second in utilitarian philosophy.[2] Adherents of the first view speak of *natural rights*, inherent and usually inalienable features universal to all human beings and knowable through human reason. Such rights normally include life, freedom, pursuit of well-being, and protection from unjustified punishment; various theories encompass additional characteristics as well. These rights are considered natural endowments either because they are thought to be God-given or, in a non-theistic approach, because they are held to be, by nature, a part of the very makeup and definition of what it means to be human. Morris R. Cohen and Lon L. Fuller are among the recent legal theorists advocating a revived version of the natural rights approach.

The alternative, utilitarian theory envisions only *positive rights*, which are explicitly enacted and enforced by law, i.e. by positive law rather than by some postulated natural law. Ever since Jeremy Bentham referred dismissively to rights as "rhetorical nonsense,—nonsense upon stilts" (501 [Article II, Sentence 1]), his utilitarian heritage has tended to regard rights in terms of especially compelling interests, which people choose through law to protect and maximize. Legal positivism, a descendant of utilitarianism, now holds a dominant position in legal theory; John Austin, Hans Kelsen, and H. L. A. Hart are representative of this tradition. To the natural law position that legal rights can only be grounded in natural rights, positivists respond that numerous laws and governmental actions do in fact exist without any basis in rights. For positivists, laws and legal rights stem from society and not necessarily from nature, and their legitimacy derives from their social parentage and not from their congruence with some putative divine or natural law. Even if there may be natural rights, they argue, it is altogether possible that they are not determinative for a given society's laws since the people may choose not to enact them as law.

There is a substantial range of theories and nuances within these two schools of thought, and as might be expected each tradition advocates a very different assessment of the relation between law and morality. Positivist theories, with their emphasis on legal analysis, logical reasoning in legislation, and laws as products of the ruling body, tend to dispute

---

[2] To be sure, legal philosophy includes a much wider variety of theories and approaches than just these two. Yet while such schools of thought as legal realism, idealist theories of law, sociology and anthropology of law, and Critical Legal Studies offer varying perspectives on law, fundamentally their respective positions on rights are formulated in relation to or in reaction to either the natural law tradition or the positivist tradition. Ronald Dworkin, who seeks an alternative route by emphasizing the importance of interpretation, hermeneutics, and the social construction of principles, is an example of a theorist whose considerations are firmly based on a critique of the debate.

any *necessary* connection between law and morality. As stated by Hart (1961:181–82), "it is in no sense a necessary truth that laws reproduce or satisfy certain demands of morality, though in fact they have often done so." Such a view differs markedly from the classical and modern natural law positions, according to which a law that is immoral is not to be considered a law, or conversely: law, i.e. positive law, is intrinsically moral, there being no separation between "is" and "ought." For our purpose in the present discussion, we will not dwell on these two different jurisprudential approaches but will instead take a tact that draws primarily on the fields of the sociology and anthropology of law and politics. By focusing on the social and economic dimensions of political and legal action, with special attention to roles, functions, and class, we may find it possible to move beyond the issues dominating the natural law–positivism debate on legal rights—a debate, in fact, that Ronald Dworkin (1986:98) observes has actually been "a contest between different political theories" inasmuch as rival groups in society contend with each other over the validity of statutory law.

What then are we to make of political rights specifically? The same division between the natural law theory and the legal positivist theory pertains for the identification of political rights and the moral basis of such rights. Are humans by nature endowed with certain rights concerning their political self-determinacy, or are any such rights they may enjoy simply theirs not by nature but by the people's own assertion and enactment? More specifically, are political rights legitimated by reference to natural rights? For our analysis of Israelite politics, we will examine these questions not in the abstract but in specific terms, restricting ourselves to four fundamental areas of action or protection that can in a society have the status of political rights. The most general is the right of *self-determination*, the prerogative and power to choose or affirm one's type of political system and to participate, whether directly or indirectly, in the ongoing administration of government, including the making and enforcing of laws. The corollary is the right of *citizenship* itself: who is considered a citizen, who is not, and on what grounds? Third is the right of *protection* from inappropriate state intrusion and from injury at the hands of others. Fourth is the right of *dissent* or, more specifically, civil disobedience, openly breaking a law that one considers morally corrupt. Various societies and theorists have affirmed numerous other political rights, many as elaborations of the abovementioned, but at least these four seem to be foundational.[3] Although they are stated here as

---

[3] Isaiah Berlin has proposed the now well-known division between two types of freedom, one positive and the other negative. Positive liberty consists of an individual's desire to be the primary determiner of one's own goals and life, whereas

if they were natural rights, my intention is rather to present them heuristically in order to inquire whether or not any of these substantive points appeared or functioned as rights in the political systems of ancient Israel. We should not expect to find them identified as rights, but we may be able to make certain inferences about their substance on the basis of Israelite sociopolitical contexts as well as biblical texts, particularly those which represent an attempted check on the abuse of political power. Moreover, it is also important to note the grounds on which any appeal is made on behalf of these "rights" or against their abuse.

One further point emerges in this context, viz. the connection between rights and power. At a practical level it would seem that those persons with power have rights, while those lacking power also lack rights. Certainly, privileging one group—e.g., males—means the potential marginalization of other groups—in this case, of course, females, but probably also children if the privileged males are primarily adults, and perhaps even elderly males if their status has diminished by virtue of their lesser involvement in the life of the community. Power tends to be used as a means of self-preservation, for by asserting their rights those in power can eviscerate a reform movement; Bartlett and Kennedy, eds., present multiple examples relating to the legal status of women. Power can thus designate the ability or likelihood of persons to effect their will, even against resistance. It is the ability to achieve a result, and in the political arena it often becomes power over power, i.e., the capacity to marshall other power groups toward some end. Max Weber distinguishes power from authority, the latter being the socially legitimated exercise of control (e.g., by bureaucrats) and the former referring to the actual capacity to realize one's will even against resistance (1947:152–53, 324ff.; also 1946:159–264; Meyers [40–45] applies this distinction in her study of female status in ancient Israel). Although often wielded by an individual, power adheres especially to groups according to economic class, social status, and political party.[4] Power may manifest itself in raw terms but more often works through subtle and indirect means. The "hermeneutics of suspicion," which aims to expose ulterior motives of control, is

---

negative freedom is the absence of outside interference with or obstruction of one's own actions. In terms of this dichotomy, the first two political rights mentioned above embody primarily positive freedoms while the latter two rights comprise mainly negative freedoms.

[4] See the extended discussion of powers and privileges in Lenski, particularly pp. 189–296 on the state in agrarian societies. While monarchy and its effects in ancient Israel have been much examined, the theme of political power has not received much explicit attention in Hebrew Bible studies. See, however, Walsh; and Lind, who focuses though on "divine politics" as an antidote to the negative aspects of human power.

warranted at all levels, not only in criticizing society—ancient and modern—but also in reading the biblical texts. To a significant degree, the Hebrew Bible in its present form represents the canonization of power and deserves to be scrutinized as such.[5] While earlier strata and especially oral traditions may well reveal the viewpoints of broader segments of the population, the few who had a hand in the final production of the text were largely members of the elite class, who had their own interests at stake as they sought to define the norms for all others. Thus the very character of political power, just as that of religious orthodoxy, requires that we learn to be suspicious of such norms, asking who benefits from them and who suffers loss, who becomes legitimated and who becomes excluded or controlled. Only through examining the evidence in such a manner can we hope to identify the realistic political options possessed by various groups and individuals across the full spectrum of Israelite society. By so doing we should reach some understanding of "rights" and powers, and thereby also aspects of the value systems at work in that ancient culture.

One of the distinct achievements of the field of political anthropology[6] has been a reconsideration of the very nature of politics on the basis of comparative data. No longer is it acceptable to regard only the "higher," complex state systems as being political in character, for societies without a state apparatus are equally political, only in different ways. In our examination of political rights and powers in ancient Israel, we will focus on the two primary political levels during the period of the Israelite monarchy, the national state and the local context, the latter typified by the village but represented also in lower-class urban neighborhoods with lineage or professional cohesion. One should avoid the common distinction between center and periphery because it sets the center as the point of reference: other regions are considered peripheral to it. Such a duality tends to diminish the experiences of those not located in the seats of national power. From the perspective of villagers, of course, their own contexts constitute the heart of life in the whole region, and the capital city and urban culture are marginal and anomalous in comparison.[7] We

---

[5] The ideological character of literature has come under analysis recently. See, e.g., various works by Terry Eagleton (especially 1976, 1983, 1991); and for the biblical literature: Jobling and Pippin, eds.

[6] For basic treatments of political anthropology, see the following and the bibliographies they contain: Vincent; Balandier; Cohen and Middleton, eds.

[7] Edward Shils, who has conducted instructive sociological analyses of the multi-leveled society, explicitly associates the center with the elites and the periphery with the hinterland populations over whom the elites exercise authority. While such groupings and dimensions in society certainly exist, in historical and theoretical scholarship such characterizations as central/peripheral can easily prejudice the

will use the terms "national" or "centralized" to designate the level of government that seeks to control the whole region politically, economically, and ideologically, and "local" will refer to the level of sociopolitical life more restricted to smaller geographical areas, usually only a village or neighborhood or perhaps several of these situated contiguously.

NATIONAL POLITICS

Once the state had emerged on the Israelite scene—and for what reason and through what process will need to be left untouched at this point—the balance of power shifted radically, and with it the exercise of political "rights" and privileges. Even though there never was a time when power was fully and equally diffused throughout the population, the presence of royalty and the machine of state had an unrelenting, inexorable impact on the populace. The vast majority of the people had their options limited by virtue of the demands the state could make of them in terms of taxation, production, military or labor conscription, property, and more. Let us look in sequence and in summary fashion at the four political rights mentioned above.

1. Self-determination and Participation. First Samuel records two traditions concerning the founding of the monarchy, one "promonarchical" (9:1–10:16) which is thought to be early and the other "antimonarchical" (8:1–22; 10:17–27) which is generally held to be later, probably Deuteronomistic (or, rather, from the later redactor DtrN; see Veijola). While the two stories depict diametrically different divine assessments of royalty, there is actually no direct conflict in terms of popular sentiments: if Israel demands a monarchy in one account, they do not resist when God volunteers it in the other narrative. It is quite reasonable to expect that a move toward the familiar political structure of a kingdom, "like all the

---

discussion in favor of the center, the intellectual power base to which the present-day researchers and writers themselves typically belong. Another example of biased terminology is the common distinction between the Great Tradition and the Little Tradition, the former "cultivated in schools or temples" while the latter "works itself out and keeps itself going in the lives of the unlettered in their village communities. The tradition of the philosopher, theologian, and literary man is a tradition consciously cultivated and handed down; that of the little people is for the most part taken for granted and not submitted to much scrutiny or considered refinement and improvement"—to cite Redfield's description in his influential study (1956:70). Rainer Albertz is among the growing list of biblical scholars who seek to acknowledge with appreciation the religious pluralism present in ancient Israel at the various levels of society. For general comments and cautions about scholarly assessment of Israelite "popular religion"—and a similar evaluation could be made of Israelite "popular morality"—see Berlinerblau.

nations" (1 Sam 8:5), would have been appealing to many; how extensively is impossible to say. To view it as a plebiscite is too simplistic and anachronistic. In all likelihood a centralized state emerged gradually, with a type of chieftaincy preceding the monarchy (Flanagan). For our purposes it is enough to assume that the people willed it, or at least did not oppose it. On the other hand, if they exercised some political right in the establishment of the kingdom, they effectively abdicated their sovereignty thereafter. The monarchy became the status quo, the only remaining question being succession. Despite the claims to the contrary (Alt), there was no charismatic—let alone "democratic"—principle at work in the Northern Kingdom as opposed to a dynastic principle in the South (Ishida: 171-82; Buccellati: 200-8). The tendency in a monarchy is to perpetuate itself, and the coups d'état in the North under Jeroboam I, Omri, and Jehu did not seek to introduce a different type of political structure but only to place an individual outside the line on the throne; thereafter the dynastic ideal prevailed again. Certainly the notion of the "assembly" is greatly overplayed in our minds.[8] If it ever served as a check on monarchic absolutism (McKenzie: 539), that must certainly have occurred only as an ad hoc intervention by the elite, not as an act of a standing, authorized, widely representative body, much less as a political convention to choose a successor or to arbitrate a treaty. The Hebrew Bible occasionally depicts all of the people as being explicitly in support of their kings (e.g., 1 Kgs 12:20 [concerning Jeroboam I]; 14:22-24 [Rehoboam]; 16:16-17, 21-22 [Omri]; 2 Kgs 11:17 [Jehoash]; 14:21 [Azariah]; 23:2-3 [Josiah]). While we might suspect that there was some measure of popular backing for individual kings and that the kings would have found it expedient to solicit such support especially among their officers, their clients, the central priesthood, and others in powerful

---

[8] Several studies, especially Jacobsen, Wolf, and Gordis, have associated the assembly with a type of "primitive democracy." Note, for example, Gordis's assertion (387) concerning the assembly: "It is uniquely characteristic of Israel that unlike other Semitic peoples, it retained the strong democratic impulse derived from the nomadic stage in the agricultural and urbanized culture of monarchical days"—and thereafter, in fact, this "positive democratic spirit" continued to survive and eventually "entered the fabric of Western civilization" (388). This basic thesis is flawed at many levels, two points being particularly relevant for the monarchic period: If the members of the assembly were, as is admitted, only "the free, adult, male citizens without distinction of fortune or class" (Jacobsen: 159; also Wolf: 98), then the elimination of women and non-free groups would make this political type patriarchal not democratic, and unequal on the basis of class or standing as well. Secondly, one must distinguish between the assembly of males at the local levels of society—in villages, for example— and the putative gathering of males at the level of national politics, which is likely to have been more of a literary fiction than a historical reality. In de Boer's words, "Israël n'a jamais été une démocratie" (227). See also Sutherland.

positions in the country, at the same time these statements certainly served the Deuteronomistic historians' aim of seeing that the people were implicated with their leaders and deserved the same punishment or approbation as the kings received. From what we know about such monarchies, the people at large would have enjoyed little if any right of participation, whether directly or indirectly, in the ongoing administration of government, including the making and enforcing of laws. The Hebrew Bible displays a massive effort to legitimate the king politically and religiously (Mettinger), even to the point of suggesting a special relationship between the king and Israel's God. From such efforts, however, one might infer that the people were not always enamored with their monarchy and needed repeated persuasion to comply with its expectations.

2. *Citizenship.* If by citizenship is meant the power and right to participate fully in the political processes of the state, then there were few members in Israel's national political community. To be sure, everyone living within its borders was subject to the dominion of the government, but the number who actually had the capacity to effect change at the national level was surely meager, probably not more than a few percent of the total population. This governing class—the royal family, the courtiers, high military and civil officials, large landowners, wealthy merchants, leaders in the priesthood, and others—controlled the economic well-being as well as the legal and political viability of the rest of the country's inhabitants, whose status and political options would have been slight in comparison.9 In all likelihood, the group called עם הארץ ("the people of the land") during the monarchic period, who according to the Hebrew Bible wielded political and economic influence alongside the kings, consisted of the elite class, not the people as a whole. To call the Israelite political structure a "participatory monarchy" (Talmon: 16) as opposed to a despotic monarchy may have some validity so long as it is understood that those "participating" with the king were not the people at large, nor even all the landed free males, but essentially only the members of the small upper class close to the king. Anyone who possessed power in such a situation did so at the pleasure of the monarch. Reformers, such as some of the prophets, might have been able to wield substantial power—but on the basis not of rights but of their religious and moral authority. Thus in such a political system citizenship carried, at best, only limited meaning.

---

9 For a recent discussion of those groups holding political and economic power in Israel, see Kessler, especially 132–207. The question of social class in ancient Israel has often been neglected; see now Gottwald 1993, 1992.

3. *Protection.* Ever since Montesquieu's description in 1748, the image of "Oriental despotism" has become synonymous with harsh and absolute power applied by a totalitarian regime. Whether or not the reign of kings in the ancient Near East amounted to "total terror—total submission—total loneliness," as Wittfogel (127) describes this political type in his controversial study, can be debated. Montesquieu sought to distinguish between a monarchy and a despotic regime: The former is more complex, being governed by the rule of law and the traditions of an honorable monarch and having a range of political and social institutions to modify the actions of the ruler. The classic "Oriental despot," on the other hand, has sole and total grasp of power, with all subjects serving essentially as slaves. If these two types of hierarchical government are the only options, then it would seem that "Oriental despotism" has only limited and occasional relevance for our subject. The legal tradition prominent in the ancient Near East suggests certain restrictions, or at least ideals, under which the monarchs ruled, and substantial institutions—religious, commercial, artisan, tribal, legal—complicated the execution of a king's arbitrary will. Presumably, the monarchs would normally abide by the customs of the land, which conveyed a sense of order and obligation basic to social living. But such protection could easily wear thin for a subject who stood in the way of a king's desire. Two stories in the Hebrew Bible that demonstrate this situation graphically and poignantly are, first, David's actions against Bathsheba and Uriah and, second, Ahab and Jezebel's expropriation of Naboth's land: David respects no limits regarding Bathsheba and then makes Uriah unknowingly carry his own death warrant, and Jezebel engages successfully in a judicial sham. Here is no illusion of citizen rights; rather, subjects in the kingdom were on the alert that ultimately they could hope for no legal protection or recourse against the king's will. Direct elimination of rival threats to the throne certainly transpired with no show of due process. The biblical texts predicting *ex eventu* that the monarchs would exploit the population (1 Sam 8:11–17; Deut 17:16–20) reflect the actual recurring experiences of the people. Thus the phrase משפט המלך (1 Sam 8:9, 11) refers not to the kings' rights in the sense of natural or divine endowments but to the customary practices and privileges which they, backed by the power of their office, were able to implement. Similarly, the משפט הכהנים (Deut 18:3; 1 Sam 2:13; similarly כמשפטם in 1 Chr 6:17; 24:19; 2 Chr 30:16) designates not so much certain natural rights but powers or prerogatives developed by the priests themselves for their own benefit (viz. the portions they were to receive of the sacrifices), or the customary duties which they chose to assume in the cult. The powers of the kings, priests, and other elites were socially constructed—not directly by the people at

large, but by the individuals or groups standing to gain the most from them. On a national scale, the prophets are the only known political advocates of the oppressed groups of ancient Israel, those who were especially vulnerable because they did not have a family network of support (the widows and orphans), or equal legal standing in the community (slaves and foreigners), or economic flexibility (the poor). The prophets invoked the divine will and the communitarian ideal in order to protect these groups. Interestingly, in Israel it is the prophets and not the rulers who are most often presented as the proponents of justice and compassion, whereas in neighboring countries the monarchs and overlords are occasionally pictured as the protectors of the disenfranchised (e.g., Hammurabi in the preamble to the Code; Daniel in the Legend of Aqhat; various powerful individuals in Egyptian funerary inscriptions and prayers).

4. *Dissent.* We can hardly speak of a political right of dissent or of civil disobedience under the monarchy. The better question is whether or not the people ever engaged in such protest and, if so, on what grounds and with what effect. Unfortunately our literary sources pose special limitations on our ability to answer this question, for the Hebrew Bible records essentially the viewpoints that were in some way favorable, or at least tolerable, to the power groups who preserved and canonized the literary heritage. There were plausibly any number of individual or group acts of dissent that are lost to history. Many such instances of opposition might have been veiled, and perhaps are still present in our texts but difficult to decode. David Daube (52–59) has suggested, for example, that slaves in Rome and Greece would couch their political critique in the form of fables, which they could repeat among themselves and even to their masters' households with little risk of punishment. Similarly, women are frequently depicted in the Hebrew Bible as undermining or countering the status quo through acts of deception vis-à-vis governmental officials: the two midwives lied to the Egyptian pharaoh (Exod 1:15–19), Rahab deceived the king of Jericho (Joshua 2), and the woman of Tekoa spoke falsely to David, while Bathsheba (1 Kgs 1:11–31) and Esther (Esther 5–7) connived against their royal husbands (see Craven; Fuchs). Here and elsewhere, the biblical tradition condones acts pitching someone against the state if religion or morality is at stake; the conflicts involving prophets such as Elijah and Jeremiah demonstrate this well. We can be assured that the kings in question, as well as their supporters, did not share this favorable assessment. The monarchic state would have considered any dissent as an undermining of the total power on which the government rested. Not only the royal house but also others in the elite—the wealthy landowners, high officials, priests—would have been equally intolerant of

threats to the status quo. Again the prophets epitomize such opposition to oppressive practices, although they presumably acted not alone but with circles of support among the people (Wilson 1980). Several recent studies have proposed cryptic revolutionary backgrounds for certain texts dealing ostensibly with other matters, e.g., that Genesis 2-3 depicts Adam and Eve as peasants who revolt against established authority and are justly punished for it (Kennedy); or again, that this same text is an allegory of David's rise to power, followed by the weakening of his control over the kingdom (Rosenberg); or again, that the Elohistic texts in the Pentateuch represent the North's justification of Jeroboam's great revolt against the Davidic house (Coote). The point is that, while we can find no explicit right of protest in the monarchic period, it is reasonable to assume that dissent did occur—occasionally in public, much more frequently in private, and probably not seldom hidden in the text.[10]

LOCAL POLITICS

In his portrayal of life in contemporary Near Eastern villages, C. A. O. van Nieuwenhuijze distinguishes between the ways in which state authority and local authority operate. When governmental officials appear on the scene, their interests focus on enforcing state decisions, and the villagers typically accord them reluctant and minimal compliance at best. As he states, "it may well be that what is peace and order from the central government viewpoint (or that of its representatives) is not identical with peace and order from the village viewpoint" (306; see Mendenhall [97] for a comparable observation concerning the situation in ancient Israel). The difference is significant enough that we can speak of two distinct political systems, the national and the local—the latter varying to some degree throughout the land, but its greatest contrast evident nonetheless in comparison with national politics.

In terms of sheer numbers the local context was by far the more populous. Probably between 80% and 95% of the country's total inhabitants lived in non-urban settings. Villages were small, perhaps some 200-300 persons in each but frequently fewer. So many villages dotted the landscape that in most of the habitable regions they were often only 2-4 km apart from each other. Given this predominance of the peasant population, the relatively little attention paid by historians to village life reflects, as much as anything, the bias of the historians themselves. Cities, almost by definition, constituted the locus of public,

---

[10] For further discussion of dissent and rebellion, see Crüsemann 1978; Carroll; Parker; and Tadmor.

wide-ranging, and powerful interests, the driving force behind national politics and economics. In contrast, villages thrived socially on their relative isolation from the wider universe of the nation-state, and indeed from urban life in general,[11] although city and village were economically intermeshed. Parallel to archaeologists' earlier preference for the monumental and the affluent, historians have tracked the ups and downs of cities rather than the fate of villages, which were less likely to produce impressive artifacts of "high culture." For our understanding of Israel's rights and powers and thus political ethics and in light of the disproportionate demographics, however, local politics deserves equal if not significantly more attention than does state politics.

But first a word of caution. Anthropologists have long shown interest in small-scale societies, frequently contrasting village and city as two distinct types of social networks. Following his 1926–27 field study of the Mexican village of Tepoztlán, Robert Redfield (1930, 1941, 1947) introduced the ideal-type of the "folk society," and scores of other researchers have followed his depiction of peasant village life. In 1943–44, 1947, and 1948, however, Oscar Lewis revisited Tepoztlán and returned with a very different description. Whereas Redfield, he wrote, had given a "Rousseauan" impression of "a relatively homogeneous, isolated, smoothly functioning, and well-integrated society made up of a contented and well-adjusted people," Lewis's own findings emphasized "the underlying individualism of Tepoztecan institutions and character, the lack of cooperation, the tensions between villages within the municipio, the schisms within the village, the pervading quality of fear, envy, and distrust in inter-personal relations" (Lewis: 428–29). Redfield responded (1955:132–48) that, while some of the differences in the descriptions were probably due to the significant social and economic changes that occurred in the seventeen years between their studies, the deeper reason for the contrast lay in the dissimilarity between the two investigators—their training, research methods, type of data gathered, and personal sentiments. Taken together, he argued, the two views comprise a dialectic that is necessary for an adequate comprehension of the community as a whole.[12] For our purposes, this dispute counsels against facile conclusions

---

[11] Eckart Otto has recognized this separation between rural and urban contexts in his assessment of the origin of many Israelite laws: while individual legal practices may have been indigenous to the villagers' administration of justice, these principles were certainly formulated and codified in urban contexts where the influence of cuneiform law would more likely have been felt.

[12] Redfield (1955:136–37) cites a similar contrast in the interpretations different anthropologists have offered of the Pueblo Indians of the American Southwest, and he attributes the contrast to "the approval the first anthropologists gave to the moral unity of Pueblo life, and . . . the disapproval the second group of anthropologists gave

about the supposed idyllic, harmonious society of peasants. Israelite villagers were quite successful in developing a workable and sustainable social organization, but that should not suggest that politically and economically they achieved an equitable, consensual arrangement.

1. *Self-determination and Participation.* At first glance it would appear that the political system of the village was informal whereas the politics of the state ran along fixed and formal lines. Such an interpretation, however, underestimates the social fabric of the village. Lacking the apparatus of state, the local communities operated according to patterns of behavior, status, honor, and custom that together functioned more tenaciously than a monarch could hope to achieve for the policies of state. The key was inculcation and socialization, reinforced by sanctions. With power distribution thus set by tradition, political self-determination or complicity become moot points: an individual's inclination to alter the system was generally doomed to fail. Ongoing participation in the political community was another matter, with potentially all adults either directly or indirectly involved, depending on status and other traditional criteria. If we are to assume that some type of segmentary lineage system prevailed throughout the monarchic period, we are thrust into the complex network of kinship and politics in these villages. The acephalous segmentary society relies on the principle of descent to define the various segments and their relations with others at the same levels, families to families, clans to clans, and with ever-increasing concentric circles so long as the groups claim a common ancestor. Israel's centralized monarchic state may seem to have displaced this structure, but actually it was only superimposed on the segmentary society, which could continue to function as powerfully as ever—and to the frustration, probably, of state officials.

2. *Citizenship.* The segmentary society is not as egalitarian as is often described. Indeed, one of the most important corrections made by anthropologists to this model has been to observe stratification within it (Balandier: 74–75). In ancient Israelite village life, kinship relations, gender, age, profession, and property affected the political standing of persons and groups. In the most basic of the social segments, the

---

to the authoritarianism and repressions of Pueblo society. It appears that both accounts are true." One might wonder, however, whether Redfield's notion of a dialectic represents too easy an accommodation of these divergent assessments. For example, did the putative "moral unity" result from the "authoritarianism and repressions," or are the latter largely anomalous reactions in a basically homogeneous society? The researcher needs to try to resolve such questions rather than merely attribute the social phenomena to the varying perspectives of the observers, as important as the latter are in the process of interpretation.

household or בית אב, the male head possessed the primary authority, even over any other adult males who might have resided in the household. It is quite likely, as Carol Meyers has suggested, that women actually exerted considerable power, especially because of their essential roles in production, food preparation, and procreation, and also because of their substituting for their husbands when the men were conscripted into the military or labor gangs. As a group, the male heads of the households comprised the local body of elders, who made necessary decisions regarding judicial, cultic, commercial, and other matters. Presumably, although we have little indication of it except in latifundial situations, property conveyed some measure of status at the village or clan level as well. Honor/shame sanctions could also affect one's standing (Gilmore, ed.; Bechtel; Stone). In sum, the political system at the local level was, despite its cohesiveness and cooperation, founded no more on a community of equals than was its counterpart at the national level. In both cases, the structure was predominantly hierarchical, although the group in power was proportionately larger in the villages than in the nation-state.

3. Protection. In the tightly knit local society individuals could count on protection so long as they conformed to the social norms, expressed in mores and customary law. As Robert Wilson (1983) has shown, disputes in a lineage system are handled more effectively at the lower local levels where lineage unity is strong, than at the tribal or national levels where communal consensus is more elusive. In villages the legal apparatus was community based, with the elders as the adjudicators. Restitution in the case of torts aimed to restore the injured party to a position of viability. Kinship provided the guarantee of protection in the first instance, as evidenced by the practices of redemption and blood vengeance. Those least protected, such as widows and orphans, were the ones who lacked an immediate family base. Resident aliens held some but not full legal rights, while slaves depended largely on the good will of their masters. On the whole, a certain equilibrium characterized the segmentary society, especially at the lower levels. Community approbation or shame served as a powerful motivator and corrective.

4. Dissent. Did individuals or groups in these local communities have appreciable options to dissent from these political structures, i.e. from the political system within the villages (in other words, quite apart from any dissent at the national level)? It might appear so if violation of a law constituted a form of protest, for the laws according to which the local societies operated were for the most part direct reflections of their social values. But other motives or factors than dissent could be at stake in breaking laws. As we saw for the national level, some biblical stories of deception seem indicative of opposition to traditional customs or restrictions: Rebekah's trickery against Isaac in order to secure his blessing on Jacob (Genesis 27); Jacob's conniving against Laban for the livestock and then Rachel's lying to her father about the household gods (Genesis 30-31); Judah's failure to fulfill the levirate obligation, and then Tamar's seduction of him because she was left defenseless (Genesis 38); Samson's ruin because of his wife's and later Delilah's complicity with the Philistines (Judg 14:15-20; 16:4-21); and, although issues of state were also at play, Jonathan's and Michal's siding with David against their father (1 Samuel 19ff.). Directly and not deceptively, the daughters of Zelophehad challenged the male-oriented law of inheritance (Numbers 27; see also Numbers 36). Mieke Bal's reading of the book of Judges shifts the focus from the seemingly dominant theme of wartime violence to the more fundamental violence within the social, domestic order, a violence that "seems to be the inevitable consequence of a social structure that is inherently contradictory" (231), particularly in its treatment of women. Feuding within a society based ostensibly on an ideology of equity can be another indication of fundamental rifts along economic and political lines (Black-Michaud). On the whole, we should note, it is impossible for us to know how extensive the dissent might have been within the local political community, for the bulk of our literature from the monarchic period focuses on the rulers, their intrigues, and their wars. Probably any such opposition should be regarded as ad hoc responses rather than as fundamental challenges to the prevailing political and legal systems. The local network of norms and sanctions exerted power often subtly and according to traditional warrants, and consequently its strategies were more effective in determining social viability than were the egregious acts of the state and the wealthy.

CONCLUSION

Political as well as social inequality persisted throughout Israel's history. The strength of the centralized state was disproportionate to its numbers in comparison with the rural population. Power at the local level was too diffused to resist the monarchy effectively or to exert a comparable set of controls at the national level. On the other hand, local power was most felt—if not in its geographical reach, then in its intensity—in its regulation of the everyday lives of its members. Structurally, a hierarchy of control prevailed at both the local and the state levels, in neither case driven by a philosophy or theology of rights. Nonetheless, humans were held to have high worth (Greenberg 1966;

Knight 1989)—even if in a rather utilitarian sense at the state level from the perspective of the ruling class—but this high valuation of persons was not connected to an explicit notion of the rights with which all are endowed or which could be ensured by positive law. In the local contexts the well-being of the community and the continuation of its customs were paramount, and any "rights" adhered primarily to the social organism, the harmony and survival of which were not to be jeopardized. A communitarian ideal of sorts can be extrapolated from the segmentary society, but more as a result of tradition and social coherence (or, as Bal suggests, counter-coherence?) than due to a rights theory.

What remains for us is an open question: What can positively be said about Israel's hierarchical political and social structures, especially with respect to distribution of wealth, authority, and responsibility? Did these structures even approximate Rawls's second principle of justice, viz. that "while the distribution of wealth and income need not be equal, it must be to everyone's advantage, and at the same time, positions of authority and offices of command must be accessible to all" (61)? For all practical purposes, such accessibility did not obtain at either the national or the local level in Israel's political systems. Viewed nationally, the distribution of wealth and authority under the monarchy could scarcely have benefited the masses, who were subject to the whimsical moves of the elite. The village contexts, with their own variety of hierarchy, may have fostered more of an economically integrated, communitarian system, although the literature indicates that powerless and disadvantaged individuals were also to be found.

Whatever our own assessment of political and economic power in the modern world, the Hebrew Bible manifestly opts in favor of a hierarchy in terms of divine, royal, and familial relations, a hierarchy reinforced by the notion of order set at creation and, perhaps, basic to a type of "natural theology."[13] Interestingly, though, the biblical tradition also preserves voices of serious dissent concerning God's reign (especially in the wisdom literature) and the kings' rule, but only occasionally concerning the power and privileges of the pater familias. Political ethics, it would seem, is oriented toward order, traditional roles, and maximization of interests. Even with power concentrated proportionately in more plentiful hands at the local level and in much fewer hands at the national level, we must not be deceived into supposing that anything approaching democratic polity prevailed in ancient Israel—in any context. Nonetheless, the vast majority of the population certainly experienced more of a sense of political

---

[13] Cautious use of the categories "natural theology" or "natural law" with respect to ancient Israel seems to be warranted. See Barr 1990, 1993:81–101; Horst; Gehman; Barton; Collins; Knight 1985.

involvement and responsibility in their local community than was possible for them in the centralized state. Yet such involvement was not defined according to certain "rights" with which they were endowed, nor were rights explicitly enacted by law and grounded in natural rights. The terms of action were set by social norms and traditions, and not everyone enjoyed the same privileges. However, to the extent that individuals or groups could effect their will or express their dissent in public arenas, they had—if not rights—at least some political options.

WORKS CONSULTED

Albertz, Rainer
1978   *Persönliche Frömmigkeit und offizielle Religion: Religionsinterner Pluralismus in Israel und Babylon.* Calwer Theologische Monographien, 9. Stuttgart: Calwer.

Alt, Albrecht
1967   "The Monarchy in the Kingdoms of Israel and Judah." Pp. 312–35 in *Essays on Old Testament History and Religion.* Trans. R. A. Wilson. Garden City: Doubleday, 1967. German original in 1951.

Austin, John
1832   *The Province of Jurisprudence Determined.* Reprinted with an Introduction by H. L. A. Hart: London: Weidenfeld and Nicolson, 1954.

Bal, Mieke
1988   *Death and Dissymmetry: The Politics of Coherence in the Book of Judges.* Chicago and London: The University of Chicago Press.

Balandier, Georges
1970   *Political Anthropology.* Trans. A. M. Sheridan Smith. New York: Pantheon Books. French original in 1967.

Barr, James
1989   "Ancient Biblical Laws and Modern Human Rights." Pp. 21–33 in *Justice and the Holy: Essays in Honor of Walter Harrelson.* Ed. Douglas A. Knight and Peter J. Paris. Homage Series, 12. Atlanta: Scholars.
1990   "Biblical Law and the Question of Natural Theology." Pp. 1–22 in *The Law in the Bible and in Its Environment.* Ed. Timo Veijola. Publications of the Finnish Exegetical Society, 51. Helsinki: The Finnish Exegetical Society; Göttingen: Vandenhoeck & Ruprecht.
1993   *Biblical Faith and Natural Theology: The Gifford Lectures for 1991 Delivered in the University of Edinburgh.* Oxford: Clarendon.

Bartlett, Katharine T., and Rosanne Kennedy, eds.
   1991   *Feminist Legal Theory: Readings in Law and Gender.* Boulder and Oxford: Westview.

Barton, John
   1979   "Natural Law and Poetic Justice in the Old Testament." *JTS* n.s. 30:1–14.

Bechtel, Lyn M.
   1991   "Shame as a Sanction of Social Control in Biblical Israel: Judicial, Political, and Social Shaming." *JSOT* 49:47–76.

Bentham, Jeremy
   1791   *Anarchical Fallacies.* Pp. 489–534 in *The Works of Jeremy Bentham,* vol. 2. Ed. John Bowring, 1838–43. Reprint: New York: Russell & Russell, 1962. Originally in French.

Berlin, Isaiah
   1958   *Two Concepts of Liberty.* Oxford: Clarendon. Reprint: Pp. 118–72 in *Four Essays on Liberty.* London: Oxford University Press, 1969.

Berlinerblau, J.
   1993   "The 'Popular Religion' Paradigm in Old Testament Research: A Sociological Critique." *JSOT* 60:3–26.

Black-Michaud, Jacob
   1975   *Cohesive Force: Feud in the Mediterranean and the Middle East.* New York: St. Martin's.

Boer, P. A. H. de
   1955   "'Vive le roi!'" *VT* 5:225–31.

Buccellati, Giorgio
   1967   *Cities and Nations of Ancient Syria: An Essay on Political Institutions with Special Reference to the Israelite Kingdoms.* Studi Semitici, 26. Rome: Istituto di Studi del Vicino Oriente.

Carroll, Robert P.
   1977   "Rebellion and Dissent in Ancient Israelite Society." *ZAW* 89:176–204.

Cohen, Morris Raphael
   1953   *Reason and Nature: An Essay on the Meaning of Scientific Method.* 2d ed. Glencoe: Free Press.

Cohen, Ronald, and John Middleton, eds.
   1967   *Comparative Political Systems: Studies in the Politics of Pre-Industrial Societies.* Garden City: The Natural History Press.

Cohn, Haim H.
   1984   *Human Rights in Jewish Law.* New York: Ktav.

Collins, John J.
   1977   "The Biblical Precedent for Natural Theology." *JAAR* 45/1 Supplement, B:35–67.

Coote, Robert B.
1991   *In Defense of Revolution: The Elohist History*. Minneapolis: Fortress.

Cover, Robert M.
1987   "Obligation: A Jewish Jurisprudence of the Social Order." *Journal of Law and Religion* 5:65–74.

Craven, Toni
1989   "Women Who Lied for the Faith," Pp. 35–49 in *Justice and the Holy: Essays in Honor of Walter Harrelson*. Ed. Douglas A. Knight and Peter J. Paris. Homage Series, 12. Atlanta: Scholars.

Crüsemann, Frank
1978   *Der Widerstand gegen das Königtum: Die antiköniglichen Texte des Alten Testamentes und der Kampf um den frühen israelitischen Staat*. WMANT 49. Neukirchen-Vluyn: Neukirchener Verlag.
1992   *Die Tora: Theologie und Sozialgeschichte des alttestamentlichen Gesetzes*. Munich: Chr. Kaiser.

Daube, David
1972   *Civil Disobedience in Antiquity*. Edinburgh: Edinburgh University Press.

Dworkin, Ronald
1977   *Taking Rights Seriously*. Cambridge: Harvard University Press.
1986   *Law's Empire*. Cambridge, MA, and London: Belknap, Harvard University Press.

Eagleton, Terry
1976   *Criticism and Ideology: A Study in Marxist Literary Theory*. London: Verso.
1983   *Literary Theory: An Introduction*. Minneapolis: University of Minnesota Press.
1991   *Ideology: An Introduction*. London and New York: Verso.

Flanagan, James W.
1981   "Chiefs in Israel." *JSOT* 20:47–73.

Fuchs, Esther
1985   "Who Is Hiding the Truth? Deceptive Women and Biblical Androcentrism." Pp. 137–44 in *Feminist Perspectives on Biblical Scholarship*. Ed. Adela Yarbro Collins. SBLBSNA 10. Chico: Scholars.

Fuller, Lon L.
1958   "Positivism and Fidelity to Law." *Harvard Law Review* 71:630–72.
1969   *The Morality of Law*. Rev. ed. New Haven and London: Yale University Press.

Gehman, Henry S.
1960   "Natural Law and the Old Testament." Pp. 109–22 in *Biblical Studies in Memory of H. C. Alleman*. Ed. J. M. Myers, O. Reimherr, and H. N. Bream. Locust Valley, NY: J. J. Augustin.

Gilmore, David D., ed.
  1987   *Honor and Shame and the Unity of the Mediterranean.* American Anthropological Association Special Publications, 22. Washington: American Anthropological Association.

Gordis, Robert
  1950   "Democratic Origins in Ancient Israel—The Biblical 'ēdāh." Pp. 369–88 in *Alexander Marx Jubilee Volume, on the Occasion of His Seventieth Birthday.* New York: The Jewish Theological Seminary of America. Reprint: "Primitive Democracy in Ancient Israel." Pp. 45–60 in *Poets, Prophets, and Sages: Essays in Biblical Interpretation.* Bloomington and London: Indiana University Press, 1971.

Gottwald, Norman K.
  1992   "Social Class and Ideology in Isaiah 40–55: An Eagletonian Reading." *Semeia* 59:43–57.
  1993   "Social Class as an Analytic and Hermeneutical Category in Biblical Studies." *JBL* 112:3–22.

Greenberg, Moshe
  1960   "Some Postulates of Biblical Criminal Law." Pp. 5–28 in *Yehezkel Kaufmann Jubilee Volume.* Ed. M. Haran. Jerusalem: Magnes. Reprint: Pp. 18–37 in *The Jewish Expression.* Ed. J. Goldin. New Haven and London: Yale University Press, 1976.
  1966   "The Biblical Grounding of Human Value." Pp. 39–52 in *The Samuel Friedland Lectures, 1960–1966.* New York: The Jewish Theological Seminary of America.

Harrelson, Walter
  1980   *The Ten Commandments and Human Rights.* OBT 8. Philadelphia: Fortress.

Hart, H. L. A.
  1955   "Are There Any Natural Rights?" *Philosophical Review* 64:175–91.
  1958   "Positivism and the Separation of Law and Morals." *Harvard Law Review* 71:593–629
  1961   *The Concept of Law.* Oxford: Clarendon.

Horst, Friedrich
  1950/51 "Naturrecht und Altes Testament." *EvT* 10:253–73. Reprint: Pp. 235–59 in *Gottes Recht: Gesammelte Studien zum Recht im Alten Testament.* Ed. Hans Walter Wolff. TBü 12. Munich: Chr. Kaiser, 1961.

Ishida, Tomoo
  1977   *The Royal Dynasties in Ancient Israel: A Study on the Formation and Development of Royal-Dynastic Ideology.* BZAW 142. Berlin and New York: Walter de Gruyter.

Jacobsen, Thorkild
  1943   "Primitive Democracy in Ancient Mesopotamia." *JNES* 2:159–72.

Jobling, David, and Tina Pippin, eds.
  1992   *Ideological Criticism of Biblical Texts. Semeia* 59. Atlanta: Scholars.

Kelsen, Hans
  1946 *General Theory of Law and State.* Trans. Anders Wedberg. Cambridge: Harvard University Press.
  1967 *Pure Theory of Law.* Trans. Max Knight. Berkeley and Los Angeles: University of California Press.

Kennedy, James M.
  1990 "Peasants in Revolt: Political Allegory in Genesis 2–3." *JSOT* 47:3–14.

Kessler, Rainer
  1992 *Staat und Gesellschaft im vorexilischen Juda vom 8. Jahrhundert bis zum Exil.* VTSup 47. Leiden: E. J. Brill.

Knight, Douglas A.
  1985 "Cosmogony and Order in the Hebrew Tradition." Pp. 133–57 in *Cosmogony and Ethical Order: New Studies in Comparative Ethics.* Ed. Robin W. Lovin and Frank E. Reynolds. Chicago and London: The University of Chicago Press.
  1989 "The Ethics of Human Life in the Hebrew Bible." Pp. 65–88 in *Justice and the Holy: Essays in Honor of Walter Harrelson.* Ed. Douglas A. Knight and Peter J. Paris. Homage Series, 12. Atlanta: Scholars.

Lenski, Gerhard E.
  1984 *Power and Privilege: A Theory of Social Stratification.* Chapel Hill and London: The University of North Carolina Press. First published in 1966.

Lewis, Oscar
  1951 *Life in a Mexican Village: Tepoztlán Restudied.* Urbana: The University of Illinois Press.

Lind, Millard C.
  1970 "The Concept of Political Power in Ancient Israel." *ASTI* 7:4–24.

McKenzie, John L., S.J.
  1959 "The Elders in the Old Testament." *Bib* 40:522–40.

Mendenhall, George E.
  1960 "The Relation of the Individual to Political Society in Ancient Israel." Pp. 89–108 in *Biblical Studies in Memory of H. C. Alleman.* Ed. J. M. Myers, O. Reimherr, and H. N. Bream. Locust Valley, NY: J. J. Augustin.

Mettinger, Tryggve N. D.
  1976 *King and Messiah: The Civil and Sacral Legitimation of the Israelite Kings.* ConBOT 8. Lund: CWK Gleerup.

Meyers, Carol
  1988 *Discovering Eve: Ancient Israelite Women in Context.* New York and Oxford: Oxford University Press.

Montesquieu, Charles de Secondat, Baron de
  1748 *De l'esprit des loix.* Reprinted in *Œuvres complètes de Montesquieu,* vol. 1. Ed. André Masson. Paris: Nagel, 1950. First English translation by Thomas Nugent, *The Spirit of Laws,* 1750. New translation: *The Spirit of the*

Laws. Trans. and ed., Anne M. Cohler, Basia Carolyn Miller, and Harold Samuel Stone. Cambridge: Cambridge University Press, 1989.

Nahmani, Hayim Simha
1964   *Human Rights in the Old Testament*. Tel Aviv: Joshua Chachik.

Nieuwenhuijze, C. A. O. van
1962   "The Near Eastern Village: A Profile." *The Middle East Journal* 16:295–308.

Otto, Eckart
1993   "Town and Rural Countryside in Ancient Israelite Law: Reception and Redaction in Cuneiform and Israelite Law." *JSOT* 57:3–22.

Parker, Simon B.
1976   "Revolutions in Northern Israel." SBLSP 10:311–21. Ed. George MacRae.

Rawls, John
1971   *A Theory of Justice*. Cambridge: Belknap, Harvard University Press.

Redfield, Robert
1930   *Tepoztlán—A Mexican Village: A Study of Folk Life*. Chicago: The University of Chicago Press.
1941   *The Folk Culture of Yucatan*. Chicago: The University of Chicago Press.
1947   "The Folk Society." *The American Journal of Sociology* 52:293–308.
1955   *The Little Community: Viewpoints for the Study of a Human Whole*. Chicago: The University of Chicago Press; Stockholm: Almqvist & Wiksell/Gebers Förlag.
1956   *Peasant Society and Culture: An Anthropological Approach to Civilization*. Chicago: The University of Chicago Press.

Rosenberg, Joel
1986   *King and Kin: Political Allegory in the Hebrew Bible*. Bloomington and Indianapolis: Indiana University Press.

Shils, Edward
1975   *Center and Periphery: Essays in Macrosociology*. Chicago and London: The University of Chicago Press.

Stoljar, Samuel
1984   *An Analysis of Rights*. New York: St. Martin's.

Stone, Ken
1993   "Sexual Practice and the Structure of Prestige: The Case of the Disputed Concubines." SBLSP 1993:554–73. Ed. Eugene H. Lovering, Jr.

Sutherland, Ray K.
1986   "The Political Role of the Assemblies in Ancient Israel." Ph.D. dissertation, Vanderbilt University.

Tadmor, Hayim
1982   "Traditional Institutions and the Monarchy: Social and Political Tensions in the Time of David and Solomon." Pp. 239–57 in *Studies in the Period of David and Solomon, and Other Essays*. Ed. Tomoo Ishida. Winona Lake: Eisenbrauns.

Talmon, Shemaryahu
    1979   "Kingship and the Ideology of the State." Pp. 3–26 in *The World History of the Jewish People*, vol. 4/2: *The Age of the Monarchies: Culture and Society*. Ed. Abraham Malamat. Jerusalem: Massada. Reprint: Pp. 9–38 in *King, Cult and Calendar in Ancient Israel: Collected Studies*. Jerusalem: Magnes, The Hebrew University, 1986.

Veijola, Timo
    1977   *Das Königtum in der Beurteilung der deuteronomistischen Historiographie: Eine redaktionsgeschichtliche Untersuchung*. Annales academiæ scientiarum fennicæ, B:198. Helsinki: Suomalainen Tiedeakatemia.

Vincent, Joan
    1990   *Anthropology and Politics: Visions, Traditions, and Trends*. Tucson: The University of Arizona Press.

Walsh, J. P. M., S.J.
    1987   *The Mighty from Their Thrones: Power in the Biblical Tradition*. OBT 21. Philadelphia: Fortress.

Weber, Max
    1946   *From Max Weber: Essays in Sociology*. Trans., ed. and with an Introduction by H. H. Gerth and C. Wright Mills. New York: Oxford University Press.
    1947   *The Theory of Social and Economic Organization*. Trans. A. M. Henderson and Talcott Parsons. Ed. Talcott Parsons. New York: Oxford University Press, 1947. German original in 1921.

Wilson, Robert R.
    1980   *Prophecy and Society in Ancient Israel*. Philadelphia: Fortress.
    1983   "Enforcing the Covenant: The Mechanisms of Judicial Authority in Early Israel." Pp. 59–75 in *The Quest for the Kingdom of God: Studies in Honor of George E. Mendenhall*. Ed. H. B. Huffmon, F. A. Spina, and A. R. W. Green. Winona Lake, IN: Eisenbrauns.

Wiltshire, Susan
    1992   *Greece, Rome, and the Bill of Rights*. Norman and London: University of Oklahoma Press.

Wittfogel, Karl A.
    1957   *Oriental Despotism: A Comparative Study of Total Power*. New Haven: Yale University Press; London: Oxford University Press.

Wolf, C. Umhau
    1947   "Traces of Primitive Democracy in Ancient Israel." *JNES* 6:98–108.

Wolfson, Susan A.
    1992   "Modern Liberal Rights Theory and Jewish Law." *Journal of Law and Religion* 9:399–427.

KINGS AND CLIENTS:
ON LOYALTY BETWEEN THE RULER AND THE RULED IN ANCIENT "ISRAEL"

Niels Peter Lemche
University of Copenhagen

ABSTRACT

It was formerly believed that the system of patrons and clients was peculiar to Roman society, and in fact that it was more or less invented by the Romans. This is hardly the case. On the contrary, patronage may have been a well-known feature of ancient Near Eastern society, including Israelite society, thus being the basis of solidarity between ruler and subjects. In the Amarna letters from Syria and Palestine we possess a number of indications of the importance attached to this concept of loyalty, and also a number of Hebrew Bible passages testify to the significance of the concept. In this connection the Hebrew root חסד is especially important. However, the study of patronage may also contribute to the understanding of the biblical idea of the covenant, which may not be as exclusively Deuteronomistic as envisaged by, for example, Lothar Perlitt.

In the first scene of the movie "The Godfather" (I), the old Don Vito Corleone, the head of an established mafia-family in New York, gives audience to whomever among his followers has an application to put forward. Among the applicants appears a very shy person, asking for revenge because some youngsters have mishandled his daughter. They were arrested by the police, but in their appearance before the judge they got a very mild and—according to the girl's father—absolutely insufficient sentence. The content of the dialogue which follows is especially interesting. Don Corleone opens with a forewarning, first because the applicant had gone to the police and not to the Godfather; he mentions that the applicant has been inattentive and not shown him respect, and further that the applicant has never wanted his friendship because he has never wanted to owe the Godfather a service and thus be in his debt. As the scene continues, the Godfather refers to the fact that the applicant needed no protection because he believed that the court would provide him with protection. Only now, because this was certainly not the case, the applicant asks the Godfather to give him justice, but without respect, as the applicant still does not offer his friendship to the Godfather and is still not prepared to address Don Corleone as the Godfather. And when the applicant offers to pay for the service, the offer is simply refused as being disrespectful. The applicant should have come at once when he was offended, and the scoundrels would already have suffered. Finally, the Godfather offers his friendship to the applicant and promises that any enemy of the applicant will at the same time be the enemy of the Godfather himself and will therefore always fear the anger of the Godfather. The scene comes to an end when the applicant agrees to become the client of the Godfather, a relationship symbolized in his kissing the hand of Don Corleone and greeting him as the Godfather. The applicant is at the same instance warned that, although the present favor is given to him as a gift, the Godfather may want his services at a later occasion—which soon comes to pass, as the movie continues.

This scene embodies in an excellent way the essentials of the concept of patronage, that is, the special relationship that is supposed to exist between a patron and his clients, or between a ruler and the ruled in traditional societies, which is the subject for discussion here. Patronage is, to be short, best defined as the type of relationship to be found between people of different standings not only in non-centralized but also in partly centralized political societies or in centralized states that are beginning to fall apart. It is therefore my conviction that, more than any other system, the patronage system governs the political interplay between the various members of such societies.

Formerly, patronage as an acknowledged institution was considered to be peculiar to Roman society, being indeed a lawful and accepted ingredient of that society.[1] As is well known, the great families of Rome collected around themselves a vast following of retainers, not only in order to promote their own interests but also to fight rival families and their retainers. The patronage system was invoked even at the highest level when the Roman state itself introduced and made use of the concept on a large scale, as its veterans were promised land and safety in foreign, often newly conquered provinces: they were supposed to create Roman *colonies* subordinate directly to Rome and not to the local authorities, thus helping to establish centers of Roman influence all over the empire, places that could later be considered particularly loyal to the Roman state. However, clientship could also be used to bind selected local communities, mostly in the form of cities or city states, directly to the Roman authorities in a kind of friendship that was supposed to exist between these cities and the city of Rome itself.

---

[1] An excellent, though dated description of how the Roman system worked on all levels of society can be found in Syme.

It should not, however, be argued that the Romans themselves were the inventors of this system; they only organized it on a large scale and made it renowned. The influence of the great and noble families of Rome was so extensive that the system on the private level as well obtained official recognition—and not just as another sub-system lying below the surface of the official society and its authorities. The intention behind the system was, however, not exclusively to provide the members of the Aemilian, Julian, Claudian, or other families with advantages; it also provided security and safety for the common person who, when in trouble, could always appeal to the patron family for help. As such, membership in this political system made life tolerable under conditions that would otherwise be considered unbearably harsh and difficult. Especially in connection with the distribution of justice, patrons could be of extraordinary importance because they possessed the ability and means to secure the rights of the poor members of their *clientela*, their personal group of clients, including paying any expenses connected with the judicial process or even fines imposed on their clients. On the other hand, without a patron the poor individual stood alone, and no official institutions were readily available that could ensure fair treatment when, for example, the conflict was with more influential members of society.

It is obvious that the mafia-organization referred to at the beginning of this essay should be considered a late form of this patronage system. Don Corleone very precisely diagnoses the situation of the person who applies for help. The man asks for justice because he could not—in his own opinion—obtain it when he turned to the official authorities. In this manner the Godfather was obliged to act as a substitute in the role of the good judge, a role the applicant at first believed belonged to the officers of the state in which he lived.

The problem connected with the modern patronage organizations as they can still be found in the Western world, however, is firstly that the state authorities are generally ready to provide the services and safety arrangements that were formerly part of the patronage system, and secondly that the patronage system in modern times has developed into a caricature of itself, being criminalized to a great extent—indeed organized crime is almost its sole object today. In this way, the patronage system has turned not into a protective organization to provide justice for its members, but into a criminal institution bringing harm and disaster over the larger society surrounding it. It is thus obvious that the system has been marginalized rather than being at the center of the socio-political organization of life; it has been removed to the fringe of modern society. It is, nevertheless, also clear that the organization will continue to operate— at least theoretically, but presumably also to some extent in real life—to the benefit of its members according to the rules that were original parts of the system.

Another factor inherent to this system is the notion of loyalty, which must be considered fundamental to the organization and which should not be limited to the notorious *omertá* (my Italian dictionary: the "solidarity that exists among criminals," but the essence of the concept is actually the obligation placed on the members not to talk). Loyalty is a governing concept, and without it the organization will have no chance to survive. It is in this connection important that Don Corleone expressly demands to be called "Godfather" because, like a real god, he promises to fulfill his obligations and expects to be obeyed without question. As usual when loyalty forms the basis of a relationship, with its obligations often publicly expressed by both parties in the form of a vow, the penalty imposed on members who do not live up to their duties will have to be severe, more often than not the death penalty, frequently in combination with torture, corporal molestations or the like, pains that are inflicted not so much in order to be cruel against transgressors as to frighten other "faithful" members of the organization and prevent them from deserting.

It is my conviction, however, that this system, which has sometimes been called a Mediterranean social organization, is likely to be present in most—if not all—societies that are not governed by strongly centralized institutions belonging to a state. Moreover, it is the organizing system that appears in many kinds of societies, including embryonic states similar to the ones we are likely to confront when dealing with the history of Palestine in antiquity, but including also, in somewhat altered form, the feudal political organizations of the Near East as well as of Europe in the Middle Ages.

It is a system in which both parties, the patron as well as the client, are bound together by mutual oaths of loyalty. It is a system that, in principle, works to the benefit of both parties. It is, however, a political system that has been adequately described neither by students of the ancient Near East nor by modern sociologists who have been working in the Middle East, although occasionally we get a hint of how this system even today can be considered a subsystem below the surface of the seemingly modern states in that part of the world. It immediately shows up when such states are being torn apart by conflicts, as for example Lebanon in recent times.

The shortage of studies of the extensive patronage systems likely to be found in most, if not all, modern Middle Eastern societies points to negligence on the part of the social anthropologists who have been working in this part of the world. I would maintain that it is precisely their presuppositions and their methodological assumptions that have prevented them from accepting the presence of a system that runs counter to their general notions, according to which the dominant political factor in traditional society is reckoned to be the family system.

Thus, if one is prepared to get involved in a survey of post–World War II ethnographic treatises on Middle Eastern society, one will most likely be struck by the importance attached to the family system. Most descriptions of traditional Middle Eastern society will contain an extensive survey of the family organization under the rubric of "social structure," providing a fair impression of the life and whereabouts of the nuclear family and of the lineage as well, together with some comments—often rather vague—on the clan system if such a system is present, which is not always the case (or so the ethnographers frequently maintain). Such treatment of the family system will generally close with an extensive but often not too well organized discussion of the importance of tribes. It is a general feature of such treatises that the family and the lineage are invariably considered to form the most important basis of the life of a Middle Eastern person—that the family and the lineage constitute the solidarity group on which each individual can count in times of crisis.

Although the nuclear family certainly plays a decisive role, such a group is far too small to provide effective protection for its members, apart from the most commonplace kinds of problems. It is, on the other hand, a strange fact that on the higher level, among the members of one and the same lineage, it is difficult to point to practical examples of the "solidarity" which putatively binds its members together; indeed, the solidarity is far less pronounced than might be expected if this organization really functions as importantly as is generally assumed. Most anthropologists stress that the individual family forms an economically independent group in traditional societies, irrespective of whether we are speaking of a tribal or a centralized society. There are, of course, examples of impoverished lineage members who may get some help in order to survive physically, but they can hardly ever count on assistance from the lineage to restore their fortune or to support their survival for long. Thus a very conspicuous process found in nomadic tribal societies, which should otherwise be considered the epitome of tribal solidarity, is that poor families who for some reason have lost their livestock are generally being forced to settle down and to survive as hired workers. To be sure, some may be "luckier" in finding employment as herders for rich members of their own lineage—often, however, without being properly paid![2]

---

[2] This section builds on arguments in Lemche (especially 209–44), where the relevant anthropological studies are discussed. The analysis presented there seems to have gone unchallenged by Hebrew Bible scholars. A sad fact of negligence on the

In descriptions of such societies it is very unusual to find comments on other kinds of political organization than that based on family relationship. I cannot remember having found a proper discussion dealing with patronage, except some very general comments on the relationship between the rich and the poor. Some anthropologists, like the late Jacob Black-Michaud, have questioned the importance of family solidarity, and they have at the same time referred to other political structures that are to be considered more important. However, not even Black-Michaud, who presented us with vivid descriptions of the "tyrannical" use of the concept of family solidarity to suppress unlucky members of one's own family and lineage (1972), ever discussed the subject of patronage to a satisfactory extent.

There are several reasons for this state of affairs. In comparison it is much easier to describe the family organization, and local informers are generally ready to offer explanations about the tiniest details of the family system or to present the all-too-happy ethnographer with age-long genealogies, tracing such societies and their lineages back to ancient ancestors living at the beginning of history. However, when it comes to the more clandestine lines of patron–client relationships, these informers generally have very little to say—if they have been asked at all. At the minimum, they may not have been prepared to guide the ethnographer into the various political alliances of their communities, simply because it is an ingredient of the system itself that it should not be too openly known, and certainly that it should not be known to persons outside the given society.

Another reason for this situation may reside in the fact that anthropologists have generally not been very interested in ideological matters. A system as important as patronage will most likely be present on the ideological level, and if scientific caution prohibits tracing its presence in the traditional communities of the Middle East, it should at least have left its mark on the tradition, although not necessarily in the form of fully exposed systems. One should not expect to find the system

---

part of Hebrew Bible scholars when it comes to social-anthropological matters—and this is still to be found in current work—is the attention that continues to be paid to the stereotype of the extended family supposedly encompassing scores of members. As was already explained in Lemche, such families simply do not exist except on the dynastic level or among the few rich families likely to be present in a traditional Middle Eastern society, the reason simply being that no poor family can afford to support so many members. As I have previously described, it is truly remarkable that general confusion persists among modern scholars concerning the difference between, on the one hand, an extended noble family counting as many as *twenty* persons and, on the other, the *lineage*. For an archaeologically based study that concurs with and differs from various of my arguments, see Stager.

described "sociologically" or systematically in Middle Eastern traditional folklore, but one should at least be able to discover vestiges of it in literature and tradition. As a matter of fact, such indications will be plentiful as soon as one realizes that they may be present.[3]

We will limit ourselves here to the situation in the Hebrew Bible. Nowhere in the text do we find a full description of the structure of so-called "ancient Israelite" society, only very schematic and superficial layouts—for example, in the short text of Jos 7:16–18, which divides society into, respectively, families, lineages, and tribes, or in the extensive reports of a census such as Numbers 26. However, if we move to the ideological level, another world opens up before our eyes: references to concepts are readily available that can be joined together to form the basis of my hypothesis, namely that the society that produced the biblical literature was also organized according to lines following the patron-client relationship.

As already described, we find at the very center of the system the notion of "loyalty," that is, a loyalty that binds patron and client together—at least on the ideological level—in an unbreakable relationship. In combination with this idea of loyalty, other subconcepts such as friendship, respect, and fear appear. The patron asks the client to be a friend, to "love" and show the patron respect, which is certainly not a passive part of the deal but a very active way of expressing subordination to the patron. "Fear," on the other hand, is not a part of the relationship between patron and client but is the general attitude of foreigners who are experiencing the negative effects of the system, for example in a confrontation between two rival patronage groups.

Fortunately, in this case we do not need to break entirely new ground, although we will in the present context need to limit our discussion. Several scholars (e.g., Glueck; Sakenfeld; Clark) have already published analyses of a few technical Hebrew expressions that obviously refer to the ideology underlying the patronage system. Among such studies, Nelson Glueck's old German dissertation from 1927 on the term חסד may count as one of the major contributions and should still be able to hold its position in spite of Gordon R. Clark's new examination of חסד. Glueck's study is divided into three parts, the first devoted to the human sphere alone, the second to the attitude of humans toward God, and the third to the use of חסד to express the attitude of God toward humans.

While Glueck is not explicitly addressing patronage in his small volume, some of his conclusions point directly toward the existence of such a concept. Let me quote from his first section of conclusions: "חסד ist

---

[3] As an example of what can be done in this field, see Meeker.

die einem Rechts-Pflicht-Verhältnis entsprechende Verhaltungsweise. ...
Versteht man חסד als eine solche Verhaltungsweise, so erklärt sich die
früher festgestellte Tatsache, daß nur diejenigen, die in einem Rechts-
Pflicht-Verhältnis stehen, חסד empfangen und erweisen können" (20).
These statements by Glueck, in fact, articulate precisely the very essence
of patronage! The rest of his book simply elaborates on this theme; the
essentials are all contained in these two first statements. It is thus self-
evident that a number of concepts can be introduced as components of
Glueck's relationship characterized by obligations and duties; he himself
immediately points to the concept of אמת (20). It is also obvious that his
two subsequent chapters, which broaden the perspective to include the
world of the divine being, contribute in fundamental ways to the
understanding of the concept. They do not change its content in any
important respect, apart from the fact that the relationship between
patron and client will necessarily be clearer under such circumstances
where one party is God and the other is God's creatures.

It is meaningful and perceptive, however, that Glueck also includes in
this connection the concept of "knowledge of God" ("Gotteserkenntnis")
and "fear of God" ("Gottesfurcht") (34). The first can without difficulty be
compared to the idea of friendship mentioned above as part of the system,
and the second to the demand for respect for the patron. A number of
Hebrew expressions are close at hand; here I shall only refer to the idea of
"knowing God", expressed by the Hebrew verb ידע (see also Huffmon),
and of course and above all the "fear of God", in Hebrew יראת אלהים.

It is also interesting that these terms in combination inevitably force
us to direct our attention to the concept of covenant theology. As already
explained by Glueck, the establishment of a חסד relationship can be
effectuated by a ceremony including a solemn oath. When two parties
decide to establish such a relationship, what is more natural than to
conclude it formally in some kind of ceremony? As soon as we speak of
an agreement of this kind, combined with such symbols as the
pronouncing of oaths and claims, we find ourselves in the middle of a
discussion on the concept of covenant. It is no accident that, in the 1960s
when the discussion about the role of the covenant in ancient Israel
reached its highest point, numerous technical terms and ideas relevant to
the present argument, including those mentioned above, were central to
the debate.

The discussion of patronage may thus stimulate a renewed interest in
the importance of the covenant concept among the ancient Israelites. This
inquiry can, however, now be kept on a more realistic level than was
previously the case. The old debate almost closed down when in 1969
Lothar Perlitt published his study of "Bundestheologie," which he

claimed was a Deuteronomistic concept. By and large, Perlitt is right. In most places in the Hebrew Bible where we find the specific expressions of the divine covenant, these are without doubt Deuteronomistic ideas and concepts or ones inspired by Deuteronomistic ideas and concepts. However, this Deuteronomistic covenant theology is only narrowly connected to the Hebrew term ברית, which is certainly a solemn technical expression for "covenant." The debate has overlooked the fact that this term may not be exclusive to the extent that all kinds of covenants must perforce include it. Other terms may be sufficient as expressions of the essence of the covenant relationship, be this between the divine and the human world or between human beings alone.

At this point we can leave the basic question of whether or not חסד expresses the essentials of the patronage system seen as a covenant arrangement of some sort. The next step involves a broader view of the old covenant discussion. Generally, ancient Near Eastern documents touching on the concept of covenant concern two different types of arrangement: on the one hand, compacts that regulate the connections between persons of the same standing; on the other, agreements that include persons on different levels. As patronage explicitly belongs in the second category, this will be the more promising subject to discuss in the present connection.

In 1955 when George Mendenhall started the discussion of covenant ideas, he initially referred to parallels to the biblical concept to be found in Hittite international treaties of the second millennium BCE, and rightly so because these treaties—mostly vassal treaties that bind vassals in Syria or Asia Minor to their Hittite overlord—can with certainty be considered expressions of the basic notions attached to the system of patronage. On this level there can be absolutely no doubt that such a system existed, at least between states of unequal standing. In formulating such covenants, the patron, the king of Hatti, imposed his will on the vassal, who for all future time was supposed to belong among his personal retainers, to appear before his lord every year in the capital, and to swear loyalty to his overlord. The vassal was obliged to perform a number of ceremonies that expressed comparable notions.

In this way the vassal treaties of Hatti contained all the above-mentioned elements. They firmly established a patronage relationship between local kings and the great king himself. Such treaties can be considered arrangements that curtailed the aspirations of the vassal. At the same time, they acted as a guarantee for the survival of the vassal and his family. It is well known to most Orientalists that the Hittite system survived the fall of Hatti. Almost the same system of vassal treaties also flourished in the first millennium BCE, not the least in those areas governed by Assur.[4] There is therefore no reason to assume that it would have been unknown to the kings of the two petty states of Israel and Judah.[5] Nor should we assume that allusions to the system found in the Hebrew Bible should necessarily have anything to do with the Hittite evidence, except sharing its ideas. Mendenhall was certainly right and wrong at one and the same time.

The Hittites did not invent the system of patronage, which in this case existed presumably only on the highest level, regulating affairs between states. Rather, they were elaborating on a system that was already widespread and known to all parties involved. This cannot be inferred from the Hittite treaties themselves but becomes evident when surveying documents from other parts of the Near East that did not belong to the Hittite empire in the Late Bronze Age. The Amarna letters, which originated in the Egyptian sphere, are of special interest in this regard.

More than twenty-five years ago in a marvelous article dealing with the difference between the political ideas of Egypt and the political habits of its provinces in Asia, Mario Liverani demonstrated how this difference had been the cause of many misunderstandings between the Egyptian administrators and their Palestinian and Syrian subordinates. It is clear that the local Palestinian kings all considered the relationship between themselves and their overlord, the Pharaoh, to be a kind of patronage relationship: they themselves being the clients and the Pharaoh the patron. They expected the Pharaoh to protect them once they paid their duties to the king of Egypt. It is, however, also clear that the Egyptian ruler had another idea of the relationship: the Palestinian princelets were mere low-ranking Egyptian bureaucrats and should be treated like such persons, that is, like employees who had to fulfill their duties and would then receive compensation—although a compensation quite different in kind than what was usual according to the West Asiatic patronage system, where the patron *owed* the loyal client a recompense.

It is impossible in the present context to continue much further along this line. However, I believe that I have at least formulated a theory of one

---

[4] The Assyrian treaties are now easily available in Parpola and Watanabe.

[5] In fact, the terrible fate of Zedekiah in comparison to the lenient treatment of Jehoiachin may be seen as a consequence of what was likely to happen when a Judean king deserted his overlord. While Nebuchadnezzar merely confined Jehoiachin to a "golden prison" in Babylon, Zedekiah was treated by the same Babylonian king in the harshest possible fashion. In contrast to Zedekiah, Jehoiachin was no vassal of Babylon, having been installed by the Egyptian king, whereas Zedekiah had been placed on the throne by the very king who was later to dispose of him. Nebuchadnezzar, therefore, had no legal rights to punish Jehoiachin, and he certainly treated him in a most gentle way—considering the manners of the time—whereas he may have felt it absolutely correct to destroy Zedekiah, who had betrayed him.

of the governing ideas of political life—if not, in fact, *the* governing one—that of patronage, the relationship between client and patron. If this was also in force in Palestine in the first millennium BCE—and I believe that a fairly strong case in favor of such a suggestion can be made—then the relationship between the kings of Israel and Judah and their subjects must have been regulated according to such lines, as the kings were simply to be considered the patrons of their state whereas the common persons acted as their clients, from whom the kings were entitled to expect and demand absolute loyalty but whom they also had to recompense for their service.

A number of ideological matters concerning the status of the king point in the same direction, not the least being the notion of the "just king," who was supposed to have his place in the city gate where he was to distribute justice among his people—of course a rather impractical idea for the ruler of a state, but nevertheless part of the popular image of the just king in Israel, as elsewhere in the ancient Near East. Another related fact supports this impression of the king as the high judge acting as the personal patron of every single citizen of the state who may apply for help in critical situations, and that is the peculiar fact that no laws have ever been uncovered in Israel, apart from the absolutely non-royal sections of the Book of the Covenant in Exodus with all its implied Near Eastern parallels. As a matter of fact, it is a strange fact that no written law has ever appeared in the archives of a city in Western Asia, not even in the highly centralized states of the Bronze Age (see also Liedke: 57). The reason for this circumstance is obviously that no one could force patrons to act against their own judgment. The patron was, seen from this angle, surely a despot in the Marxist meaning of the word, and the system may be called despotic because the rulers were the only persons who had in their power the ability to make final decisions which no one could dispute. It was, at the same time, also believed that the rulers would always act as just arbitrators between their subjects.

This belief was rooted in the understanding that the kings of Israel, like their colleagues in other parts of the ancient Near East, were at the same time clients themselves, not necessarily always the client of some great king (although this was certainly often the case) but always of the God of Israel. It is a well-established fact that at least from the days of the Amorite dynasties at the beginning of the second millennium BCE this notion formed a central part of the royal ideology not only in Western Asia but also in Mesopotamia—not, however, in Egypt where the king was believed to be the god himself. The god—whoever this god might have been—was at the same time considered to be the personal patron of the king and the royal family, but the god did not accept this obligation for nothing; on the contrary, the king was always in the god's debt and had to fulfill the duties imposed on him by his patron, the god. Thus the relationship between god and king was likely to be arranged as a covenant relationship—in fact exactly as described in the Hebrew Bible, where we find ample evidence that such a royal covenant must have formed the basis of the Davidic dynasty's claim to be the rightful royal family of Judah and Israel.

There is no reason to elaborate further in this connection. It should be enough to maintain that this relationship between king and god can be seen as the reverse of the normal relations between king and subjects, and the clearest example of the interchangeability of these notions may be the description of the royal covenant which according to 2 Kgs 11:17 was concluded at the end of Athaliah's reign. According to this narrative, the high priest Jehoiada made a covenant between YHWH and the king and people, and between the king of Judah and the Judean nation.

What happened when the patronage system failed to operate according to the expectations of the system? We have no hard evidence of a commoner's reaction against the king in such a circumstance, although the Deuteronomistic history contains a number of passages that border on this question, such as the incident of Naboth's vineyard (1 Kings 21) or the confiscation of grazing land for the royal horses during periods of famine (1 Kgs 18:3–6). A just king is certainly not expected to react in this way, and the complaints against the king are in both cases very severe. However, Psalm 89, for example, represents a much more vivid expression of the reaction of the client when the patron–client relationship broke down, although in this case the relationship was one between God and king.

Psalm 89, without doubt, provides a first-rate impression of what may have been the usual reaction under such circumstances, and there is reason to pay special attention to the psalm's use of the Hebrew word חסד, discussed above. In fact, the concept of חסד may be considered the governing issue in the psalm, from the very first word of the psalm's text to its end.

At the beginning it is stated that the divine חסד has been established in heaven as an everlasting quality, and on the basis of this quality the covenant between YHWH and David was concluded. The mighty hymn that follows (vv. 6–19 [English: 5–18]) merely stresses that חסד is a creation of the divine being and as such should forever be considered an established fact. However, the plot of the play is that God, the patron, has deserted his client, who has done no harm to him and has not broken his oath and covenant. The only thing to hope for in the future will be that the correct relationship will some day be reestablished, thereby securing the right of the Davidic dynasty to sit on the throne of Israel.

I cannot say whether, according to ancient beliefs, the normal expressions of patronage were also considered to be founded in heaven, but such a likelihood can certainly be argued since kingship itself was, as the Babylonians expressed it, established in heaven and justice was a matter of the gods. Be this as it may, the best conclusion to the present discussion is simply to quote the famous words of King Hammurabi of Babylon, who in the prologue to his codex (*ANET*: 164, translation by Theophile J. Meeks) states:

> When lofty Anum, king of the Anunnaki,
> (and) Enlil, lord of heaven and earth,
> the determiner of the destinies of the land,
> determined for Marduk, the first-born of Enki,
> the Enlil functions over all mankind,
> made him great among the Igigi,
> called Babylon by its exalted name,
> made it supreme in the world,
> established for him in its midst an enduring kingship,
> whose foundations are as firm as heaven and earth—
> at that time Anum and Enlil named me
> to promote the welfare of the people,
> me, Hammurabi, the devout, god-fearing prince,
> to cause justice to prevail in the land,
> to destroy the wicked and the evil,
> that the strong might not oppress the weak,
> to rise like the sun over the black-headed (people),
> and to light up the land.

WORKS CONSULTED

Black-Michaud, Jacob
    1972   "Tyranny as a Strategy for Survival in an 'Egalitarian' Society: Luri Facts versus an Anthropological Mystique." *Man* n.s. 7:614-34.

Clark, Gordon R.
    1993   *The Word* Hesed *in the Hebrew Bible*. JSOTSup 157. Sheffield: Sheffield Academic.

Glueck, Nelson
1927   *Das Wort ḥesed im alttestamentlichen Sprachgebrauche als menschliche und göttliche gemeinschaftgemäße Verhaltungsweise.* BZAW 47. Gießen: Alfred Töpelmann.

Huffmon, Herbert B.
1966   "The Treaty Background of Hebrew Yāda'." *BASOR* 181:31–37.

Lemche, Niels Peter
1985   *Early Israel: Anthropological and Historical Studies on the Israelite Society before the Monarchy.* VTSup 37. Leiden: E. J. Brill.

Liedke, Gerhard
1971   *Gestalt und Bezeichnung alttestamentlicher Rechtssätze.* WMANT 39. Neukirchen: Neukirchener Verlag.

Liverani, Mario
1967   "Contrasti e confluenze di concezioni politiche nell'età di El-Amarna." *RA* 61:1–18.

Meeker, Michael E.
1979   *Literature and Violence in North Arabia.* Cambridge Studies in Cultural Systems, 3. Cambridge: Cambridge University Press.

Mendenhall, George E.
1955   *Law and Covenant in Israel and the Ancient Near East.* Pittsburgh: The Biblical Colloquium.

Parpola, Simo, and Kazuko Watanabe
1988   *Neo-Assyrian Treaties and Loyalty Oaths.* State Archives of Assyria, 2. Helsinki: Helsinki University Press.

Perlitt, Lothar
1969   *Bundestheologie im Alten Testament.* WMANT 36. Neukirchen: Neukirchener Verlag.

Sakenfeld, Katharine Doob
1978   *The Meaning of ḥesed in the Hebrew Bible: A New Inquiry.* HSM 17. Missoula: Scholars.

Stager, Lawrence E.
1985   "The Archaeology of the Family in Ancient Israel." *BASOR* 260:1–35.

Syme, Ronald
1951   *The Roman Revolution.* Rev. ed. Oxford: Oxford University Press.

THE END OF THE OMRIDE DYNASTY: SOCIAL-ETHICAL OBSERVATIONS ON THE SUBJECT OF POWER AND VIOLENCE*

Hannelis Schulte
Ruprecht-Karls-Universität Heidelberg

ABSTRACT

In light of the immense amount of deadly violence accompanying the end of the dynasty of Omri, one may raise a question about its causes. Which political and socio-cultural changes created the tensions that were resolved in these violent acts? The person of Jezebel clearly reveals how closely the religious issues were bound with the social and political ones. The short miracle stories of the Elisha tradition present a non-violent alternative, which, however, was not to be of consequence. By supporting Jehu's military putsch, Elisha himself contributed to the use of violence. The change of government in Samaria was to bring no amelioration of the situation of the lower classes. It did, however, usher in a political change and consequently led to the loss of royal authority and to the downfall of Israel.

In our days, at any rate here in Germany, there is much talk of change. Times of change are times of uncertainty, of shifts in orientation. Old values lose their validity; new standards are hard to find. How does a society or an individual deal with such change?

The ninth century BCE, the middle years of which constitute the period of our concern, belongs in many respects to such a time of "change." First, the change from tribal state to royal state, in other words, the origin of monarchy, is characteristic of the Iron Age—as Mario Liverani (654–60) has described it—in the whole of the Syro-Palestinian area, not only in Israel. To this institution belongs a system of taxation, a bureaucracy, and the like. Furthermore, in the region of Palestine we see the increase of a settled peasantry and the disintegration of clans ("Sippen") into small family units in secure possession of house and land.

These general sociological changes went hand in hand with the political. The superpower Assyria launched a campaign to conquer the small kingdoms along the Mediterranean coast. The small states were able to resist this threat only by forming a coalition. Thus there came into

---

* Translated by Carl S. Ehrlich.

being a political tension: On the one hand was the coalition between Aram, Tyre and the other city-states of the Phoenician coast, Israel, Judah, the Philistine cities, and the Transjordanian kingdoms, which led to a political and military union, economic cooperation, cultural exchanges, and open borders. On the other hand, opposing it was an already existing or newly awakening nationalism, an insistence on one's own, a self-definition recoiling from that which was foreign.

The general sociological developments together with this political change led to acrimonious tensions between "traditionalists" and "modernizers." These tensions expressed themselves in social-ethical and religious spheres (Liverani: 674).

Kingship was supposed to be the guarantor of peace vis-à-vis foreign countries. It was also to ensure justice, that is, domestic peace, protecting the weak against the strong and arbitrating in such a manner as to wean people from taking the law into their own hands, thus also from blood vengeance, and to cause them to seek justice from a judge instead. Thus arose at the outset a state monopoly on violence, one that severed the individual and the family from their right to violence. The king, who represented this monopoly on violence, was supposed to have clean hands on which no blood was to be found, as it is expressed by the advocates of the royal ideology of 1 Samuel 25 (David, Nabal, Abigail).

The social-ethical problem that I would like to discuss is the relationship between power and violence in a crisis situation. Upon what basis does the power of the king as the representative of state authority rest? On the power of weaponry? On inherited legitimacy? On personal authority? On his "innocence" (in the sense of 1 Samuel 25) as an arbitrator? On the support of his political program by the people or the "princes" (officers, bureaucrats, heads of the large clans)? How does the opposition express itself? What possibilities exist for alternatives when there are groups that do not agree with the official political program? Are there any options other than a military putsch to change the regime? If all arguments concerning a correct political agenda are settled by military might, then what does this imply for the authority of the king and the existence of the state?

My point of departure in the following discussion is the individuals who appear in the narratives from the time of the downfall of the Omrides.

ATHALIAH

What moved me to reflect on this subject were the biblical reports about the brutal execution commands issued by King Jehoram of Judah and his wife Athaliah.

According to 2 Chr 21:2-4, when Jehoram became king in Jerusalem, he had his six brothers and some of the princes of Judah executed. This report is missing in Kings. How believable is it? Since it does not appear to belong to the typical fabrications of the Chronicler, I accept it at face value. Yet, how could such an order of execution come about? Chronicles hints at Jehoram's envy of his brothers. Why then the death of some of Judah's princes? This latter would appear to be more a dispute between various parties, in other words, a political conflict. Jehoram had served for a number of years as regent in place of his sick father Jehoshaphat (2 Kgs 8:16; cf. Levin: 84). Did such strong tensions arise between Jehoram and his brothers, as well as between him and the leaders of some of Judah's clans, that following the death of his father he felt that the only way in which to solve the question of authority was the removal of his opponents (Gray: ad loc.)? What role did his wife Athaliah, who was from the house of Omri, play in this? Was there a connection to the tensions in the Northern Kingdom, which would lead three years later to Jehu's military putsch?

Who was Athaliah? In the Hebrew Bible she is referred to as both the daughter of Omri (2 Kgs 8:26) and the daughter of Ahab (2 Kgs 8:18).[1] I am inclined to view her as the daughter of Ahab and Jezebel, which would fit the chronology of the period.[2] She would have been born ca. 879 BCE, would have married Jehoram of Judah, who was about three years older than she, in ca. 864, in the following year would have given birth to her son Ahaziah, who was to become king of Judah in 842 following the death of his father, only to be killed that same year by the hand of Jehu. Subsequently Athaliah was to reign as queen for six years until her own assassination (ca. 842–836 BCE). Her marriage to Jehoram certainly served

---

[1] Supporting an interpretation as Omri's daughter are, among others, Miller, Katzenstein, Levin, Minokami, Thiel. Viewing her as Ahab's daughter are, among others, Montgomery, Gray, Soggin ("wahrscheinlich"), Clauss, Metzger. In Würthwein's commentary she is both Ahab's daughter (1977:202) and Omri's daughter (1984:323). The strongest argument in support of "Omri's daughter" is the nature of the sources: 2 Kgs 8:26 is taken from the Judean royal chronicles, while 2 Kgs 8:18 stems from the Dtr–commentary (Thiel). In my opinion, the common dynastic appellation "house of Omri" could have led to the mistake in the Judean chronicles.

[2] If Ahab and Jezebel were born ca. 900 BCE and were married between 885 and 881, then Ahaziah was born in 881, Joram in 880, and Athaliah in 879. The latter could have married Jehoram (born ca. 883) in 864, so that their son Ahaziah was born in 863 and became king in 842 at the age of 22 (2 Kgs 8:26).

a political purpose: it strengthened the political bonds between the house of Omri and the Jerusalemite house of David.

According to 2 Kgs 11:1ff., after the report of the death of her son Ahaziah had reached her, Athaliah had all the male members of the royal house of Judah executed, including her own offspring. This execution order is so monstrous that it has been proposed that it was an invention of circles opposed to Athaliah. As Levin (85) has argued, if she had issued the order, she would only have hurt herself since it would have robbed her of any legitimacy as queen mother. Würthwein (ad loc.) also suspects that the information is not factual. Similarly, the rescue of the young prince Joash by his aunt Jehosheba is also regarded as an invention. This is explained on the basis of the textual and factual problems of 2 Kgs 11:2–3.[3] In my opinion, however, these problems can be solved and thus pose no obstacle to assuming the historicity of the events.

If we are not to take the easier path of relegating Athaliah's orders of execution and the rescue of the prince to the realm of fable or political propaganda, then there remains the more difficult task of explaining her actions. Was Athaliah a cruel person? There is no other evidence for this assumption. Did she "go crazy" at the news of the murder of her son? If so, she would not have been able to reign for six years in Jerusalem. Was there a "rational" or political reason to murder the princes?

The eradication of the whole of the opposing family after a putsch is otherwise attested in the Hebrew Bible (1 Kgs 15:29; 16:11; 2 Kgs 10:1–7). It was motivated on the one hand by fear of blood vengeance by the remnants of the conquered clan, on the other by the desire to leave no one behind who might have a claim on the throne. However, what Athaliah ordered was much worse since she could not have been motivated by fear of blood vengeance nor concerned about securing her own legitimacy.

---

[3] Levin (29ff.), who espouses this position, bases his argument in part on the textual difficulties of 2 Kgs 11:1–3. There it is written concerning prince Joash, who is saved by his aunt Jehosheba: "And he remained with her for six years, hidden in Yahweh's house" (11:3). Chronicles (2 Chr 22:1) and the LXX have turned Jehosheba into the wife of the priest Jehoiada in order to allow her to reside in the temple. However, this cannot have been the case, for if she were married it would have been mentioned when she was first introduced (11:2). As an unmarried princess she resided in the royal palace, in which she could not have dared to hide the prince for six years. Therefore Levin deletes "in Yahweh's house," while still viewing the whole as pure invention on account of the inconsistency. There is, however, a simple solution: Jehosheba—especially as a princess!—was a קְדֵשָׁה. In this case she would have been allowed to reside in the temple compound. The reason why this information is missing in the text of Kings can easily be surmised. I solve the textual difficulty in 11:2 by translating "out of the bedchamber": an original מ was accidentally or on account of a variant textual tradition changed into ב.

Once again: Was there a "rational" motive for her act? Were there political reasons for her orders to exterminate? And if so, what relationship is there between her deed and her husband's command to execute his brothers and some of the princes of Judah? We will return to these questions after we have considered the whole situation of that period.

JEHU

How were political battles fought at the time, in the middle of the ninth century BCE? It appears to me that we are able to deduce from a few texts in Isaiah (see especially Isa 28; 30:1-5; 31:1-3) what was debated in Hezekiah's royal council at critical times. However, the prophetic stories of the ninth century tell only of religious battles and of wars against hostile powers. Texts that derive from royal chronicles deal with political conflicts only—and then indirectly—when they led to acts of violence, to military putsches, or to the extermination of the vanquished. For this reason we are forced to rely on circumstantial evidence in forming an image of the political conflict underlying the reported acts of violence. Concerning Jehu's assumption of power, I believe that it could only have succeeded because a large part of the population welcomed it. What is surprising about the account in 2 Kings 9-10 is that one individual together with the crew of his battle chariot is able to undertake a rebellion and be successful.

Let us examine the situation. Israel's army was engaged in battle against Aram in or near Ramoth-Gilead, an important border town that had either been besieged or conquered by the Arameans. King Joram of Israel was nursing his wounds in Jezreel. Some army officers proclaimed their commander Jehu king. He had to fight for power, but could not withdraw the army from the border. So he ordered utmost secrecy and departed in his chariot in the direction of Jezreel. Everything depended on a surprise effect. Thus he was personally able to murder both kings, Joram of Israel and Ahaziah of Judah. Everything was well calculated and precisely executed.

It is astonishing that he was also able to bring the nobles of the capital city, Samaria, on his side by writing them two letters. He was even able to have them eliminate the dependents of the royal family residing in Samaria. They surely knew that he was unable to pull the troops away from the border. There must have been strong anti-Omride sentiments at large in Samaria or in the land as a whole. In my opinion there is no other way to explain this process. Even when Jehu pulled into Jezreel and Jezebel confronted him at the window, he was able to reckon with supporters in her vicinity, whom he then successfully urged to cast the queen mother down.

THE POLITICS OF THE OMRIDE DYNASTY

The surprising manner in which Jehu succeeded in carrying out his putsch and thereafter apparently enjoyed broad support among the people presents us with another question. Why were the rulers of the house of Omri—at any rate the last one, Joram, and his mother Jezebel—rejected by the people?

According to Soggin's description (1984:191–92), Judah in the middle of the ninth century was a very poor land, subsisting on livestock breeding and cut off from the major trade routes. Israel, on the other hand, had highly developed crafts and commerce, as well as a rich urban culture with international trade connections. On account of this the North was a prized object of plunder and, hence, at much greater risk than Judah. The impetus to unite was, therefore, more likely to come from the South. When the two states buried their ancient enmity—perhaps since Baasha but certainly since Omri—and established friendly relations, the North was clearly the superior partner. Thus Soggin reconstructs the picture.

However, Israel's relationship to Phoenicia was analogous to the relationship of Judah to Israel. Poorer Israel had a natural inclination toward the rich and highly cultured maritime trading center. According to Liverani (693–713), the powerful cities of the Phoenician coast were pursuing a politics of grand coalition, the aim of which was to include all regions that belonged to their hinterland and with which the Phoenicians were related: Aram, Transjordan, and Palestine, including Philistia. The standard of living was increased, and cultural achievements could be shared owing to a lively international trade. While the rulers held onto their thrones, in other words while the individual realms retained a measure of independence, the peoples came into contact with each other across open borders. Thus they de facto formed an empire, such as was the case—albeit on a smaller scale—with the Philistine cities. Whether the impetus for the formation of this coalition was economic or whether the Assyrian threat already served to bring these peoples together is a question that I will leave open. At any rate, the coalition proved itself militarily in 853 BCE at the battle of Qarqar and managed to put a temporary halt to Assyrian expansion.

When one takes this policy of the Phoenician cities into account, then one can speculate about the possibility that Omri's putsch against Zimri was perhaps directed by Tyre and that the Tyrian princess Jezebel was for this reason given to Omri as a wife for his son Ahab. In any case, Omri and after him Ahab followed a political policy of open borders with Tyre, and hence also with Aram, Transjordan, Judah, and Philistia. This does not mean that the relations were always free of violence, as the conflict with Moab indicates (cf. 2 Kgs 3:4–5 and the Mesha Stele). This policy promised economic and cultural development, and as a side benefit also protection against Assyria. Omri's grandson Joram continued this policy, especially since he stood under the influence of his mother Jezebel. However, this would seem to be contradicted by the war against Aram over control of Ramoth-Gilead. This change in policy could either be the result of pressure from the military or more probably the consequence of the change of regime in Damascus, where Hazael ascended the throne and changed the course of politics.[4]

The founding of the city of Samaria and, for example, the ivory carvings discovered there indicate the success of this policy of open borders as early as the reign of Omri (ca. 882–871 BCE). However, increasing wealth is not always shared with the common people. It can be hoarded by society's upper classes, which causes an increasing inequality in the social situation. As a result, the poor tend to blame the "foreigners" for their misfortune, as well as the royal house that had opened the gates. Thus there can ensue a defensive reaction against the foreigners, in addition to criticism of the new international policy. Since the state of being different can also be expressed religiously, it is often difficult to decide whether nationalistic or religious sentiments play the major role.

Fundamentally, however, the difficulties lay elsewhere. As indicated above, the Iron Age was a time of great social upheaval. Among other factors were the changeover from a tribal to a royal state and the attendant division of people into modernists and traditionalists, which was expressed in religious and social-ethical realms. The people were unable to comprehend these cultural and societal changes. They focused on that which was before their eyes: the politics of their royal house. They saw the foreign queen Jezebel, experienced the newfangled cultic practices derived from Tyrian models, were amazed at the luxury of the upper class, and reacted to the influx of foreign elements with a heightened nationalism and a new religious consciousness: Yahweh, our God.

---

[4] 2 Kgs 8:7–15. This would apply even if the account is in its particulars non-historical. I view the mention of the name Ahab in 1 Kings 20 and 22 as secondary.

The "Nonviolent" Elisha

There are a few texts in the Hebrew Bible that—if I have interpreted them correctly—do contain information concerning the social situation of the common people of that era. I am referring to the short miracle stories in 2 Kings 2–6 and 13.

But first a few remarks about Elisha. According to 1 Kgs 19:19–21 he was the son of a well-to-do farmer. In other words, he belonged to the class that profited from the economic changes of that period. His heeding of Elijah's call without hesitation can be attributed to his guilty conscience vis-à-vis the people who suffered under those economic realities. Even if this succession narrative is the product of a later period, Elisha's position as the scion of rich farmers must be taken into account.

In these short stories we encounter him as the head of a group of people who are designated the "sons of the prophets." They seem to have lived in a commune, although there were married members with their own houses among them (2 Kgs 4:1–7). Poverty was their major problem. In order to cut down a tree, they had to borrow an ax (2 Kgs 6:5). When they had nothing else to eat, they had to cook a stew of vegetables that they gathered in the wild (2 Kgs 4:38–41). In the time before the new harvest they were especially short of sustenance (2 Kgs 4:42). They "sit before Elisha" (2 Kgs 4:38), who probably taught them either how to meditate or how to induce ecstasy, or both (as emphasized by Schmitt: 170). In modern scholarly studies the poverty of the group is normally attributed to their religious lifestyle: they meditated, therefore they did not work, therefore they had nothing. What, however, if it was the reverse? Could they not have been "communes of the unemployed"? Could they not have been released debt slaves without land and property, or people who had been driven from their homes and could no longer count on normal means of subsistence?

The story of the woman who was supposed to hand over her two sons to a creditor indicates that old tribal ties offered no more protection (2 Kgs 4:1–7). Otherwise she would have been able to turn to her or her husband's kinship group, rather than to the man of God. Without a doubt clans were being broken up into smaller units at that time, into family units with their own land and homes. Even so, relatives would have helped those in distress, had poverty not assumed the upper hand in the agricultural realm, overtaxing the clan's ability to redeem debts.

In earlier times there were others who had been left in the lurch or been driven out by their clans—Jephthah and David come to mind in this connection (Judg 11:2; 1 Sam 22:4), both of whom escaped into the mountains and became brigands. In Elisha's time, however, many more people were affected. The social situation of the mid-ninth century was somewhere between the free farmers of the pre-state and early state period and the massive poverty that we encounter in the writings of the eighth-century prophets. The people who gathered themselves around Elisha did not go into the mountains, nor did they endeavor to seize by force that which they had been denied. Rather, they attempted to come to grips with their poverty by means of their communal lifestyle. Meditation is a good way to make hunger palatable. However, as these stories show, a complete lack of food cannot be endured. Their life was a non-violent variant of the mountain brigands' life. That the commune grew—they had to build themselves a larger house—is a consequence of the spreading misery. So much for these Elisha traditions.

THE "VIOLENT" ELISHA

Other traditions show us Elisha in completely different circumstances. As Elisha approached death, the king called out, "Israel's chariotry!" (2 Kgs 13:14; cf. Minokami: 162–63). Elisha initiated Jehu's putsch (2 Kgs 9:1ff.). He intervened in the war with the Arameans (2 Kings 6–7; 13:14–19). Were there two Elishas? Or was there a break in the life of the one Elisha? Did he come to the realization that his community was unable to cope with the growing misery? Did he become an opponent of the Omride dynasty out of solidarity with the common people? Did he attribute the holes in the social net to the political policy of open borders, of international relations, especially with Tyre? Of course he could not realize that completely different upheavals—the change from a tribal society to a monarchy, the disintegration of the extended families, the new concept of personal possession of property, the imperial politics of Assyria—were the actual causes. Did he think, as many of his fellow citizens undoubtedly did, that "Beforehand, when Israel was on its own, things were better for us; but ever since the foreigners, such as this queen mother Jezebel, came into the land, ever since everything became oriented toward Tyre and Aram, ever since we have had these imported wares and nothing has been good enough for the younger generation, ever since these new international political policies, everything has been going downhill"? Did Elisha subscribe to this nationalism of the commoners, which had arisen out of their social situation? Was this the reason that he entered the political arena and felt that a new king would improve everything? Did he expect that Jehu would change the country's course by 180 degrees?

JEZEBEL

In contrast to the Elijah traditions, the Elisha tradition includes no battle between Baʻal and Yahweh, no rejection of the Baʻal cult. Nor is the story of 2 Kings 9 interested in this issue. The account of 2 Kings 10 is concerned with it only if one assumes that vv. 18–27 are original. There are commentators who want not only to eliminate the clearly Deuteronomistic passages[5] from 2 Kings 9, but also to deny the chapter any relevance to religious questions. In that case it is not only the introduction to the chapter, in which Elisha sends his followers from Gilgal (?) to Ramoth-Gilead in order to anoint Jehu king, which is viewed as a later prophetic addition (see especially Würthwein: ad loc.), but also Jehu's statement justifying his murder of King Joram: "Why peace? There 'still' exist the prostitutions of your mother Jezebel and her many sorceries!" (2 Kgs 9:22b).[6]

I consider both the introductory section and this statement by Jehu to be indispensable parts of the narrative.[7] If they are excised, the story loses

---

[5] 2 Kgs 9:7–10a is generally viewed as a Deuteronomistic addition. In the case of 9:25–26, it is debated whether it is a pre-Deuteronomistic insertion or a typical Deuteronomistic notation of fulfillment.

[6] In favor of the originality of the passage I would list the following arguments:

(a) There is no evidence of Deuteronomistic language in the remark. זנונים never occurs in Deuteronomy or the Deuteronomist, and זנה is present only in the phrase "to go whoring after other gods." כשפים "sorcery" is never found in Deuteronomy or the Deuteronomist; the "sorcerer" in Deut 18:10 has been taken from the Covenant Code in Exod 22:14.

(b) Its brevity fits the situation, while the excessive length of 9:25–26 does not fit the context.

(c) The argument that זנונים is used here as a metaphor for apostasy from Yahweh, just as it is a century later in Hosea, and hence cannot be original is not convincing. First, Hosea could have used an older expression; and second, זנונים does not need to carry this metaphorical connotation.

(d) I consider completely irrelevant the argument of Würthwein and others—that the sentence is redundant in the context of the story since King Joram would have already realized Jehu's evil intentions by the tone of his voice in answer to the question, "Is it well?" In a real-life situation this could be argued, but not in the context of a good Hebrew narrative that has been written down. The narrator would not have had the reader guess the tone of a passage, but would have spelled it out in a manner clear to all, even if we today have to guess at its meaning.

[7] In my opinion 2 Kgs 9:1–6, 10b belongs to the whole narrative of chaps. 9–10, which has its origin in civil or official circles (thus Steck: 47). Arguments in favor of this position include:

(a) Elisha is not referred to as "man of God," as is otherwise the case in passages stemming from his school, but as "prophet."

(b) The officers call the prophet's disciple a "madman." This does not reflect the self-understanding of the prophets but rather the court officials' assessment of their character.

(c) A prophetic author would have let the prophet himself appear.

integral structural elements. The introduction leads us to Ramoth and establishes the figure of Jehu until his departure. Then the narrator transplants us to Jezreel and lets us experience the situation from the perspective of the recuperating king. At the moment when the two protagonists encounter each other on their chariots, Jehu tersely justifies his act of murder. By doing so, he also introduces the queen mother Jezebel, whose demise will eventually be recounted, into the equation. This elaborate structure should not be marred by arbitrary deletions.

What, however, does this say about Jezebel? What judgment does it pass on the queen mother? The answer resides in two terms: זנוני and כשפים. Most commentators assume that she is not being accused of adultery in a literal sense. But if it is a metaphor, what does it mean? Some exegetes see evidence here of Hosea's pictorial language, which presupposes the notion of the marriage between Yahweh and Israel (Montgomery: ad loc.). Serving other gods would then be akin to adultery or harlotry. On the other hand, John Gray writes in his commentary on 2 Kgs 9:22: "The 'harlotries' ($z^e n\bar{u}n\hat{e}$) of Jezebel refers to ritual prostitution as a rite of imitative magic in the fertility cult of the Canaanite Baal. Her 'sorceries' ($k^e\check{s}\=ape\d{h}\=a$) may refer to the seductive arts, i.e. the allurement which those rites had for the common man." I belong to those interpreters[8] who insist on eliminating the concept of sacral/cultic prostitution from the language of exegesis, since such a phenomenon never existed. However, this is not to deny the existence of fertility rites among the indigenous Canaanite cults. That would not appear permissible on the basis of Hos 4:13-14 and the archaeological evidence.[9] Therefore I assume that Queen Jezebel, who as a member of the royal house of Tyre was most probably herself a high-ranking priestess, participated in such rites and also possessed the mantic capabilities that belonged to such a position. "Prostitution" and "sorcery" would then refer to the Canaanite fertility cult with its sexual and mantic manifestations (Steck: 35 n. 1).

This "foreign woman" (Soggin 1981) was not only a symbol for the politics of the Omrides, for the coalition with Tyre and Aram, for the influx of foreign wares, techniques, and thoughts, but also for a type of

---

(d) Eliminating the introduction would destroy the narrative structure of the chapter.

[8] I refer here to Eugene Fisher, Tikva Frymer-Kensky, and Joan Goodnick Westenholz, to name only a few important works.

[9] On this question see Keel and Uehlinger: chaps. VI and VII. Nevertheless, it is striking that in Iron IIB Palestine, i.e. in the eighth and ninth centuries BCE, not only do pictorial representations of the goddess become rarer, but her symbols and attributes (animals) become less sexual in comparison to earlier times (see e.g. Keel/Uehlinger: 208).

religiosity that was foreign to the faithful Yahwists. Disassociation from her reflected the disassociation of the Yahweh religion from fertility rites. Jehu's reproach of Jezebel was hence of a religious nature and indicates that he stood in contact with those who considered themselves loyal Yahwists. His actual motivations may have been ambition and hunger for power, but as a clever tactician he secured the support of the circles of loyal Yahwists, including those around Jehonadab son of Rechab and Elisha (2 Kgs 9:1–6, 10b; 10:15ff.). For their part, these Yahwists viewed him as the bearer of hope vis-à-vis Queen Jezebel and all that she embodied religiously and politically.

ONCE AGAIN ATHALIAH

Jehu's putsch and the change from a coalition politics to a pro-Assyrian and anti-Aramean orientation meant the end of a discussion that had lasted for years, not only in the Northern Kingdom but also in the South, in Judah. Its king, Jehoshaphat, had allied himself with King Ahab of Israel, had won the latter's daughter (or sister) Athaliah as wife for his son Jehoram, and enjoyed the enthusiastic backing of the population of Jerusalem for this new policy. For it meant economic improvement and cultural ties with the "big world." Like Jezebel in the North, Athaliah in the South was the symbol of this policy of open borders. Parallel to the developments in the North, an opposition to this influx of foreign influence formed in the South. It probably consisted of the large clans of the countryside, not of the inhabitants of Jerusalem, and was spearheaded by the priests of the Jerusalem temple. If 2 Chr 21:2–4 is correct in noting that King Jehoram had his six brothers and some of Judah's princes murdered when he came into power, and if this act is to be interpreted as the elimination of political opposition (see above), then it can be concluded that the rural clans and the priests had supporters among the royal family. In such a case, to use Liverani's terminology (see above), traditionalists would have opposed modernists, or in other words nationalists would have opposed internationalists. King Jehoram of Judah, determined to continue the politics of his father and certainly standing under the influence of his wife, the Omride Athaliah, knew of no other way to ward off this opposition than by issuing the order of execution (see above). Athaliah's expressed intent and order to annihilate the Davidic clan would have been devised in accord with the same considerations.

How could she have perceived the situation when she received the report that Jehu had assassinated her son Ahaziah, who had briefly been king after the death of Jehoram? She had to deal with strong pro-Davidide opposition in the land, an opposition that needed to be intimidated. She could no longer rely on the alliance with Samaria since Jehu was in power there, and she saw herself cut off from the Phoenician homeland of her mother (or sister-in-law) Jezebel. Her only hope could be that Jehu's reign would not long endure. Previously, when Zimri had toppled Elah, he himself had soon died as a result of Omri's counter-putsch (1 Kgs 16:9ff.). Jezebel had alluded to this when she called out to Jehu, "Is all well with Zimri, the murderer of his master?" (2 Kgs 9:31b). Thus Athaliah, too, did not reckon with a long reign for Jehu. Completely unaware then of the total extirpation of the Omrides, Athaliah could have handed the reins of government over to an avenger from within her family. In the interim, she herself had to hold onto power. Seen in this regard, she considered her order of execution well grounded and sensible. Whether or not it was so according to higher standards also is another question.

CONCLUSION

Violence—deadly and destructive violence—is the thread that dominates and runs through all the biblical texts that we find from the mid-ninth century BCE. It is no different in the stele of the Moabite king Mesha, which is permeated in a similar manner with Moabite nationalism and its god Chemosh, as well as in the annals of the mighty kings of Assyria. In this context the commune at Gilgal seems an exceptional idyll, one in which misery was dealt with through communal life, meditation, and ecstasy. I assume that these poor people, the victims of the social changes of that time, became increasingly aware of their impotence vis-à-vis the conditions which were constantly producing fresh poverty. They and their leader, Elisha, wanted not only to heal the wounds but also to fight their causes. In Samaria different political policies should be pursued—not the politics of foreigners, of the queen (or queen mother) Jezebel, not the politics which opened the gates to foreign influence, but a national politics characterized by loyalty to the ancient God of Israel, Yahweh. To effect this shift they had a champion, Jehu the commander of the army. If he were to become king, everything would be good once again, just as in old times. De facto, however, nothing at all improved. The reason lay not only in the fact that Jehu apparently acted mainly out of personal ambition, that he consequently took advantage of the national and religious sentiments in the land, and that he was not particularly concerned about the lot of the commoners. It was also not only that his pro-Assyrian, anti-Aramean policy plunged the land into the devastating Aramean wars. On the contrary, the reason was that the social situation of the common people did not at all depend on one political policy or the other in Samaria, but rather on wholesale structural changes in the social configuration.

The problems of the common people could only have been solved or at least alleviated by a king who would have confronted his own state apparatus, the officers and tax-collectors, the large landowners and leading merchants, as an advocate for the poor, one who sought equity and justice. For this, however, one did not need a new dynasty. The poor could have demanded this of the Omrides.

Yet, was the monarchy of this period an institution that could provide justice, one capable of effecting social equity? The Omrides, also with bloodied hands, had come into power by military means and were first and foremost interested in holding onto that power. They were certainly concerned about the economic welfare of the country. But they regarded the affluence of only a single class, the elite who supported them, as if it were representative of the well-being of all. They did not see what was transpiring below this level.

For their part, the poor did not go to Samaria to demand equity and justice from the king. They relied on violence, on another king, to topple the old dynasty and pursue a domestically oriented political line. This was the mistake in their calculations, the mistake in Elisha's reckoning.

That the change of power from the Omrides to the dynasty of Jehu brought the common people no improvement is indicated by the social criticism of the eighth-century prophets. The power of the state to impose its will by force had so little authority a century after Jehu's putsch that Hosea was able to speak of the king and the princes with scorn and derision (Hos 3:4; 7:3; 9:15; 13:10) and that neither Amos nor Micah nor Isaiah considered appealing to the king for the rights of the poor against the upper class. Jehu's murders and—if I may say so—Athaliah's counter-putsch robbed the monarchy of a large part of its legitimacy. Elisha gave Jehu the religious sanction for this. That the God of Israel was not to be used for such a political policy by a prophet such as Elisha is evident in the verdict conveyed through the prophet Hosea (1:4):

Give him (i.e. your son) the name Jezreel,
for soon I will requite the blood of Jezreel on the house of Jehu
and bring the kingdom of Israel to an end.

Works Consulted

Clauss, Manfred
1986 Geschichte Israels: Von der Frühzeit bis zur Zerstörung Jerusalems (587 v. Chr.). Munich: C. H. Beck.

Dietrich, Walter
1972 Prophetie und Geschichte: Eine redaktionsgeschichtliche Untersuchung zum deuteronomistischen Geschichtswerk. FRLANT 108. Göttingen: Vandenhoeck & Ruprecht.

Fisher, Eugene J.
1976 "Cultic Prostitution in the Ancient Near East? A Reassessment." BTB 6:225-36.

Frymer-Kensky, Tikva
1992 In the Wake of the Goddesses: Women, Culture, and the Biblical Transformation of Pagan Myth. New York: Free Press.

Gray, John
1977 I & II Kings: A Commentary. OTL. 3rd ed. London: SCM; Philadelphia: Westminster.

James, E. O.
1959 The Cult of the Mother Goddess: An Archaeological and Documentary Study. London: Thames and Hudson.

Katzenstein, H. J.
1955 "Who Were the Parents of Athaliah?" IEJ 5:194–97.

Keel, Othmar, and Christoph Uehlinger
1992 Göttinnen, Götter und Gottessymbole: Neue Erkenntnisse zur Religionsgeschichte Kanaans und Israels aufgrund bislang unerschlossener ikonographischer Quellen. QD 134. Freiburg: Herder.

Levin, Christoph
1982 Der Sturz der Königin Atalja: Ein Kapital zur Geschichte Judas im 9. Jahrhundert v. Chr. SBS 105. Stuttgart: Katholisches Bibelwerk.

Liverani, Mario
1988 Antico Oriente: Storia, società, economia. Rome: Editori Laterza.

Metzger, Martin
1983 Grundriß der Geschichte Israels. 6th ed. Neukirchen-Vluyn: Neukirchener Verlag.

Miller, J. M.
1967 "The Fall of the House of Ahab." VT 17:307–24.

Minokami, Yoshikazu
1989 Die Revolution des Jehu. GTA 38. Göttingen: Vandenhoeck & Ruprecht.

Montgomery, James A.
    1951   *A Critical and Exegetical Commentary on the Books of Kings.* Ed. Henry Snyder Gehman. ICC. Edinburgh: T. & T. Clark; New York: Charles Scribner's Sons.

Schmitt, Hans-Christoph
    1972   *Elisa: Traditionsgeschichtliche Untersuchungen zur vorklassischen nordisraelitischen Prophetie.* Gütersloh: Gütersloher Verlagshaus Gerd Mohn.

Soggin, J. Alberto
    1981   "Jezabel, oder die fremde Frau." Pp. 453–59 in *Mélanges bibliques et orientaux en l'honneur de M. Henri Cazelles.* Ed. A. Caquot and M. Delcor. AOAT 212. Neukirchen-Vluyn: Neukirchener Verlag; and Kevelaer: Butzon & Bercker.
    1984   *A History of Ancient Israel.* Trans. John Bowden. London: SCM; Philadelphia: Westminster.

Steck, Odil Hannes
    1968   *Überlieferung und Zeitgeschichte in den Elia-Erzählungen.* WMANT 26. Neukirchen-Vluyn: Neukirchener Verlag.

Thiel, Winfried
    1992   "Athaliah." *ABD* 1:511–12.

Timm, Stefan
    1982   *Die Dynastie Omri: Quellen und Untersuchungen zur Geschichte Israels im 9. Jahrhundert vor Christus.* FRLANT 124. Göttingen: Vandenhoeck & Ruprecht.

Westenholz, Joan Goodnick
    1989   "Tamar, Qĕdēšā, Qadištu, and Sacred Prostitution in Mesopotamia." *HTR* 82:245–65.

Würthwein, Ernst
    1977   *Das Erste Buch der Könige: Kapitel 1–16.* ATD 11/1. Göttingen: Vandenhoeck & Ruprecht.
    1984   *Die Bücher der Könige: 1. Kön. 17 – 2. Kön. 25.* ATD 11/2. Göttingen: Vandenhoeck & Ruprecht.

RESPONSES

THE QUEST FOR HEBREW BIBLE ETHICS: A JEWISH RESPONSE

Peter J. Haas
Vanderbilt University

As I began work on this essay, I noticed that I had been given two different working titles for the volume: "Political Ethics in Ancient Israel" and "Ethics and Politics in the Hebrew Bible." Those two titles reflect what appears to me to be a major, and I think unresolved, question that lurks behind the entire collection: are we interested in the ethics of ancient Israelites, in the diverse ethical visions presented in the various books of the Hebrew Bible, or in the ethical assumptions that guided the final redaction of the biblical corpus? As we shall see, some essays implicitly assume one perspective, and others another. Because of this, the essays included here sometimes talk with each other, sometimes against each other, and sometimes past each other. In the end we have a collection of voices and perspectives and are left to draw conclusions on our own as to what it all means. In a curious way, then, the collection before us replicates somewhat one of the salient features of the Bible itself.

I want to begin my comments by calling attention to the essay by Robert Wilson. In his contribution Wilson notes what seems to me to be a central and crucial caveat, namely, that the study of ethics in the Hebrew Bible is fraught with methodological problems. In his short article he does us a public service by pointing out what at least some of the major areas of difficulty are. I hardly need to go over that material again here. The fact is that nearly all of the other contributors to this project end up in one way or another going over ground that he has mapped for us. Unfortunately, many then proceed to do just what he warns against, namely, ignore or discount the methodological problems and, after a brief review of some of the data, draw broad conclusions about "Bible ethics." In part, I suppose, this is a necessary consequence of the way the question is asked. Some of the essays in the collection seem to posit that the Hebrew Bible is a coherent and self-contained entity with a more or less single ethics and politics therein. From this beginning position a number of unarticulated assumptions flow. It is to these that I wish to address myself in the remainder of this response. I propose to do so by setting forth another plausible set of assumptions, a set derived from a traditional Jewish understanding of the Hebrew Bible (or Tanakh) about the nature of the biblical text and the community it represents. My goal is not to argue that the operative model in these essays is wrong and that the alternate that I am posing is correct. Rather, by highlighting an alternative paradigm I hope to bring into relief the unarticulated, and in some cases possibly the unconscious, choices and decisions that undergird and structure the essays before us.

The whole enterprise of studying the "ethics of ancient Israel" or "the ethics of the Hebrew Bible" takes on an entirely different meaning when approached from the perspective of Judaism rather than from the perspective of Christianity. The difference grows out of the different place that biblical literature holds in the two communities. For much of Christian moral thinking, the Bible is canonical in the sense that it is regarded as a complete and internally coherent body of revelation handed down to a collective body of "prophets." For much of Western Christian, essentially Protestant, theology this body of material is the sole foundation for religious and moral thought and dogma. Judaism has always regarded the biblical texts in a much more complex and dynamic way. To begin with, traditional Jewish literature and thought have never considered the Tanakh to constitute the entire "canon." In fact the written Torah, which comprises the Hebrew Bible, is held to be but a small portion of the Sinaitic revelation, the bulk being made up of the Oral Torah. This oral tradition is held to be just as authoritative as, and in fact more comprehensive than, the written part of the revelation. Indeed, it is taken as a matter of course that the written Torah cannot be fully comprehended without the aid of the Oral Torah. Beginning in ancient times, this larger and more comprehensive part of divine revelation has been slowly committed to writing in the form of rabbinic literature: Mishnah, Talmud, midrash, commentaries, and so on. These writings have not by any means exhausted the content of the revelation, and the process of writing down the revelation continues to this day, constantly adding to the canonical literature. In short, there is no closed "biblical" canon in Judaism. The Tanakh or Hebrew Bible, as one small and embryonic part of the available canon, cannot be isolated, excised, and treated as an independent self-standing statement. To talk about "the" ethics of the Tanakh as a self-contained system makes no sense from a Jewish perspective.

But this is only one of the difficulties that this alternate perspective presents to the project before us. Another is the fact that the Tanakh itself hardly need be regarded as a single, uniform, monolithic block of revelation. To be sure, the first section of the Tanakh, the Torah, is considered authoritative in a somewhat strict sense. But the rest, the Prophets and the Writings, is understood for the most part as what it seems to be, namely, a melange of diverse writings by different people in different times chronicling the history of the Israelites and how they understood, interpreted, and absorbed the Sinaitic revelation. This history involves a number of different voices and perspectives. Further, this history of appropriation did not stop suddenly with Malachi. It continued in unbroken succession down through the Second Commonwealth and into the rabbinic period and beyond. The Tanakh, then, is but a part of that early history of the interpretation of the divine revelation at Sinai, a history of interpretation that stretches down into the present.

Viewing the Hebrew Bible in this light gives it a much different character, and so authority, than what has been assumed by many of the non-Jewish efforts to investigate and identify "biblical ethics." As is pointed out by John Barton, the Hebrew word "torah" does not mean "law," but rather "teaching" or "instruction." That is, the canonical literature of Judaism (all of which can be called Torah) does not so much tell us what to do as it teaches us how to think about what to do. It is, then, neither descriptive of how all ancient Israelites acted, nor is it directly normative, a series of behavioral models to be adopted by us. Rather, it presents us with situations and events that illustrate how certain decisions in certain circumstances have molded subsequent events. Seen in this way, turning to the Tanakh (or worse, just to the Pentateuch) to find a full set of immediately applicable answers to our present-day moral or ethical questions would be like making legal decisions in the United States today by looking only at the Federalist Papers and the Constitution without considering the history of understanding, interpretation, appropriation, and experience encapsulated in Supreme (and other) Court decisions. It is in effect to take one moment out of an ongoing process and declare the literature of that moment to be comprehensive, definitive, and sacred.

An example of the consequences of this approach may be found in a statement Bruce Birch makes at the beginning of his article. He writes that "ethics in the Hebrew Bible is inextricably bound up with the entire theological witness of the biblical story to a god who becomes known in relation to the people Israel." Let us take a moment to unpack the assumptions of this assertion. Now there is no member of the people of Israel that I am aware of who is ready to claim that Israel's relation to G-d was worked out in any complete or final fashion solely in the pages of Tanakh. At best we have the first few chapters of the first volume of how Israel and G-d have interacted—and still are interacting. This does not mean that the witness of the Bible's literature is of no consequence or concern. It was and still is tremendously rich and suggestive. Yet, if one takes the Bible to be the full and encompassing witness of how the divine revelation has been appropriated by the people of Israel, then everything that follows is seriously flawed. If ethical enquiry for Christians, as Birch says, is to be based on G-d's call and the response of G-d's people, then closing the investigation in the ancient Persian period (that is, when the Hebrew Bible is "closed") has the effect of arbitrarily, and I think fatally, compromising the body of available evidence. To be sure, Birch is aware of the problem and tries at least obliquely to neutralize it by claiming that the canon reflects "the intention of the biblical text as we now have it to transcend its originating social contexts" so as to address itself to "community formation through succeeding generations." To the extent that this means for Birch that the text is not authoritative in and of itself but needs an interpreting community, I have no argument. But if it means that this text alone is to be treated as though it conveys the full story of G-d's interaction with the people Israel, then Birch has seriously undermined his own enterprise on at least two counts. On the one hand, as we said, he is distorting the nature of the text. On the other, he is calling for moderns to ignore centuries of postbiblical Jewish interaction with G-d, thus forcing them to reinvent the wheel, that is, to repeat rather than learn from centuries of human experience.

Even if we grant that the literature in the Bible is a fair representation of a community's relationship to the divine, we are not home free. Another philosophical and methodological problem, touched on by Eryl Davies, is concealed here. The problem is how to describe what it is that the Bible is telling us. For example, is the Bible informing us of the Israelites' interaction with G-d, that is, how Israelites actually behaved, or is it, in Davies's words, "a statement of the principles or ideals of behavior generally considered to be desirable"? In other words, are we to take the biblical stories to be descriptive of ancient Israelites, or normative like a book of law? If the former is the case, then we must assume first of all that the biblical stories are accurate representations of how actual people behaved. While not an impossible position, it is certainly one that would have to be argued in light of current understandings of how the biblical text came into being. But if we grant that this is so, we still have to ask why it is that the way this ancient people happened to have conducted themselves ought to be paradigmatic for us. Why does their political conduct in particular instances need to be conveyed to us? What does it teach us that we could not learn from other civilizations or literatures, or even from observing modern politics? Are we, too, to adopt animal sacrifice and the stoning of criminals? This position holds only if we assume that biblical characters lead exemplary lives, an assumption that the Bible constantly undercuts. Alternatively, we could look at the Bible as normative, that is, as legislating the view of G-d, or some elite, as to how people ought to behave. The biblical stories are then shaped to show us what happens if we act one way or the other. This means, of course, that we must proceed on the assumption that the thoughts and values of the actual Israelite population did not always necessarily coincide with the "official" view expressed in our texts. We cannot simply assume without further comment that the laws of Leviticus represent Israelite morality, for example. Rather, we can only assume at the outset that these laws reflect the view of some priestly writer or group of writers in perhaps the sixth or fifth century BCE. These laws are indeed important, but they must be seen as the party line of one group at one moment in the history of a people's developing moral and ethical tradition. It also means, as Davies points out, that we have to see the Bible as potentially expressing a multiplicity of views as different voices speak through different books, as Davies himself advocates.

Such a multiplicity should warn us against broad generalizations of "biblical ethics" or the "morality of biblical Israel." In this regard, Davies performs a valuable service. He notes that "some consideration must be given to the possibility that a 'natural law' type of ethic functioned in ancient Israel." By this he does not mean that all of biblical or Israelite ethics was based on a natural-law perspective. Rather, he means simply to alert us that some exempla of biblical law were (or could be conceived to have been) based on a natural-law perspective and so we must not close off that (or, by extension, any other) hermeneutic possibility. In short, at least some of the essays in the first part of the volume implicitly, and in some cases explicitly, bring into question the very foundational assumptions on which the study as a whole rests.

I wanted to lay out this alternate understanding of the Hebrew Bible, as I said, because I think it helps highlight some of the underlying assumptions that animate much of the discussion in the present volume. Despite some disclaimers and with a few exceptions, all the essays in the first part tend to see the Hebrew Bible as a single, coherent body of literature that is self-contained and essentially internally consistent. In short, there is an assumption that there is "an" ethic in "the" Hebrew Bible. With these assumptions in mind, I think we are in a better position to see more clearly and evaluate more fully what results these efforts have yielded.

This brings us to the second half of the collection, which does not look at "the" Bible, but rather at individual stories, events, or themes. The question now is whether or not we in fact can derive ethics, or an ethical view, or even anything specifically Israelite (Judean?) from any of these texts. The answer to all three questions seems to me to be "No." Let me explain.

I want to begin by reading two of these articles side-by-side, namely, Douglas Knight's analysis of rights and powers in monarchic Israel and Niels Peter Lemche's study of patronage ("*ḥesed*"). In juxtaposition, these highlight one of the fundamental problems of doing any study of this type, namely, what questions are appropriate to ask. Knight wants to know how monarchic society in Israel dealt with the distribution of rights and power. He recognizes, of course, that these are modern concerns not addressed explicitly in the biblical texts. Nonetheless, he wants to include the experience of biblical Israel in the discussion. He asks the same questions—about participation, citizenship, protection, and dissent—of both the "national" and the "local" levels. His conclusions are that the biblical system favored hierarchy and the powerful over the powerless but that, nonetheless, common people had a certain level of political influence, usually at the local level. This, he says, was never justified or enacted by reference to "rights" but was a matter of social norms and traditions. Lemche makes roughly the same point, but from within the linguistic horizon of the biblical text itself. The political relationship between the ruled and the rulers Lemche speculates to be described by the term "*ḥesed*," a term which, he argues, refers to the relation between client and patron. In this kind of patronage situation the client, of course, does have certain rights and, to say the same thing in a different way, the patron does have certain obligations. These may not be spelled out as "natural rights," but they are binding nonetheless. So both Knight and Lemche come to essentially the same conclusions. But the common answer arrived at by two different means still leaves a host of fundamental questions unanswered. Let us assume for a moment the patron–client relationship as described by Lemche and evaluated by Knight. Even if we grant everything they maintain, we still do not know exactly how such a patron–client system worked. I am aware that we cannot retrieve what actually transpired between a supposed patron and his (or her?) client in a village in biblical Israel in, for example, the middle of the eighth century BCE. But it would seem that drawing conclusions about rights, duties, and obligations would require just such knowledge. We do, of course, have access to how similar political relationships and obligations function in rural village life. There are innumerable studies of "village politics" from Latin America (a scant sample of which appears in Knight's "Works Consulted"), Europe, Africa, and the Middle East. Lemche's discussion of the scene from "The Godfather" is highly suggestive, I think, of the kind of human relationship that could have gone on in Israelite villages, a model that anthropological studies have found to be repeated in its essentials in villages all over the globe. This in no way proves that Israelite life was this way, but it may help us to determine what questions are appropriate to ask. In many ways, I am sometimes convinced, the patronage system may give its clients more access to power at crucial times than does a commonly shared citizenship in a vast yet democratic bureaucracy. To be sure, it all depends on the client, the patron, and the situation in which the patron does his or her work. We have precious little access to that kind of information for biblical Israel. As a result, looking at this overall scheme for moral guidance may be a poor strategy. We simply cannot see the workings of the system with sufficient clarity and nuance.

Even if we knew more about how the patron–client system worked at some point in the life of biblical Israel, it is hardly clear what that knowledge would mean in terms of our own situation. There is ample ground for both praising the system and condemning it. The biblical text really does neither; it simply assumes the relationship (if Lemche, et al., are correct). So what does that tell us about what we are to do? What political, or social, ethics are being conveyed? I doubt that anyone would take seriously the proposition that because the Bible takes a patron–client relationship in a "monarchy" for granted we are called upon by G-d to do the same.

One possibility is to ask more modest questions. If biblical ethics are to be useful for us today in our setting, maybe we should look not at grand schemes of overall political organization but at specific uses of power. This brings to mind Hannelis Schulte's piece on the end of the Omride dynasty. The discussion in the article of the various political pressures and options is good—so good, in fact, that it seems to undermine the premise of the entire collection. The issue as it emerges from Schulte's pen is not one of simple right or wrong. What we have in the violent downfall of the Omride dynasty is a classic political confrontation. The diverse actors each had his or her own perspective on matters and acted to achieve what at the time seemed to be the overriding interests at stake. But this is what all politics is really about. To be sure, we can stand back after the dust has settled and evaluate how things in fact worked themselves out in the long run and in that light pass judgment on the parties involved. But matters are never so simple or clear to political actors who are engaged in the struggle. They have to work with the reality they experience, with the resources they perceive to be at hand, and for the constituencies on whom they rely. What we see, through Schulte's analysis, in the struggles surrounding the fall of the Omride dynasty and the roles played by Athaliah, Elijah, Elisha, and others is a more or less typical political struggle in which various viewpoints come into conflict and representatives of each push their own interests. What we may learn from this struggle, as Schulte presents it, is how certain types of political struggles play themselves out. But there is nothing particularly Israelite or biblical or divine about the results of our investigation of this struggle. We could achieve the same insights, I submit, by studying Roman or English politics.

Schulte does not end on this note, however. The article concludes that the violence that accompanied the putsch was not acceptable to G-d and in fact eventually weakened the monarchy it was supposed to protect. So for Schulte, and maybe even the biblical redactor, there is a moral to the story. But we have to keep in mind that this was a moral written (or read) into the story by some later observer and interpreter. We are reading not history's moral, necessarily, but a redactor's conclusions. We are back to the earlier question of why this particular redactor's view should be binding or paradigmatic for us. And of course we still have the problem of translating the redactor's evaluation of this episode to the political struggles with which we are faced.

This point about the redactor's (or author's) evaluation is important because the assumptions we make about how and why the text came into being will tell us how to evaluate its evaluations. This thorny issue is touched upon both by Frank Crüsemann and Frank Frick. Crüsemann makes it clear that the shaping of the Jacob narrative was heavily influenced by later political realities, that is, that the relationship between Jacob and Esau in the narrative was structured according to later perspectives and realities. The narrative served as a kind of propaganda, a way of justifying what had already happened. If there is a lesson to be drawn from how the Bible treats these events, it may be that moral evaluation cannot take place until after the event is over and its consequences have emerged.

The notion of biblical histories as propaganda raises a whole series of questions for the stated theme of this collection. There are the obvious literary questions of who wrote it, for what audience, and how the audience was to be exposed to this piece of propaganda (do we assume that everyone had a copy of the Deuteronomistic History, that it was circulated among the sympathetic, that it was read out in village squares?). Beyond that, we have to ask the heuristic question: if the Deuteronomistic History is propaganda, then how are we to derive ethics from it? From a complex political struggle à la Schulte, a propagandistic reading will only give us one side—if that. Because this one side will reflect certain interests and developments, how do we extract from it any transcendent truths about political behavior at all times and in all places? If the biblical writings stem from a particular time and place and represent only a particular point of view, possibly one that formed only generations after the events they are discussing, then what can it mean to be looking for the ethics of the Hebrew Bible?

In the end we are left with the question with which we started: are we looking for the ethics of ancient Israelites, the ethics of the Hebrew Bible, or the ethics of the final redactor and/or that redactor's community? It seems from our considerations that it is either impossible or trivial to retrieve the ethics of ancient Israelites. It seems also that to treat the entire Hebrew Bible as a single and complete moral treatise is historically naïve and unacceptable. If anything, we are left with the view shaped for us by the final redactional activity. This, however, hardly seems to provide a coherent picture of what constitutes political ethics—unless, of course, that is just the point. In the complex collection of materials that we regard as Bible, we are being called upon not simply to have answers but to consider the full complexity of human relationships with each other and with G-d. The Bible is not about answers but, as the Judaic tradition would have it, about what questions still need to be asked.

OF AIMS AND METHODS IN HEBREW BIBLE ETHICS

Eckart Otto
Johannes Gutenberg-Universität Mainz

PRELIMINARY REMARKS

The mail carrier brought the papers of this volume just when I was reading the proofs of my recently finished *Theologische Ethik des Alten Testaments*. So I divided my days. In the morning I continued my hunt for the demon of misprints; in the afternoon I read these papers and wrote my response, eager to learn what others think about writing an ethics of the Hebrew Bible. It consoled me to learn that I was not the only one to have great difficulties with the task. How does the subject of an ethics of the Hebrew Bible differ from the subject of a theology of the Hebrew Bible? How should one organize the abundant materials relating to the different ethics of different social groups in different periods of Israelite and Judean history, and what purpose does such an ethics have in our present world? In 1982 I signed the contract to write the ethics of the Old Testament, but it took me twelve years, including several years when I thought that it was an enterprise too difficult to accomplish, before I could complete a manuscript. When I read the papers of this volume, I had the feeling that it was not I who was responding to the papers but they who were responding to me.

At the outset, I should explain one of my presuppositions based on a fundamental exegetical decision: I do not follow the canonical approach, which Brevard S. Childs has once again (1993) worked out so impressively, because I believe that if we want to understand a given text we also must understand its history. Moreover, I maintain that the text of the Hebrew Bible can still address our entire society and not solely the Christian or Jewish communities. Just as the intellectual shape of modern societies is not uniform but full of tensions and differences, so also that of the ancient Israelite and Judean societies was pluriform. The exegete discovers the discourses and discussions of these ancient societies in the literary history of the biblical texts. The canonical approach diminishes this perspective—and in fact curtails not only dialogues within the Bible but also those between the Bible and surrounding cultures of the ancient Near East. I fear that it also depreciates the necessity to understand the biblical text as a dialogue partner in our discourses about truth in modern society and in our conversations with the so-called Third World (Otto, 1988b). Scholars who are more interested in only the internal perspective of Christianity or Judaism, I admit, may come to a different conclusion.

The ethics of the Hebrew Bible can be structured according to three basic problems: (1) the interpretation of the systems of legal and ethical rules; (2) the biblical legitimation of these rules, i.e. the answer to the question of why one in ancient Israel should follow these rules even if it meant renouncing one's own (temporary) advantage; and (3) the consequences of moral conduct, i.e. the expectation that there is a mediation between moral conduct and a successful life, between "Ethos und Glückseligkeit" (Kant).

THE HISTORY OF LEGAL AND ETHICAL RULES

The contribution of Douglas Knight concerning the political rights and powers in monarchic Israel underscores the fact that the actual behavior of Israelites and Judeans cannot be the subject matter of an ethics of the Hebrew Bible—not only because of the fragmentary sources we have for reconstructing how people really lived and acted, but far more because the sources show that the people of Israel and Judah were living under social conditions that can no longer serve as a model for a modern society and are not even meaningful under a cultural-historical perspective. To the extent that Israel can be regarded as the cradle for modern industrial and bureaucratic societies (Weber), it was far ahead of its time not so much in terms of its actual social life but in terms of its great religious ideas (Schluchter 1979, 1981; Otto 1982).

The legal collections form one of the pillars of an ethic of the Hebrew Bible. In my view, the primary subject matter of an ethics of the Hebrew Bible, in contrast to a theology of the Hebrew Bible or a history of Israelite and Judean religion, is the system of legal and ethical rules in the Covenant Code, Deuteronomy, Decalogue, and the post-priestly Holiness Code.

In the Covenant Code we can perceive the origin of an ethic apart from the law (Otto 1988a:38–44, 69–75). Exod 22:20–26[*1] constitutes one of the oldest statements giving divine legitimation to the law. God's concern for the poor, who were crying for help, has its background in God's function as divine king (Boyce: 27–42; cf. Psalms 15 and 24). The mixture

---

[1] Exod 22:20aβb, 23, 24b are post-Deuteronomistic additions to the Covenant Code. For a different view, cf. Lohfink 1990a. In accord with scholarly convention, an asterisk signals that reference is being made to only a part, not the entirety, of the verse or verses named. Hebrew versification is followed throughout this essay.

of casuistic and prohibitive-apodictic formulations, the parenetic tone, and the fact that one could not appeal to a court to sue for solidarity with the poor show that these rules had become separated from a strictly juridical setting. God alone, not a human court of justice, enforces these rules. With this explicit divine legitimation, ethical rules developed out of the law. When Judean society was in danger of fragmenting into rich and poor classes because of social differentiation, a theological theory was presumably needed to base the integration of society no longer on genealogy or political power but on God's will that responsibility be shared for the weak and poor in society. This was the starting point of the ethics of the Hebrew Bible. The ethics of social solidarity was related to community—but it was the whole Judean society that should be kept together. The ethos of social solidarity subsequently developed into an ethos of solidarity with the enemy in Exod 23:4–5 (Barbiero: 72–130). This ethical rule formed the center of the collection of procedural laws in Exod 23:1–3, 6–8, which are framed by "social-privilege laws" in Exod 22:28–29 and 23:10–12. These privilege laws, stipulating what is to be set apart for God, are cast mostly in a 6/7 scheme to symbolize the assignment to God's realm, and in this manner they functioned as divine legitimation. This legitimation determines also the basic redaction of the Covenant Code, framing it with slave laws (Exod 21:2–11) and fallow-year and Sabbath regulations (Exod 23:10–12). The religious-ethical rules (Exod [20:24–26] 21:2–11; 22:20–26*, 28–29; 23:4–5, 10–12 [14–19]) forms a framework that theologically legitimates the legal provisions for capital delicts (Exod 21:12–17 [22:17–19a]), bodily injuries (Exod 21:18–32), property damages (Exod 21:33 – 22:14), family law (Exod 22:15–16), and court procedures (Exod 23:1–3, 6–8).[2] All fields of daily life were subjected to God's will.

The literary history of the biblical law codes is comprised of a continuous history of their exegetical rereading. Deuteronomy was a modernizing interpretation of the Covenant Code with cultic centralization as its hermeneutical key. The structure of pre-Deuteronomistic Deuteronomy was derived from the Covenant Code. Deuteronomy 12*, an exegesis of the altar law of the Covenant Code (Lohfink, 1984; Levinson: 169–232), opens Deuteronomy with a foundational regulation ("Hauptgebot"). The social-privilege laws (Deut 14:22 – 15:23 [cf. Hamilton]; 26:2–13*) form a framework for Deuteronomy 16–25* and subject festivals (Deut 16:1–17), court procedures (Deut 16:18 – 18:8*), and law systems (Deut 19:2 – 25:1) including family laws (cf.

---

[2] For the process of theologization of casuistic laws in the Covenant Code, see also Schwienhorst-Schönberger: 284–414.

Pressler), i.e. all aspects of cultic and daily life, to the reign of God.[3] Again one of the main aspects of the redaction is solidarity with the poor in society. The Deuteronomistic redactions reinterpret the preexilic Deuteronomy as a program for postexilic New Israel, which is to be a society without marginal groups (Deut 15:4-6; Lohfink 1990b). The intensive Deuteronomistic concern in Deuteronomy for the poor provokes the question of whether the sparse use of terms for the poor in the Deuteronomistic History itself (see the contribution of Frank Frick in this volume) was not so much a matter of the social prejudice of the Deuteronomists as it was a function of the narrative books in relation to Deuteronomy, the constitution of the New Israel after the exile.

When the Deuteronomistic History was connected with the priestly Tetrateuch, the Deuteronomistic Horeb-revelation had to be harmonized with the priestly Sinai-revelation. While according to the Deuteronomistic theory of Deuteronomy 5 and 9-10 the Decalogue was directly revealed to the people of Israel and Deuteronomy 12-26 to Moses at Horeb, the Decalogue in Exodus 20 (Hoßfeld: 163-213) along with the Book of the Covenant was inserted into the Sinai-pericope. Yet there were numerous laws in Deuteronomy, especially among the family laws, without any correspondence in the Covenant Code, and a number of contradictions between Deuteronomy and the Covenant Code also existed. The answer was the Holiness Code (Leviticus 17-26), which was an exegetical harmonization of the Priestly Code, the Decalogue, the Covenant Code, and Deuteronomy. The structure of the Holiness Code has its two primary pillars in Leviticus 19 and 25. Leviticus 19 develops an ethical program for the individual that has its center in the command to love one's neighbor, including the enemy, as one loves oneself (Lev 19:17-18; Mathys: 1-142; Barbiero: 205-96). Leviticus 25 is a program of social ethics (cf. Fager) based on social solidarity.

It is my basic thesis that law normally precedes its narrative context. The Covenant Code became part of the Sinai-pericope after the formation of Deuteronomy and the priestly Tetrateuch. The preexilic Deuteronomy originally had no narrative frame. The law codes formed the backbone in the development of the Pentateuch, and only with the mirrored image adopted by the canonical approach could this literary-historical relation of the law codes and narratives be reversed.[4]

---

[3] Deuteronomic theology was a counter-reaction against the Judean tendency toward secularization in the seventh century BCE—and not an exponent of it. For a different view, cf. Weinfeld: 191-243.

[4] Methodological care is especially necessary for ethical interpretation of narratives if they do not provide a direct hint about the ethical or legal rule involved. Otherwise there is a danger that speculation or even misinterpretation can prevail. In

What is the significance of this effort to discern in the biblical systems of legal and ethical norms God's will for us today? The social-hermeneutical differences between the modern technological world and the ancient agrarian societies of Judah and Israel make it impossible to apply ethical rules of the Hebrew Bible directly to our world. If their validity were to be restricted to contemporary religious communities, it would lead to these communities' isolation from the rest of modern society. However, there is a point of convergence between biblical law and modern society that is relevant for Christians and Jews with respect to their responsibility for our society. The law codes of the Hebrew Bible were stamped by a continuous process of presenting divine sanction for legal and ethical precepts, with the result that they integrated daily life into God's will. Modern industrial societies are dominated by just the opposite process of disintegration of different sectors of society, i.e. economy, state administration, cultural activities, and the like, and it becomes more and more difficult to reflect the ethical unity of all these sectors, which are acting according to their own often unethical logic. In the Hebrew Bible the ethical integration of the different sectors of society was effected by the theological interpretation of law and ethics.

In view of various contributions in this volume (Frank Frick, Douglas Knight, Niels Peter Lemche, Robert Wilson), there remains one central question: what was the sociohistorical function of such an ethical program in Israelite and Judean history, and what does it mean for the ethics of the Hebrew Bible if we come to the conclusion that they were priestly ideologies legitimating the behavior of the upper class? I think it is impossible actually to prove that these texts had such a function in direct contradiction to the texts' own words and meanings. It is too narrow an approach to suppose that only texts that were produced by lower-class circles could in fact favor an egalitarian solidarity. We can learn a more appropriate approach from Max Weber, who recognized the fundamental meaning of intellectuals in Judean social history who were not bound by a class standpoint. It seems likely to me that these ethical programs were the result of intensive theological work by intellectual circles of priests who were not concerned with controlling the moral and religious values or the economic options of large portions of the population, nor with legitimating upper-class behavior. Rather, they were concerned with the social crisis of Judean society and wrote against their own class standpoint. This is a most important ethical theme: programs written by priests in favor of the poor. If this supposition is correct, then a social-

---

ethical interpretation, narrative and legal or ethical rules should be kept together (Daube).

scientific and deconstructionist approach cannot suffice to write an ethics of the Hebrew Bible. We should take the ethical programs seriously and examine their attempt to solve the basic ethical questions of humankind. This does not mean that the ethics of the Hebrew Bible is disconnected with the societal context of Judean history. The ethics describes the original intentions of the idealistic ethical programs of the Hebrew Bible in their societal context and their reception in later periods. The programs, their changing legitimation, and their treatments of the unrealized ideals of society had their own history, which reflects the social history of Judah.

Wisdom literature contains a field of ethical rules distinct from those of the law codes. Its literary history was fundamentally connected to the theological discourse about the legitimation of these rules and the consequences of ethical conduct. We will deal with sapiential teachings in the next sections.

THE LEGITIMATION OF LEGAL AND ETHICAL RULES

The Covenant Code was formed out of two law collections—I: Exod 20:24–26; 21:2–22:26*; and II: Exod 22:28–23:12*. Both parts are structured by different kinds of theological legitimation. Collection I is framed by the altar law (Exod 20:24–26) and social-ethical rules (Exod 22:20b–26*), which provide a theological accent to the whole collection with the motif of YHWH as the divine king who has an ear open for the rights of the poor and miserable. This motif has its background in the solar interpretation of YHWH as a god of justice in the priestly theology of Jerusalem:

> You shall not wrong a stranger. If you do cause affliction in any way and the stranger cries out to me, I will surely hear the cry. If you lend money to any one of my people who is poor among you, you shall give it back before the sun goes down. For it may be that person's only covering, the clothing for the body. In what else shall one sleep? When that person cries out to me, I will hear, for I am merciful. (Exod 22:20aα, 22, 24aα, 25b-26)

One is required to be merciful with the poor because God is merciful. From the very beginning of the theological legitimation of law and morals, Hebrew Bible ethics was never simply based on obedience but on insight into the character of God. The basic idea in Exod 22:20–26* is the imitation of God, a feature of Hebrew Bible ethics emphasized in the articles by John Barton and Bruce Birch in this volume. Theological legitimation intends to convince and to build on human insight and understanding. There is an appeal to the logic of human compassion in the question: "For it may be that person's only covering, the clothing for the body. In what else shall one sleep?" Human logic and theological argument are not contradictory but are interrelated. The post-Deuteronomistic addition in Exod 22:20b reflects the Deuteronomic development of the imitation argument (cf. Bultmann: 166–74). It is no longer based only on the character of God as in Exod 22:26 but on God's action in the salvation history of Israel. The addressee is identified with YHWH and should act as YHWH acts with Israel. The poor are identified with Israel as slaves and strangers in Egypt. Salvation history becomes a model for socially responsible conduct. The limits of this type of theological legitimation are obvious because it is restricted to an ethical particularism lacking the ability to develop into a universal ethics.

This is the point where the ethics of proverbs becomes especially relevant for the ethics of the Hebrew Bible. The preexilic proverbs in Proverbs 10–31 derive their ethical rules from the observation of structures of reason and consequence in nature and society. Where a certain action leads again and again to a positive or negative outcome, one could expect that there exists something like a structure. Sapiential ethics tries to recognize these structures, to adjust human actions to them, and so to lay ground for a positive and successful life.[5] This kind of "natural law," addressed in the above essays by John Barton, Eryl Davies, and Douglas Knight, is deeply theological. The structures ordering nature and society have their ontological basis in the creation of the world. Human beings possess knowledge of them not by revelation but by observation of the world. The observations were condensed into a sapiential tradition. However, the wise knew that they would never have full knowledge of the metaempirical structures in nature and society. There is always a cognitive-theoretical limit for human beings on the one hand—only God has full knowledge of creation—and, on the other hand, a fundamental freedom and remoteness of God in relation to the orders and structures of creation. The wise knew that God represented the limited character of all their wisdom, and thus that the fear of God was the beginning of all wisdom. Sapiential ethics aimed at an accord between the natural order and moral conduct because for the wise it was obvious that there was no other chance for a good life. In the final analysis, life cannot succeed against God's creation.

THE CONSEQUENCES OF MORAL CONDUCT

Sapiential thought included the notion of order in human life—that moral conduct in accordance with ethical rules should lead to a good life. The wise invested considerable effort in reflecting on the repeated contradictions to this notion in the empirical world. In postexilic wisdom

---

[5] For the material ethics of Proverbs 10–31, see Delkurt.

literature, the legitimation of ethics was changed from the inductive method dominating the preexilic text of Proverbs 10–31 to the deductive type of reasoning evident in Proverbs 1–9. According to the latter, wisdom is preexistent with God (Proverbs 8) so that no empirical experience can falsify it. But this belief was not a definitive solution to the problem that empirical experience contradicts the idea of a firm connection between moral conduct and fortune in life. Only in theory, not in practice, was the new legitimation secure from being falsified by empirical experience, for an ethical theory cannot well resist the contradictions life presents.

The Book of Job attempted to solve this problem in a different way. Although Job is a just man who fulfills the highest moral standards of his time (Job 31; Oßwald), he is surrounded by calamities and distress. God's answer to Job claims that with the creation of the world evil was overwhelmed once and for all and that metaempirically it has no power against God (Keel: 51ff.). But what does this mean for the empirical life of those in distress? The final redactor of the Book of Job did not issue a solution based on the claim that God's dominion over the powers of evil should be experienced in the context of life. Thus the redactor did not eliminate the final conciliatory scene of the Job-narrative in Job 42. However, as long as life does not follow this paradigm—and very often it does not—the theological theory of the Book of Job is unconvincing.

Consequently, Qoheleth disconnected ethics and faith in God, advocating a rational, minimal ethics that was legitimated by the insight that it was better for humans not to be alone (Krüger: 214–438). A divine order exists in the world, but humans have no insight into it. Qoheleth thus preserved God's transcendence and freedom from being falsified by empirical experience. Later, however, Ben Sira became again convinced that the metaempirical structures, including the connection between moral conduct and fortune in life (Sir 16:17–23), could be experienced empirically. Just as Proverbs ultimately failed to verify this idea, Sirach had to extend its theological basis in order to legitimate it. He did so by connecting the sapiential idea of preexistent wisdom with the legitimation of law and ethics in the law codes, and the point of connection was the idea of God's revelation in history: the preexistent wisdom found its dwelling place with Israel in Jerusalem (Sirach 24). The amalgamation of these types of legitimation expanded the horizon of the particularistic restriction inherent in the legitimation tradition of the law codes. The wisdom that had found her home in Jerusalem was the light for all the peoples of the world. On the other hand, the restrictions inherent in the sapiential type of legitimation were also removed inasmuch as the revelation of God in Israel's history—and thus not empirical experience nor metaempirically preexistent wisdom incapable of mediation through empirical experience—was the source of legitimation. But the problem of the consequences of moral conduct remained unsolved. Beside the traditional paradigms to deal with this problem there was a new idea in Sirach, namely, that the fear of God is in itself of more worth than are all kinds of superficial success in life, such as wealth and honor (Sir 10:22, 24). Moral conduct itself is the fortune, which is no longer considered merely an external consequence of moral conduct. Yet this solution could also not be fully convincing. The ethics of the Hebrew Bible is, as our survey shows, always teleologically and never purely deontologically structured. The Kantian identification of sense of duty and fortune is unacceptable for the Hebrew Bible because this idealistic identification isolates human beings from their outer world of nature and society.

In light of empirical conditions, the problem of the consequences of moral conduct could not be solved. As the Hebrew Bible was not satisfied with the identification of moral conduct and fortune, the ethics of the Hebrew Bible had to take another decisive step by integrating the eschatological dimension into its ethical reasoning. In postexilic prophetic and apocalyptic literature ethics situated its legitimation in the expectation of a new history and a new world. The Book of Daniel based this hope on a sophisticated interpretation of Israel's history (Daniel 2; 7): There is no power in the world that can prevent God's judgment of this world and installation of a new one. In the new world justice will prevail. The just will live, and there will be shame for those who do not follow the Torah (Dan 12:2–3). The ethics of the Hebrew Bible thus attained its goal with this hope for a new world of justice, a world in which moral conduct and fortune are reconciled. Apocalyptic ethics was limited by the idea that history is entirely in the hand of God and cannot be influenced by humans. Moral conduct lost its function to shape the world according to God's revealed will, and instead became an act of confession in times of total alienation from the world (Münchow: 112–42). From a Christian perspective this restricted character of human responsibility found its resolution in the idea that Jesus ushered in the new world (Schrage: 23–122).

Epilogue

This response is not and cannot be a definitive answer to all the questions raised by the papers in this volume. Discussion of the difficulties involved in the indispensable task of writing an ethics of the Hebrew Bible will continue. I am sure that there will be more and more voices taking part in this discussion, in which we as exegetes of the

Hebrew Bible will have a major role to play. If biblical exegesis is more than merely a historical enterprise but also has theological relevance for the whole of today's society, the ethics of the Hebrew Bible must count as one of the central tasks of biblical scholarship.

Works Consulted

Barbiero, Gianni
    1991   *L'asino del nemico: Rinuncia alla vendetta e amore del nemico nella legislazione dell'Antico Testamento (Es 23,4–5; Dt 22,1–4; Lv 19,17–18)*. AnBib 128. Rome: Editrice Pontificio Istituto Biblico.

Boyce, Richard Nelson
    1988   *The Cry to God in the Old Testament*. SBLDS 103. Atlanta: Scholars.

Bultmann, Christoph
    1992   *Der Fremde im antiken Juda: Eine Untersuchung zum sozialen Typenbegriff "ger" und seinem Bedeutungswandel in der alttestamentlichen Gesetzgebung*. FRLANT 153. Göttingen: Vandenhoeck & Ruprecht.

Childs, Brevard S.
    1993   *Biblical Theology of the Old and New Testaments: Theological Reflection on the Christian Bible*. Minneapolis: Fortress.

Daube, David
    1963   *The Exodus Pattern in the Bible*. London: Faber & Faber.

Delkurt, Holger
    1993   *Ethische Einsichten in der alttestamentlichen Spruch-Weisheit*. Biblisch-Theologische Studien, 21. Neukirchen-Vluyn: Neukirchener Verlag.

Fager, Jeffrey A.
    1993   *Land Tenure and the Biblical Jubilee: Uncovering Hebrew Ethics through the Sociology of Knowledge*. JSOTSup 155. Sheffield: Sheffield Academic.

Hamilton, Jeffries M.
    1992   *Social Justice and Deuteronomy: The Case of Deuteronomy 15*. SBLDS 136. Atlanta: Scholars.

Hoßfeld, Frank-Lothar
    1982   *Der Dekalog: Seine späten Fassungen, die originale Komposition und seine Vorstufen*. OBO 45. Fribourg: Universitätsverlag; Göttingen: Vandenhoeck & Ruprecht.

Keel, Othmar
    1978   *Jahwes Entgegnung an Ijob: Eine Deutung von Ijob 38–41 vor dem Hintergrund der zeitgenössischen Bildkunst*. FRLANT 121. Göttingen: Vandenhoeck & Ruprecht.

Krüger, Thomas
1990   *Theologische Gegenwartsbedeutung im Kohelet-Buch.* Theologische Habilitationsschrift. München.

Levinson, Bernhard M.
1991   *The Hermeneutics of Innovation: The Impact of Centralization upon the Structure, Sequence, and Reformulation of Legal Material in Deuteronomy.* Ann Arbor: University Microfilms International.

Lohfink, Norbert
1984   "Zur deuteronomischen Zentralisationsformel." *Bib* 65:297–328.
1990a "Gibt es eine deuteronomistische Bearbeitung im Bundesbuch?" Pp. 91–113 in *Pentateuchal and Deuteronomistic Studies: Papers Read at the XIIIth IOSOT Congress Leuven 1989.* Ed. C. Brekelmans and J. Lust. BETL 94. Leuven: Leuven University Press and Uitgeverij Peeters.
1990b "Das deuteronomische Gesetz in der Endgestalt: Entwurf einer Gesellschaft ohne marginale Gruppen." *Biblische Notizen* 51:25–40.

Mathys, Hans-Peter
1986   *Liebe deinen Nächsten wie dich selbst: Untersuchungen zum alttestamentlichen Gebot der Nächstenliebe (Lev 19,18).* OBO 71. Fribourg: Universitätsverlag; Göttingen: Vandenhoeck & Ruprecht.

Münchow, Christoph
1981   *Ethik und Eschatologie: Ein Beitrag zum Verständnis der frühjüdischen Apokalyptik.* Göttingen: Vandenhoeck & Ruprecht.

Oßwald, Eva
1970   "Hiob 31 im Rahmen der alttestamentlichen Ethik." Pp. 9–26 in *Theologische Versuche.* Ed. J. Rogge and S. Schille. Vol. 2. Berlin: Evangelische Verlagsanstalt.

Otto, Eckart
1982   "Hat Max Webers Religionssoziologie des antiken Judentums Bedeutung für eine Theologie des Alten Testaments?" *ZAW* 94:187–203.
1988a *Wandel der Rechtsbegründungen in der Gesellschaftsgeschichte des antiken Israel: Eine Rechtsgeschichte des "Bundesbuches" Ex XX 22 – XXIII 13.* StudBib 3. Leiden: E. J. Brill.
1988b "'Wir wollen den Wald und fürchten dennoch seine Geister': Beobachtungen zur Rezeption des Alten Testaments in Papua Neuguinea." *Zeitschrift für Mission* 14:204–20.
1994   *Theologische Ethik des Alten Testaments.* Theologische Wissenschaft, 3/2. Stuttgart: Kohlhammer.

Pressler, Carolyn
1993   *The View of Woman Found in the Deuteronomic Family Laws.* BZAW 216. Berlin: de Gruyter.

Schluchter, Wolfgang
1979   *Die Entwicklung des okzidentalen Rationalismus: Eine Analyse von Max Webers Gesellschaftsgeschichte.* Tübingen: J. C. B. Mohr.

1981   "Altisraelitische religiöse Ethik und okzidentaler Rationalismus." Pp. 11–77 in *Max Webers Studie über das antike Judentum: Interpretation und Kritik*. Ed. W. Schluchter. Frankfurt/Main: Suhrkamp.

Schrage, Wolfgang
1989   *Ethik des Neuen Testaments*. NTD Ergänzungsreihe, 4. Göttingen: Vandenhoeck & Ruprecht.

Schwienhorst-Schönberger, Ludger
1990   *Das Bundesbuch (Ex 20,22 – 23,33): Studien zu seiner Entstehung und Theologie*. BZAW 188. Berlin: de Gruyter.

Weber, Max
1976   *Gesammelte Aufsätze zur Religionssoziologie: Das antike Judentum*. 6th ed. Tübingen: J. C. B. Mohr. English translation: *Ancient Judaism*. Translated and edited by Hans H. Gerth and Don Martindale. New York: Free Press; London: Collier-Macmillan, 1952.

Weinfeld, Moshe
1972   *Deuteronomy and the Deuteronomic School*. Oxford: Clarendon.

AN ETHICIST'S CONCERNS ABOUT BIBLICAL ETHICS

Peter J. Paris
Princeton Theological Seminary

I welcome the editor's invitation to participate as an ethicist in responding to this volume of essays which, I am confident, will become a helpful resource for all religious social ethicists. Indeed, this book should generate much needed interdisciplinary dialogue between ethics and biblical studies. Its rich assemblage of methodological and substantive data can enhance the quality of that discourse.

Because a reciprocity of perspectives governs all genuine discussion between disciplines, scholars so engaged must attend to the prominent methods and issues in each of the fields involved. Such projects generally produce mutual enlightenment and may sometimes lead to interdisciplinary inquiry with the resources of both disciplines united for a common purpose. Cooperative ventures between biblical scholars and religious ethicists have been rare, and this volume may well be the impetus for a change in that condition.

In his introductory essay, Douglas Knight sets forth in a clear and concise way the range of methodological options presently available to biblical scholars as they analyze the textual and contextual basis for biblical ethics. In addition to the so-called *referential, literary,* and *appropriative constructs,* he describes his own special interest in a fourth method, the *sociohistorical construct,* which is distinguished from the others by its attention to the environment of the text rather than to the text as such. In differing ways these essays illustrate the contributions these constructs can make to our understanding of the ethics of ancient Israel.

Unfortunately, this collection of essays exhibits a tendency among most of its authors to submit too easily to the methodological classifications within the history of ethics and to use them as heuristic devices in determining the scope of their respective inquiries. By doing so, they not only render themselves vulnerable to anachronistic judgments but also inhibit their inquiries from yielding new knowledge. For example, John Barton's discussion of the basis of ethics in the Hebrew Bible is persuasive insofar as he describes the Hebrew ethics as *obedience to God's declared will* and *imitation of God,* but his discussion of *natural law* is much less convincing in large part because it is difficult—as he fully recognizes—to avoid engaging in anachronistic argumentation. His tentative suggestion of a *third* basis for ethics in Hebrew thought is worthy of rigorous inquiry, as is a similar idea expressed by Eryl Davies in his essay. Yet, naming that third element *natural law* and attempting to examine it without being anachronistic are tantamount to equivocation. Both Barton and Davies seem to imply that some new term should be devised to define this peculiar type of ethics more satisfactorily. I would add that adequate demonstration of its grounding in the moral world of the ancient Hebrews is essential.

Similarly, since it is difficult to find appropriate correlates in the prephilosophical Hebrew tradition for such categories as *deontology* and *teleology*, I am puzzled as to why Barton chooses to use those terms as a classification scheme for his inquiry. Would it not be more accurate and less confusing to do what he does so well in his description of the categories of *obedience to God's declared will* and *imitation of God*? In those discussions he describes the nature of moral thought among the ancient Israelites in their own terms and, hence, cannot be blamed for any possible misrepresentation of their moral ethos. This problem is clearly illustrated in Bruce Birch's argument that Hebrew ethics cannot be adequately understood as *obedience-ethics* but rather as communion with God, which he views as an entering into the life of God. Thus his conclusion—that *deontological* ethics can never capture the subtle yet radical difference between law and community—appears to be altogether correct. Interestingly, Birch quotes an earlier essay by Barton in support of his argument.

As an ethicist, I find that Birch's method is not only liberating but also productive of much greater creativity than is possible with other methods. That is to say, it seems axiomatic to me that explanatory categories of a people's moral life should be developed wholly from within their own world view. Consequently, the importation of categories from other cultures or disciplines should be strictly avoided so as to minimize the likelihood of either distortion or neglect. Following rigorous internal cultural analysis, intercultural comparative study may then proceed on a firm basis.

Thus the strongest and most convincing essays in this volume are those that analyze their subject matter from within the thought forms of the ancient Israelite culture. Rigorous study of ancient Hebrew ethics in its own terms clearly enables mutual criticism and intellectual advance in interdisciplinary discourse. For example, not only does Birch's discussion of the centrality of the Hebrew understanding of *community* and *character* enable him to acknowledge the influence of Stanley Hauerwas and others on biblical studies, but also he is from his distinctive vantage point able to offer a constructive methodological corrective to those ethicists who in his opinion tend to conflate narrative method with the function of community-building. As Robert Wilson argues so convincingly in his essay, biblical scholars are gradually making some progress in their ethical inquiries as their knowledge of the hermeneutical issues affecting the immense complexity of the biblical record increases. Hence, he concludes that much more intensive research needs to build on the nascent studies in the field.

The more substantive essays in this volume provide analyses of various political themes with considerable ethical import. Consequently, these essays are very helpful to social ethicists because they offer information about the moral life of the ancient Israelites and, more particularly, show several striking similarities of that life to moral issues of our present day. For example, Frank Crüsemann's discussion of domination and reconciliation in the Jacob narrative demonstrates the intriguing textual conflict between the theological justification of political domination on the one hand and the human capacity for thwarting the divine promise on the other. Such a pericope provides a splendid opportunity to discuss the way God's promises are related to human action—in other words, the relationship between theology and ethics. Similarly, Frank Frick analyzes not only how the language of the Deuteronomists reveals the reality of classism while concealing the systematic nature of poverty, but also how it manifests the authors' lack of interest in matters of socioeconomic justice. In short, the Deuteronomists' concern that Israel be freed from the political domination of its neighbors evidently assumes priority over the exploitation of the poor by Israel's economic elite.

These and similar essays provide a helpful resource for social ethicists because they provide moral connections that seem to span the ages. Seeing those connections enables modern readers to discern more easily how an ancient text such as the Bible can be related meaningfully to our contemporary situation. Since Jews and Christians view the Bible as an authoritative resource for matters of faith and morality, the extent to which a common morality between ancients and moderns can be demonstrated would be a most significant finding for all concerned. Not only would it provide an important moral link between the present and the past, but also it would yield vital information about the human condition as such, which is the rightful subject matter of the human sciences, including social ethics.

Yet, in order to treat the subject matter justly, the production of such evidence necessitates the use of appropriate methods. Although an essay like that of Knight's "Political Rights and Powers in Monarchic Israel" rightly aims at providing an analytical description of the prevailing moral values among the ancient Israelites, it is seriously flawed by the above-mentioned anachronistic problem, which he acknowledges by stipulating that the ancients did not have a theory of universal rights. Still, one of the strengths of the essay lies in his identification of two basic values that governed Israelite moral life: the worth of humans and the communitarian ideal. Even so, pressing modern questions onto his subject matter threatens the integrity of the latter by preventing it from emerging in its own terms. Further, some of the concerns that he places under a theory of rights need not be so defined; rather, they were also premodern concerns. For example, the ancient Greeks dealt with issues of self-determination under the rubric of self-sufficiency, and they were deeply concerned with issues pertaining to citizenship, protection, and dissent. Thus, it is erroneous to view such matters as having emerged with the birth of modernity. In short, the author should feel no obligation to cast them in the mold of a "rights" theory.

Contrary to Knight's own claim, I contend that asking certain kinds of questions about a subject is illegitimate. In order to avoid such a judgment, modern interpreters must find hermeneutical principles and investigative methods that do no possible harm to their subject matter. Instead of thinking that the questions of ethicists must always presuppose the Enlightenment, biblical scholars might well look elsewhere for guiding principles for their inquiry: principles that are premodern and, hence, do little or no harm to the inquiry into the biblical text. For example, some basic questions drawn from the empirical method of Aristotle, as he employed them in his *Nicomachean Ethics* and *Politics*, might be helpful. This is not to say that one should subject the Hebrew text to the demands of Greek methodology. That could be as problematic as the heteronomy of modernity. It is important to note, however, that in spite of the cultural divide between the ancient Greeks and the ancient Hebrews, the two share a common time-frame. Both are decidedly premodern. Hence, in my judgment little harm can be done to the subject matter by asking the questions that Aristotle asked of those he studied: What is the nature of good action? What are the historical conditions that enable good action to emerge? How can humans do the good? How can humans become good? What are the attributes of moral goodness? Can human action be morally ambiguous? What is the relation between the good person and the good community? Each of these questions requires an empirical investigation that can avoid all Greek presuppositions in favor of those of the Hebrews.[1] In principle, it seems reasonable to ask

---

[1] It should also be noted, however, that all questions are value-laden. For example, questions about moral goodness are not synonymous with questions about

whether or not the ancient Israelites confronted the kind of questions known from another culture contemporaneous with a segment of their own history. Problems such as Aristotle's are merely suggestive, and further questions culled from other premodern cultures can and should be added. The danger, of course, is that categories and questions stemming from another society of the preindustrial world, even if it is a society that existed in chronological and spatial proximity to ancient Israel, can be as foreign to Israel as are our own ways of thinking, and methodological caution must be practiced at every turn of the examination. I maintain, nonetheless, that asking premodern questions is less risky than pursuing modern issues if we hope to understand the ethics of an ancient culture such as Israel.

In spite of the difficulties I have described, Knight's study yields much richness in showing how the prophets conjoined the religious and the moral spheres in their advocacy for justice. Similarly, his analytical distinctions both between the private and the public and also between local and national politics are of great importance. In fact, when shorn of the biases of modernity, his findings are exactly what we as ethicists hope that biblical scholars will continue to provide in abundance. Niels Peter Lemche's essay, "Kings and Clients," achieves a similar result through a faithful adherence to premodern categories that are laden with ethical significance. Guided by a structural relationship, namely the patronage connection between client and patron, Lemche clearly explicates the principal features of a moral relationship that both moderns and ancients can understand and appreciate. By digging deeply into the cultural patterns of the people, he develops a theory out of that cultural context. Similarly, Hannelis Schulte's "The End of the Omride Dynasty" inquires into the moral issues pertaining to religion, politics, and violence by carefully analyzing events that occurred at that historical juncture. While the essay falls short of enunciating a theory, it raises a number of moral issues that transcend the rather limited scope of the analysis itself.

In addition to the ubiquitous question about the authority of the biblical text for contemporary ethics, many social ethicists are intensely interested in the work of biblical scholars who are engaged in empirical studies of the social world of the ancient Israelites. Their combined sociological, anthropological, political, and moral investigations undoubtedly portend the eventual yield of a major storehouse of ancient moral wisdom that may provide many insights for ethical studies in our day.

---

moral rightness. The former implies doing or becoming; the latter implies obedience to laws or norms.

It should be noted that the authors of these essays exhibit a commendable international character. We do live in a global village, and the more cognizance we give to that fact the richer our scholarly products are likely to be. Yet, the authors are, with one exception, male scholars and are all from the United States and western Europe. Collaborative projects conducted primarily by the heirs of an academic hegemony that long dominated biblical scholarship can be subject to criticism by virtue of the limited perspectives that they embody, and it would do well in the future to ensure that scholars representing diverse peoples and groups in the global village contribute to such discussions.

I do not wish to blame the writers of these essays for the things they did not do. Nevertheless, I will mention some of the concerns of contemporary ethicists with the hope that the findings of biblical scholarship might dovetail with them. During the past several decades various genres of liberation thought have sought to explicate biblical insights as foundational for their respective inquiries. In their analyses of economic structures, Latin American liberationists have emphasized the biblical biases that favor the poor. It is important to ask whether such biases inhere in the scriptures as a whole or merely reflect selected traditions therein. Perhaps these biases mirror the appropriative tradition more than the actual historical dimensions of the texts themselves. Biblical scholars can help us with this and related matters. Similarly, the black theology project and the African American church tradition have emphasized the exodus pericope as normative for their appropriation of both the Hebrew and Christian scriptures. Several womanist thinkers have dissented from that presupposition in their search for other paradigms that do greater justice to the struggles of oppressed women in the biblical tradition.

Similarly, many feminists have been struggling with the task of deconstructing the patriarchalism that is both explicit and implicit throughout much of the biblical text. They seek to determine the extent to which certain texts can be redeemed from their misogynist character. The works of biblical scholars such as Phyllis Trible, Elisabeth Schüssler Fiorenza, and others have made remarkable contributions to such an inquiry, but much more work remains to be done.

Many social ethicists are concerned with a plethora of moral issues respecting the diversity of peoples struggling in a steadily shrinking world for a life of peace and justice that they can share. Does the Bible provide moral insights that can help us deal constructively with differences between and among the races, classes, cultures, political ideologies, gays and lesbians, to mention only a few? Further, how can the Bible help us affirm and enhance our increasing awareness about the moral significance of the environment? On these and many other questions, we social ethicists seek the help of biblical scholars. Thus, we celebrate the works in this volume and sincerely hope that many similar projects will be forthcoming. We are also grateful for the stimulus for interdisciplinary discussion that this project provides.

www.ingramcontent.com/pod-product-compliance
Lightning Source LLC
Chambersburg PA
CBHW022010160426
43197CB00007B/367